THE TALISMAN

Italian Cook Book

THE TALISMAN
Italian Cook Book

By ADA BONI

Translated and Augmented by

MATILDE LA ROSA

Introduction by

PROFESSOR MARIO A. PEI

CROWN PUBLISHERS, INC.   NEW YORK

Published by Crown Publishers, Inc., 201 East 50th Street, New York, New York 10022. Member of the Crown Publishing Group.

CROWN is a trademark of Crown Publishers, Inc.

Manufactured in the United States of America

Library of Congress Catalog Card Number: 50-8521

ISBN 0-517-50387-5

36 35 34 33 32

FOREWORD

Ada Boni's *Talismano della Felicità* is universally recognized in Italy as the standard national cookbook. Its author, who is also editor of *Preziosa,* Italy's leading magazine for women, first brought out her work in 1928 in an effort to bring up to date a number of antiquated regional and national cookbooks which had been long since superseded by the expanding art of Italian cookery.

The work met with immediate and widespread success in Italy. In the course of twenty-one years, sixteen reprints and new editions have appeared, with total sales of almost a quarter of a million copies—a truly extraordinary record when one considers the limited nature of the cookbook market in Italy, for although this is a nation whose population exceeds fifty-two million people, nevertheless in this country the art of cooking is handed down as an oral tradition from mother to daughter, and written aids to cookery of all sorts are generally viewed with a mixture of suspicion and derision and it is a nation where widespread poverty is a powerful deterrent to the purchase of expensive volumes, even when they are earnestly desired. The record established by Ada Boni's masterpiece is almost fantastic.

The fifteenth edition, of which this volume is a condensed translation and adaptation, is a monumental affair of 866 pages and more than 2,000 recipes, about half being non-Italian in origin. These have been excluded from our collection, since it was deemed desirable to have a work that would deal exclusively with native Italian dishes. The remaining recipes were carefully sifted with a view to excluding those whose ingredients are totally unavailable in this country, even in the form of acceptable substitutes. On the other hand, a few recipes have been added which did not appear in Mrs. Boni's work, ones familiar to American readers who have seen these dishes on the menus of Italo-American restaurants. Several recipes are the personal contributions of the translator, Mrs. Matilde Pei, herself an experienced cook, who has found them to be very popular with her American friends. These have been indicated in the text by * following the title.

It may be emphasized that this is an Italian, not an Italo-American cookbook. The recipes here listed describe dishes which are regularly eaten throughout the length and breadth of the Italian peninsula rather than dishes which are the specialty of a single Italian region, or those which have grown up in the Italian communities in America. The corollary to this proposition is that a large number of these dishes will be almost totally unfamiliar to the American reader. All of them, without exception, are worth while trying. Some go back to the Renaissance, when Italian cookery was internationally renowned, and French

v

cooks came to Italy to learn their art. Others are comparatively modern. All are good.

The translator, Matilde Pei, was an Italian housewife, born and raised in Rome, who came to the United States at the age of 18 and was an employee of the Censorship Bureau during World War II. Her command of both languages and her own culinary skill were safe guarantees that the work of translation was accurate and well done.

The Introduction and Glossary are the work of Professor Mario A. Pei of Columbia University, author of *The Italian Language, Languages for War and Peace,* and *The Story of Language.* The Glossary gives both the dictionary definition of Italian terms used in the text and their approximate English pronunciation.

The work was done under the general editorship of Charlotte Adams, nationally known food editor and writer.

CONTENTS

INTRODUCTION

As a linguist and student of national cultures, I have often thought that there must be some intimate relationship between language and food. The countries that display the widest range of dialects are also the ones in which cookery assumes the most diversified forms; while the lands where dialectal differences are slight exhibit a certain monotony in their food.

Italy appears very close to the top of the list among countries with a wide dialectal array, and correspondingly, the food of Italy is so diversified that the cuisine of one region is practically foreign to another.

A North Italian and a Sicilian, each speaking his own dialect, have no more chance of understanding each other than an American and a German each using his own language. In like manner, a typical Venetian dinner and one concocted in Calabria have about as much in common as a meal in Paris and one in Chinatown.

The diversity of speech, food, customs, costumes, psychology, and general world outlook that one finds in the Italian peninsula and the adjacent islands may be (in fact, undoubtedly is) a very bad thing from the standpoint of national unity, co-operative teamwork and industrial progress. It probably accounts for a good deal of Italy's lack of success as a "great" nation, in the sense that physical power, economic advancement and political unity constitute greatness. But the diversity is probably just as much at the root of Italy's pre-eminence in that other, less material sphere—individual achievement, spontaneous creativeness, artistic, musical and intellectual distinction.

Variety is the spice of life. Italy has infinite variety, and infinite spice. The traveler who traverses the peninsula from end to end is struck by the differences in architectural and artistic forms, in dress, in mode of life, differences which are far greater in extent and more fundamental in kind than in any other country of comparable size. Having once seen the Italian cities, he will never confuse Venice with Florence, Milan with Rome, Bologna with Palermo, in much the same fashion that one might confuse Boston with Philadelphia, Indianapolis with Cincinnati, or Seattle with San Francisco. If he is at all acquainted with the Italian language, he will listen with growing astonishment and incomprehension to the multitude of local speech-forms that strike his ear, speech-forms which are infinitely more varied than those distinguishing Atlanta from New Haven, or Los Angeles from New York. If he has the gastronomic courage to turn his back resolutely on his first-class hotel and its international cuisine, and strike out boldly for the local eating-houses, or, better yet, manage to get himself invited to local households, he will encounter dishes whose diversity will astound him beyond measure.

We in America have contrived for ourselves a somewhat conventional picture of Italian appearance, Italian disposition, Italian ways of life, and Italian cookery. That this is partly due to the fact that the Italian immigrants who have come to our midst are mostly of southern or Sicilian origin is beside the point. The fact remains that when we speak of an "Italian type," what appears on our mind's screen is a short, dark individual with flashing eyes, a ready, tooth-revealing smile, and voluble gestures. The blond or brown-haired six-footer is common enough in Italy, particularly in the north, but since he clashes with our preconceived mental image, we refuse to believe in him. A stolid Italian is beyond our ken, yet many Italians are stolid. An Italian who does not sing "O Sole Mio" and break into a tarantella at the slightest provocation is an Italian we do not know, or perhaps even wish to know; yet there is a type of Italian who sings the hymn-like folk-songs of the Alpine passes and dances (when he does) the slow, majestic dances of Piedmont and Friuli. He uses no more gestures than the average Midwesterner, whom he resembles somewhat in physical appearance, has little use for macaroni and spaghetti, and is anything but temperamental.

The conception that most Americans have of Italian cookery has been built largely upon the traditional Italo-American restaurant, specializing in antipasto, minestrone, spaghetti, veal scaloppine and spumoni—a combination that you would have some difficulty in obtaining on Italian soil. A few Italian dishes, having landed here first, have monopolized the field, and have become far more traditional of Italy in the American mind than their Italian status entitles them to be. Not that they are not consumed in Italy (though usually not in the arrangement in which they appear in Italo-American restaurants). It is simply that they constitute a small fraction of the totality of Italian dishes, which run into the thousands, and with many of which we in America have yet to become acquainted.

There is in New York an out-of-the-way restaurant which is run by a Friulian couple, from the foothills of the Alps. They will serve you not an antipasto of the customary type (celery, olives, anchovies, pimentos and salame), but melon and prosciutto and tunnied veal. They will cook up a mess of macaroni for you if you insist, and serve it to you with a pitying glance; but if you are willing to forget your traditional ideal that macaroni *must* form part of an Italian dinner, you will get a rare type of vegetable soup, or a dish of rice with saffron sauce that is a true taste sensation. Seldom will they offer you chicken cacciatora or veal scaloppine al Marsala; instead, you will get delicately roast-

meats (two or three or four varieties) accompanied by a wealth of tasty vegetables cooked in butter, not in oil. No spumoni or biscuit tortoni, or even zabaione for dessert, but Italian cheeses in lavish profusion, with fruit in season, and a homemade pastry the like of which you have never tasted before. When I took a friend of mine to the *Friuliani*, as they are affectionately called by those in the know, he could at first believe neither his eyes nor his palate. "Wonderful!" he exclaimed. "But certainly not Italian!" I had tremendous difficulty convincing him that this was just as characteristically Italian as the Neapolitan restaurant to which he was accustomed.

It will strike many Americans as strange to hear that there is, in northern and central Italy, a broad belt where macaroni in any shape or form is seldom eaten. The low-lying valley of the Po, from Turin near the French border to Venice on the Adriatic, lends itself to cornfields and rice-growing far better than to wheat; accordingly, rice dishes and polenta (cornmeal mush) are dominant there.

An Italian friend of mine with anthropological leanings likes to speak of the two great civilizations of Italy; the wine-and-olive-oil zone and the milk-and-butter culture. In Emilia, Lombardy and Venetia the olive groves so distinctive of Liguria, Umbria and the entire south do not flourish very well, but herds of cattle do. Tuscany is the common meeting-ground of the two gastronomic civilizations of Italy, and a Tuscan of my acquaintance always uses butter and oil in equal proportions as a base for his sauces. Garlic is much favored in some regions, not at all in others. Tuscan recipes are more likely to call for onions than for garlic. The tomato, beloved and revered in the south, where it was introduced by the Spaniards who had brought it from America, is used relatively little in the north. These are only a few of the major regional differences in Italian cooking, but they serve to give the reader an understanding of the great variety of tastes that await him.

Of course, all this does not mean that a considerable amount of inter-regional exchange has not taken place, particularly in recent times. During the Middle Ages and the Renaissance, and down to the latter part of the last century, communication among the regions was difficult by reason of the mountainous nature of the country. The Apennine chain, running down the length of the peninsula from the French frontier to the toe of the boot, split the Po Valley from the verdant hills of Tuscany and Umbria, the flat Roman Campagna from the rugged Abruzzi, and the fertile, well-watered Neapolitan region from the dry Apulian tableland. People stayed at home and developed their individualistic styles, in cookery as in everything else. Railroads, automobiles and airplanes have changed all that. Today Italians travel from one to another section of their country with almost as much ease as

Americans in the New World. This has meant, among other things, an exchange of dishes. Today the menu of an Italian dining-car is almost as stereotyped as that of an Italo-American restaurant. But local specialties still thrive, on the highways and byways, in the lower-class sections of cities and in the smaller towns and villages. The process of standardization goes inexorably on, though at a slower pace than in America. A few dishes have become almost as universal as Americans think they are.

There are two ways of describing a nation's cuisine: the regional, or geographic, and the topical, or downright culinary. The first is interwoven with local customs, habits, beliefs and superstitions, and might lead us too far afield. The latter is more specific, and more in accord with the purpose of this book, which is to present Italian dishes in easy-to-understand recipes rather than as a gastronomic history of Italy.

The general classification of meal courses does not differ too greatly from country to country or from period to period. As we examine remnants of cookbooks prepared by ancient Greek and Roman writers, like the great Apicius, we discover that they, like ourselves, divided the principal meal of the day *(prandium* or *cena)* into three parts: a pregustatory or hors-d'oeuvre phase; a main course (or sequence of main courses); and a fruit-and-sweet, or dessert division. Once the arts of civilization are established, it seems normal to open the meal with food elements that stimulate the appetite, and to close it with foods of a cloying nature, which put the seal upon the tomb of departed hunger.

Between the *promulsis* (or *gustatio*, or *frigida mensa*) of the ancient Romans and the antipasto of the modern Italians many centuries have intervened, yet the general idea remains the same. Favorite ingredients of the classical *frigida mensa* were shellfish, vegetables in savory sauces, olives, mushrooms and eggs (the Romans even had an expression, *ab ovo ad mala*, "from egg to apples," to signify "from the beginning to the end" of the meal). All of these components find their way into an elaborate modern Italian antipasto.

The French expression *hors-d'oeuvre* literally means "outside of work," referring to the eating of appetite-whetting foods outside the "labor" of the main courses. The Italian *antipasto* has a more direct meaning: "before meal."

It would be a vain task to attempt to give a general description of an Italian antipasto. Its components vary from region to region, as well as with the season of the year, proximity to the sea coast and its shellfish, local tradition, and the taste of the individual. The north shows perhaps a slight preference for elaborate preparations, like cold hard-cooked eggs in a variety of sauces, stuffed mushrooms, pickled artichokes, pork products such as salame, prosciutto, capocollo (or coppa) and mortadella di Bologna (from which we get "boloney," but it's not the same thing). The south, with its abundance of vegetables, to a greater degree goes in for olives, fresh celery and fennel, lettuce, raw green peppers, scallions and radishes, or their pickled counterparts, such as the caponatina of Sicily, which can be bought in cans and which includes additional vegetables, like eggplant. Hot, peppery sausage, called salamino, is distinctive of some provinces. Sardines and anchovies in olive oil (with or without capers), pimentos, fresh cheeses such as ricotta, mozzarella and provatura, are all often added to the antipasto—the cheeses particularly in the south. The beauty of the antipasto is that it can be made as elaborate or as simple as you wish. It can range all the way from sixty varieties of fish, vegetables, meats and cheeses (almost like a Swedish *smörgasbord*) to a few simple raw vegetables sprinkled with salt.

One word of explanation: it is the custom of many Italians to dispense with the antipasto altogether and start the meal with soup or macaroni. In this respect they are like the early Greek settlers of southern Italy whose main meal consisted of two basic divisions instead of the Romans' three. Others use the antipasto occasionally, reserving it for holidays and special occasions. Do not be surprised if an Italian family by whom you are invited to dinner opens the meal with minestrone, ravioli, or risotto.

At this point, we must dispel two other favorite American illusions, fostered by the Italian restaurants in our midst. It is practically unheard of in Italy to serve minestrone (or any kind of heavy soup) *and* a macaroni dish at the same meal. Macaroni, on the other hand, is practically never served as the main course in substitution for meat or fish. The soup or macaroni (or risotto) serves as an introductory course, which may or may not be preceded by antipasto. Next comes the meat or fish, usually accompanied by vegetables and/or salad. Last comes the cheese-and-fruit course, or the dessert (seldom both, save on festive occasions). This means that the normal Italian main meal, though substantial enough, does not differ too much in quantity from its American counterpart. Italians love good food, but they seldom overeat.

The average Italian's choice of a first main course lies between soup, macaroni or rice. Unlike the antipasto, seldom do Italians skip this course. Indeed, the chief qualitative difference between the usual Italian dinner and the usual American dinner consists of the two-course nature of the former. Italians are often astonished at the American custom of starting with the roast and vegetables. They sometimes speak of the "dry" nature of the American dinner, and use the adjective

xiii

"dry" in a double connotation—the lack of wine and the lack of soup.

An interesting hypothesis is advanced by a Spanish friend of mine to account for the heavy, filling soup, macaroni and rice dishes to which Latin countries are addicted. These introductory dishes serve, he thinks, to cushion the impact that would otherwise fall with full force upon the subsequent meat course. Far more than antipasto, which primarily whets the appetite, they are meant to take the edge off the diner's hunger, disposing him to be more merciful toward the meat, which in most Latin countries is scarce and costly. If this theory is true, then the American single-course dinner is another symbol of prosperity and relatively high standard of living.

The honors of first main course are about equally shared on Italian soil by soup, rice and macaroni, with the first predominating in the central portion of the country, the second in the north, the third in the south. A good Florentine enjoys his soup far more than any macaroni dish you could set before him. The Milanese likes his *risotto*, with or without *ossobuco*. The Venetian farmer loves his dish of *polenta*, particularly if accompanied by little birds. But from Rome southward a meal is not a meal if it doesn't include a good, hefty dish of *pasta asciutta*, "dry dough," the generic name that covers the multitude of macaroni and spaghetti dishes served without broth (*pasta*, after all, can be and often is served in soup form).

Italian soups are numerous and varied. They range in quality all the way from delicate beef or chicken consommé, barely flavored by a few thin slices of vegetable or a handful of *pastina*, to the coarse, heart-warming, body-filling concoctions that go under the general name of *minestrone* ("big soup"). The Roman *stracciatella* is a beaten egg soup, easy to make and light on the stomach, made with eggs, whipped into a froth with the addition of salt, pepper, nutmeg, cinnamon and clove, and poured into boiling broth, whipped there for a second or two, and then removed from the fire. Its light, flaky consistency and spicy taste make it an ideal opener for a meal featuring heavy meats and desserts. On the other hand, dishes like *pasta e fagioli* or *pasta e ceci* (macaroni and beans; macaroni and chick-peas) constitute a complete meal in themselves. As Mayor La Guardia used to remark in his radio broadcasts during the war, "a dish of *pasta e fagioli* plus a good green salad, cheese and fruit, and you have a perfect meatless meal." In between, there are all sorts and kinds of gradations—light broths and full-bodied vegetable soups, soups that call for meat stock and leave a residue of boiled beef that is good hot or cold, and soups that eschew meat altogether, functioning on an oil or salt-pork base, plus a *soffritto*, or browned mixture of chopped parsley, celery, onion and carrot. There are fish soups which are complete seafood dinners, like the *cacciucco* of Leghorn, and fish soups in which only the clear fish broth is used, like the Roman skate-soup. Despite the warmth of the Italian climate, Italians are not partial to cold or jellied soups. The soup, which so often constitutes the opening part of the meal, should be quite hot when it comes to the table, even if you have to blow on it or transfer part of it from the soup dish to the shallow plate to cool it (but these procedures are not approved in the best circles).

The Italian rice belt extends across the northern provinces, in the great valley of the Po, whose overflowing creates ideal rice-paddies. There is not too great variety to Italian *risotto*, but northerners prefer it bright yellow, with a saffron sauce, while the tomato-loving south smothers it in tomato sauce, and the central regions compromise with a meat sauce; all top it off with grated Parmesan cheese, and eat it with a fork. The *polenta* of the corn-growing northern regions is eaten with a variety of sauces, the most characteristic being the Venetian one made with a stew of thrushes and other small birds.

Italy has an almost incredible variety of macaroni products, and perhaps it is this picturesque multiplicity of forms, sizes, and styles of macaroni which has led to the international reputation of Italians as macaroni-eaters. This reputation is well deserved by the southern Italians but somewhat exaggerated for the inhabitants of the north and center of the peninsula. The story of macaroni is an intriguing and partly mythical one.

The Neapolitans have a legend concerning a Cardinal from their city who, on being offered by his chef a novel preparation consisting of a food made from dough and served with a rich tomato sauce, exclaimed: "*Ma cari! Ma caroni!*" ("Why, the dears! Why, the big dears!"), thereby giving the new food its name at its very inception. The story gives itself away as untrue by one of its details. Tomato sauce could not exist before the introduction of the tomato, which followed by less than a century the discovery of the American continent. Macaroni, however, is specifically mentioned in Boccaccio's *Decameron* at the outset of the fourteenth century, more than two hundred years before the tomato was known in Europe. In that work, the great Florentine describes the imaginary land of Bengodi (Enjoy-yourself-well), where cooks stand on mounds of Parmesan cheese and ladle macaroni and ravioli into pots of capon broth.

The other legend concerning macaroni relates that a Chinese maiden taught her Italian sailor sweetheart the art of noodle-making, which he brought back to his own land. This pairs off with the myth of Marco Polo, who is supposed to have returned to his native Venice with coal, gunpowder and noodles from the court of the Great Khan of Tartary.

Historically, the earliest authentic reference to macaroni appears in an eighth-century version of the works of Hesychius, a Greek lexicographer, in which a food called *makaria* ("blessed things" or "food of the blessed") is described as a dish made of dough and served with a sauce (which obviously could not be tomato sauce).

Whatever the origin of the object and its name, macaroni serves today as one of the Italian staples, particularly in the south. Though all macaroni is made of the same basic wheat-flour dough, the shapes and sizes are as varied as the towns and hamlets of Italy, and size and shape influence the taste to an incredible degree. From the wire-thin *capellini d'angelo* ("angel hair") to the giant *cannelloni* ("big pipes"), macaroni sizes run the gamut of *vermicelli, spaghettini, spaghetti, maccaroncini, tufoli, ziti* and a few dozen others, while odd shapes include "butterflies" and "conch-shells." Some varieties are eaten merely with sauce; others are meant to be stuffed with meat, chopped spinach, ricotta, mozzarella and other ingredients. Ravioli are the best known in America among the latter, but there are numerous others, like the *agnolotti* ("little big lambs") of Turin, stuffed with a molten Alpine cheese called *fondua*, or the *tortellini* of Bologna, stuffed with meat and served in broth. It has been estimated that the names of macaroni products run into the thousands, but this is partly due to identical products having different names in different localities. An actual roster of shapes and sizes, however, runs well over a hundred.

Even more important than the size and shape is the nature of the sauce that accompanies the macaroni or spaghetti. Contrary to popular belief, not all macaroni sauces include tomato. There are, for instance, the "white" clam sauce of Naples, the anchovy and garlic sauce, and the *pesto* or "green" sauce of Genoa, made by grinding together with a pestle various green herbs, plus abundant garlic and olive oil. Many Italians, particularly those with weak stomachs, prefer sauceless macaroni, *al burro e parmigiano*, with butter and Parmesan cheese. Sauces in which the tomato enters as an ingredient are legion. Companion ingredients to the tomato are varied: the prosciutto of Bologna, the onion and bacon of the Roman countryside, the clams of Naples, the sardines and zucchini of Sicily, the ragout meats of Puglia, the fresh cheeses and sausage of Calabria and the fat fish of the Tyrrhenian coast.

There is almost no end to the spicy or mild concoctions devised by Italian ingenuity. The green noodles of Florence, where the dough is kneaded with chopped spinach, the giant *lasagne* of the south (broad macaroni strips, arranged in alternate layers with ricotta, mozzarella, ground sausage or tiny meat balls, covered with sauce, and set to bake in an oven), the *manicotti* ("muffs") and *cannoli* ("big reeds"), stuffed with fresh cheeses, baked, and served piping hot, are only a few of the numerous variants of that triumph of Italian cookery—the macaroni product. In connection with this, one word of caution should be voiced: all macaroni products must be cooked *al dente* ("to the tooth"); that is to say, they must be removed from their boiling water while they are still semi-solid, not after they have been stewed into a tender mush. Macaroni is meant to be chewed, not swallowed like a soft pudding.

As we have said before, not all of Italy shares the same enthusiasm for macaroni. But Italian enthusiasts are fanatics indeed. One old Sicilian of my acquaintance used to say: "First God; then *pasta asciutta*"; and Italian army recruits from the south are credited with having invented a doggerel to accompany the trumpet blare of reveille: "There's rice today! There's rice today! Why the devil don't we ever see *pasta asciutta?*" The enthusiasm of true believers is catching, and just as Americans have become steady patrons of spaghetti houses in the last forty years, many dwellers of the northern provinces have acquired the macaroni habit. The Italian who remains completely indifferent to *pasta asciutta* still exists, but he is rarer than he used to be.

Main courses in Italy, as practically everywhere else, consist of meat or fish accompanied by vegetables and salads. But before going into this matter, it may be well to speak of an item which in America is generally taken for granted though sometimes omitted from the diet in the interests of controlling one's weight. This item is bread, which in the Latin countries is truly the staff of life. The Italian saying that corresponds to "earning one's bread and butter" is "earning one's bread and wine," but the bread is taken far more literally. Another Italian expression for which there is no English equivalent is *companatico*, "that which goes with bread," any food used as a bread-filler.

Many and varied are the uses of Italian bread. In poor peasant households a dinner consisting of bread and soup is not a rarity. Workmen often carry a lunch consisting of half a loaf of good Italian bread plus a hunk of salame or a few vegetables. Lower-class Roman children are often given, for their afternoon lunch, a slice of bread dressed with oil, vinegar and salt, the name of which is *panzanella*, "little paunch," and about which a popular song has been composed. Breakfast frequently consists of black coffee with a slice of bread spread with ricotta. This Latin love of bread is traditional, and goes straight back to the Romans and Greeks.

The shapes and sizes of bread loaves and rolls as well as the proportions of whole wheat to white flour almost make Italian bread the rival of macaroni products in variety. There is, however, one predominant, traditional mold into which Latin bread is most often cast—the round, crusty loaf which is characteristic of Spain, Italy and southern France (northern France prefers the elongated loaf, which we call "French bread"). The shape and soft consistency of the American sandwich loaf is practically unknown to these people. Some scientists attribute the greater resistance to tooth decay among the Latins to the fact that the crusty loaf gives the teeth and gums exercise and stimulation which are notably lacking in the American loaf. Whether this be true or not, the Spaniard loves his *hogaza*, the southern Frenchman his *miche* and the Italian his *pagnotta*, each with a love that is rooted deep in the soil of his native land. While the average per capita consumption of bread in the Latin countries is at least double that in America, there is one food item with which Italians do not eat bread, while Americans sometimes do. That is macaroni. A moment's thought will reveal that you ought not to "double up" on your wheat products.

One characteristic product of Italy is the bread-stick or *grissino*, made familiar to us by Italo-American restaurants. Originating in the northwestern province of Piedmont (the first *grissini* are said to have been made in Turin), the bread-stick has wended its way to all parts of Italy and America.

Another bread product with which we have struck up an acquaintance is the *pizza* (sold, as most people know, in a *pizzeria*). *Pizza* is the general Italian term for pie, tart, or anything, in fact, that is round and flat and baked in an oven. One famous Italian pastry is the *pizza di ricotta*, traditionally eaten at Easter time. Another is the *pizza di polenta*, or cornmeal pie, which, sweetened and spiced, becomes a dessert; dressed with a tomato sauce, can substitute for macaroni; or simply salted, sliced and eaten hot or cold, is like our Southern cornmeal bread. But the form in which the *pizza* has come to us in America is the wheat-dough pie of the Neapolitans, baked with tomato sauce, cheese, and/or anchovies.

Italian meals show a diversity which is out of proportion to their rate of consumption on Italian soil. Italy is a poor country so far as material wealth is concerned, and meat is a rich man's food. It has been estimated that at least half of all Italian families eat meat only on Sundays, if then.

One of the effects of the relative scarcity of meat is to force people to utilize cuts which in more fortunate lands would be discarded. During the war and its accompanying meat scarcity there appeared in American butcher shops assorted animal parts—hearts, kidneys, lung, tripe, spleen, brains and entrails—theretofore disdained by most Americans. Liver, once reserved for the family cat, had already invaded the

xviii

American diet, but only by reason of a relentless campaign by medical associations concerned with vitamin content. On the other hand these "inferior" meats have long been used to the full by the frugal Italian housewife. An Italian *fritto misto* will, as a rule, contain three or four animal organs, cunningly disguised and mingled with vegetables. *Coratella*, which includes lamb's heart, liver and lung, is a delicacy. It is an Italian (and, generally, a southern European) theory that any cut of meat, however strange in its raw state, can be rendered palatable and appetizing by proper cooking and blending with such highly flavored ingredients as tomato, onion, garlic, peppers and assorted herbs. The choice of food, after all, is a matter of habit, and if one can accustom himself to locusts and rattlesnakes he can also come to view animal innards with equanimity. "The proof of the pudding is in the eating," or, to put it more bluntly in the Italian way, *"Quel che non ammazza ingrassa—*"What doesn't kill you fattens you." If you go to Italian sections in large American cities on special feast-days, you can get *capozzelle* (roasted lambs' heads), which you gnaw on till the last shred of meat is gone, and *gnummarielli* (stuffed, milk-fed lamb's entrails, roasted on the spit).

Italians are not overly addicted to steak and chops, for these are expensive. But in Florence they make a specialty of *bistecca alla fiorentina,* which is a two- to three-inch-thick cut of porterhouse or sirloin, broiled on an open grate over a charcoal fire, while Milan specializes in *cotolette alla milanese,* milk-fed veal cutlets delicately rolled in egg, breaded, and fried to a crisp, luscious golden brown. The *ossobuco* ("hollowbone") of Milan, generally served with *risotto,* the *abbacchio* (baby spring lamb) and *capretto al forno* (kid baked in the oven) of Rome are among other Italian meat dishes sure to meet with unanimous American approval.

Much use is made of boiled and stewed meats, which have a double purpose: to serve as meats and to supply the broth for soups and the meat sauce for macaroni. The ragout beef of Puglia, whose by-product supplies a rich meat sauce for macaroni, is a rewarding experience in taste. Meatballs and meat loaves *(polpette* and *polpettoni)* are also widely used. The favorite ingredients for these are ground beef and pork, in equal proportions, plus a variety of herbs, spices and even pine nuts.

Chicken and game appear in many forms, a common one being the *cacciatora* (hunter style). *Cacciatora* has two variants: the southern one in which tomato enters, and the northern and central one which uses rosemary, anchovies, vinegar, garlic, oil and herbs. The Roman *brodetto* is a dish of lamb or veal cut into small pieces and stewed in a sauce primarily composed of eggs and lemon juice.

xix

Fish is far more widely used in Italy than in America, as is natural in a country which at no point is more than 100 miles from the sea-coast. The abundance and variety of Mediterranean seafood lend themselves to fish-eating habits, but this same abundance and variety do not restrain the frugal Italians from utilizing fishes and parts of fishes which Americans discard. On a fishing trip off the Long Island coast, the main purpose of which was to gather flounders, I was amazed to see skates thrown back into the water. The large, meaty wing of the skate is the basis of the delectable French dish, *raie au beurre noir,* for which Americans pay good money and eat with gusto; but the average American who fishes for sport is not aware of the connection. Italians, instead of frying skate-wings in browned butter, prefer to boil them, draining off the broth for fish soup, and eating the boiled skate-wings with lemon juice, oil and parsley—a wholesome, easy-to-digest and extremely tasty food. Squid, cuttlefish and devilfish are fried, or stewed with rice. Strange shellfish, like the *riccio,* or sea-urchin, are consumed in Italy, though scorned by American lovers of seafood.

As for the more ordinary fish dishes, Italians consume them in vast quantities, and with a culinary variety which far outstrips anything known in America. *Pesce in bianco* (boiled fish with olive oil and lemon) is one of the Italian abstinence-day favorites. Fish soups, fish stews (like the Leghorn *cacciucco,* a doughty rival of the Marseille *bouillabaisse),* roast fish, baked fish and fish fries *(fritto misto di pesce)* are popular throughout Italy. Lobsters, crabs, shrimps and other shell-fish round out the general Italian seafood picture, highlighted by such specialties as *triglie alla livornese* (mullet in a special tomato sauce), the famous fried *scampi* (prawns) of Venice, the stewed *cozze* (mussels) of Taranto and the peppery *scungilli* (conch) of Naples.

That Italy is a land of vegetables is evidenced by the fact that we in America use so many Italian vegetable names (broccoli, zucchini, finocchi); Jerusalem artichoke is a corruption of Italian *girasole,* and kohlrabi of *cavoli-rape* ("cabbage-turnips"). The names endive, celery, chicory, radish are barely disguised from the original Italian *indivia, sedano, cicoria* and *radice.* Italians like their vegetables raw, in salad form (in which case they are usually accompanied by a dressing of olive oil, wine vinegar, salt and pepper), or boiled and left to cool (where-upon olive oil, lemon juice and garlic predominate). Many vegetables are fried (the Italian *fritto misto* includes celery, eggplant, mushrooms, artichokes and other vegetable varieties); others are skilfully blended with fresh cheeses and tomato sauce, like the eggplant *parmigiana.* The ubiquitous tomato, which figures as an ingredient in so many sauces and dishes, appears in its own right in Rome, where it is hollowed out, stuffed with boiled rice which is mixed with the tomato's own juices plus olive oil, garlic and chopped mint, then baked in the oven. The potato is used more sparingly in the Mediterranean lands than in the Nordic countries, mainly because it is rivalled as a source of carbohydrates by older and more traditional foods (bread, macaroni and rice). Cabbage, turnips, parsnips, yellow squash and pumpkin are also less popular in Italy than in the lands to the north. But green vegetables of all kinds and descriptions figure more largely in the average diet, along with dried beans, peas, chick-peas and lentils. A sailor's dish like the *baccalà e ceci* (dried cod and chick-peas) is a soul-warming affair on a cold winter night. The dried chick-peas are left to soak overnight with the dried cod, from which they absorb salt; then they are stewed with macaroni, oil and tomato sauce until a thick soup is attained, which is eaten as a first course, while the softened cod, separately stewed with oil and tomato, serves as a second course.

One is often tempted to wonder what Italian cookery would be like if the tomato had never been discovered. It is the tomato, along with olive oil, garlic and, to a lesser degree, onion, that sets the pace for the most colorful dishes of Italy. A Milanese chef might be able to get along without it, but a Neapolitan would be lost indeed without his *pommaruola* (dialectal for *pomodoro*, "apple of gold," a term that replaced the earlier *pomo d'amore*, "apple of love").

The herbs which go into the Italian cuisine are far more numerous than their American counterparts. Sage is little used, but marjoram, thyme, bay leaf, origan, and particularly basil (or *basilico*) are the order of the day. Rosemary *(rosmarino)* is spread over most Italian roasts, and does marvels for a leg of lamb or a pork roast. *Basilico*, fresh and dried, is the almost indispensable component of a good southern spaghetti sauce. In addition, Italian cooks are more generous with spices than their American counterparts. The hot red pepper that burns the tongue and causes one to drink quarts of wine is characteristic of the south, but even in the butter-civilization of the north, dishes are apt to be more spicy and flavorful than is the custom in America.

The wealth and variety of Italian cheeses are proverbial. No land, with the possible exception of France, can vie with Italy for number and quality of cheese products. The *fontina* of Piedmont, the *stracchino* ("little tired cheese") of Milan, the Parmesan and Reggiano of Emilia, the Gorgonzola and Bel Paese of the north, the Pecorino, or sheep's cheese of Rome—all are only a preparation for the greater abundance that meets us as we go southward. Central and southern Italy provide fresh cheeses: *ricotta, provola, mozzarella,* as well as sharp, pungent cheeses like *provolone, incanestrato* and *caciocavallo* ("horse-cheese," though the origin of this strange name is unknown). A peculiar Italian custom is the use of a cheese-name to designate one who is inept at a game: *mozzarella* and *provola* are typical card-game terms to characterize one's partner when he makes a blunder, for which the term *mozzarellata* has been coined. *Ricotta,* which looks like cottage or cream cheese, is the product of repeated slow boiling, as the name implies ("recooked"), of sweet milk from which the butter fat has been extracted. In addition to its uses as a stuffing for macaroni products, *ricotta* may be eaten plain, salted, with sugar and cinnamon, or it may be spread on bread like butter, particularly at breakfast, and then perhaps be dunked into a cup of black coffee.

Nature's own accompaniment for Italian cheeses is fresh fruit. The two are eaten not successively, but together, by most Italians. One curious saying that reflects this custom, as well as Italy's share-cropping agricultural system, is *"Al contadino non lo far sapere—quanto sia buono il cacio con le pere"*—"Don't let the share-cropper know how good is cheese with pears," else he will gyp you out of your share of the two products.

Italian fruit is savory and abundant, but not too different from that with which California has blessed us. It is the way fruit is eaten that differs. Fruit (with or without cheese) generally constitutes the Italian dessert, and is definitely a part of the meal. A fruitless dinner table is hard to find, even in the most modest home or inn.

Pastry, on the other hand, is more frequently reserved for festive occasions, or taken in the afternoon, with black coffee, often at an outdoor café table. Italian *pasticceria,* however, has considerable range. There are pies and cakes and tarts, all quite different from the American varieties. There are smaller pastries, similar in structure to French pastry, which include the Sicilian *cannoli* (crisp tubes filled with a rich custard); *sfogliatelle* (layer pastries, faintly reminiscent of a German *Apfelstrudel*); buns and cookies of every description; *torrone,* or nougat, a holiday delicacy of honey, nuts, almonds and other ingredients baked into a hard mass; local specialties like the *panforte* ("strong bread") of Siena; the *panettone* of Milan; the *zuppa inglese* of Rome; and the *cassata* of Sicily.

Then there are ice creams and ices, all of which had their origin in Italy, whence they spread to the rest of the world. *Aphrogala* (Greek for "foam-milk") was the name bestowed by the Swiss upon the new Italian invention when it first reached them some centuries ago. That which Americans call *spumoni* is more often known by the name of *cassata* in Italy (not to be confused with the Sicilian *cassata*, which is a rich, gooey cake). *Granita* is the Italian ice. Frozen custard was eaten in Italy long before it appeared in America, under the exotic name of "Chantilly cream."

As for Italian beverages, the most typical by far is wine, of which Italy, in common with other southern European countries, has an abundance. Italian wines range from the Barolo, Barbera and Freisa of Piedmont, the Valpolicella of Venetia, the Lambrusco of Emilia, the Chianti of Tuscany, the Orvieto of Umbria, the Frascati and Grottaferrata of Rome, the Capri and Lacrima Christi of Naples, through a variety of little-known but delicious brands of southern Italy, to the Misilmeri and Marsala of Sicily and the Malvasia of Sardinia. *Spumanti,* or sparkling wines, rival French champagne and are produced in the north; heavy, sweet wines come from the south and the islands. Italians are regular but temperate wine-drinkers. The fact that they regard wine as a food rather than an intoxicant is indicated by their giving it, in small, watered doses, to their children from the time the latter begin to partake of solid food. Very, very seldom does an Italian go on a wine-jag.

Italians shrink from strong liquor. In the place of the American cocktail they prefer an aperitif of vermouth, with a dash of bitters and a piece of lemon peel, often diluted with seltzer. (The white vermouth of Turin is a drink to remember.) Gin and whiskey are seldom used in Italy, save by people who wish to ape the Anglo-Saxons. On the other hand, there is an entire series of Italian after-dinner cocktails, including Strega, Fiori Alpini and Anisetta. There is also a potent beverage, called *grappa,* produced by distilling the lees of grapes that have been pressed for wine, which lower-class Italians use when they feel in need of a real lift. But in general, Italian social custom frowns upon drunkenness, or even over-indulgence, and Italy is accordingly one of the most temperate countries in the world.

Reference must be made at this point to Italian coffee, which is roasted black, not brown, is drunk either straight or with milk in 50-50 proportions in the morning, and is served in demitasse form with no milk at the end of an Italian meal. In cafés it is prepared by a complicated machine-urn and called *espresso.* It is quite easy to become accustomed to Italian black coffee after dinner; not quite so easy to get the habit of Italian *caffè e latte* for breakfast.

Breakfast, however, is a meal of which the Italian, like the Frenchman, approves only half-heartedly. The French and Italian words which correspond most closely to "breakfast" are *déjeuner* and *colazione,* but they serve also for "lunch." *Petit déjeuner* ("little lunch") and *prima colazione* ("first lunch") are really in the nature of afterthoughts, or concessions to international usage. Many Italians take nothing but black coffee on rising, and wait until noon to begin to eat. Others add a slice of bread, with or without ricotta or butter, or a brioche. A few gourmets add fresh fruit or preserves. It is next to impossible to get an American breakfast of the ham-and-eggs type, but when and if you get it, you will be amazed at the new gustatory sensation that you experience, because the Italian cook will fry prosciutto in butter over a very slow fire, then add the eggs so that they encase the prosciutto as they gently harden.

Such is the general gastronomic picture of Italy, but anyone thinking that it is exact, complete, or exhaustive is certainly misled. To criticize the author, the translator or this writer for having failed to include dishes which may have come to the reader's notice is useless. No living man or woman is acquainted with all the dishes of a variegated country like Italy, or, for that matter, of a far more standardized country like the United States. All that Mrs. Boni, Mrs. La Rosa or I can claim to have done is to have given a cross-section of Italian dishes that range all the way from the Alps to Sicily without, however, covering completely all the territory traversed.

> "Full many a gem of purest ray serene
> The dark unfathomed caves of ocean bear,"

said a great English poet. And we might continue, with a reverently circumspect paraphrase:

> "Full many a dish is born to blush unseen,
> And waste its savor on the village air."

MARIO A. PEI

New York
April, 1950

THE TALISMAN

Italian Cook Book

WEIGHTS AND MEASURES

(All measurements are level and standard)

3 teaspoons	equal	1 tablespoon
2 teaspoons		1 dessert spoon
1 tablespoon		½ fluid ounce
4 tablespoons		¼ cup
8 tablespoons		1 gill
2 cups		1 pint
4 cups		1 quart
4 quarts		1 gallon
16 ounces		1 pound
1 tablespoon butter		1 ounce
2 cups butter		1 pound
4 cups flour		1 pound
2 cups granulated sugar		1 pound
2⅔ cups brown sugar		1 pound
3½ cups confectioners' sugar		1 pound
1 square baking chocolate		1 ounce
7 - 8 egg whites		1 cup

1. Antipasto

General Antipasto

ARTICHOKE HEARTS IN OLIVE OIL

24 small artichokes	6 peppercorns
½ cup lemon juice	¼ lemon, cut into very thin slices
3 cups dry white wine	olive oil
2 tablespoons wine vinegar	3 bay leaves
3 bay leaves	4 peppercorns
3 cloves	

Remove outer leaves and tops of artichokes. Cut off excess stalk. Dip into lemon juice. Mix together wine, vinegar, bay leaves, cloves, peppercorns and lemon slices, add artichokes and simmer 10 minutes (time may vary a little depending on tenderness of artichokes). Drain thoroughly and place in large jar. Cover with olive oil, bay leaves and peppercorns and let stand in jar 3 days. Add more oil if needed and cover jars. Store in cool place. Will keep very well for a long time.

CANTALOUPE AND PROSCIUTTO

1 small cantaloupe	¼ pound prosciutto, sliced thin

Ice melon, cut into 8 small wedges and remove seeds. Serve with prosciutto. Serves 4.

CAPONATINA SICILIAN STYLE

4 medium eggplants	12 green olives, pitted and cut into pieces
1½ cups olive oil	1 tablespoon pine nuts
4 onions, sliced	½ cup wine vinegar
½ cup tomato sauce	¼ cup sugar
4 stalks celery, diced	¾ teaspoon salt
½ cup capers	½ teaspoon pepper

Peel and dice eggplants and fry in 1 cup hot olive oil. Remove fried eggplant from skillet, add remaining oil and onions and brown gently. Add tomato sauce and celery and cook until celery is tender, adding a little water, if necessary. Add capers, olives, pine nuts and fried eggplant. Heat vinegar in small saucepan, dissolve sugar in vinegar and pour over eggplant. Add salt and pepper and simmer 20 minutes, stirring frequently. Cool before serving. This caponatina will keep a long time in refrigerator.

3

CHICKEN LIVER CANAPE

4 chicken livers	1/8 teaspoon pepper
2 teaspoons chopped	1/2 tablespoon flour
parsley	2 tablespoons stock or water
2 tablespoons butter	2 teaspoons lemon juice
2 anchovy filets, chopped	6 slices bread, cut into triangles
dash of salt	and fried in butter

Chop livers very fine, mix with parsley and fry in butter for 5 minutes. Add chopped anchovies, salt and pepper and sprinkle with flour. Add stock or water and bring to a boil, stirring constantly. Remove from fire, add lemon juice, spread on bread triangles and serve immediately. Serves 4.

CROSTINI OF MOZZARELLA AND ANCHOVIES

8 slices white bread,	1/2 pound mozzarella cheese,
rather thin	sliced thin
16 anchovy filets	1/2 cup butter

Cut off crust of bread and cut slices in halves. Place a thin slice of mozzarella and 1 anchovy filet on each of 8 half slices of bread and cover with the other half slices to make 16 half sandwiches. Heat butter in frying pan and fry sandwiches on both sides until golden brown. Serve immediately. Very good as appetizers. Serves 2 or 4.

FIGS AND PROSCIUTTO

4 fresh figs, skinned	1/4 pound prosciutto, sliced thin

Chill figs and serve with prosciutto. Serves 2.

FRIED BREAD WITH ANCHOVIES

16 slices of bread from a long	1/2 teaspoon pepper
French loaf, 1/2 inch thick	1/2 cup flour
1/2 pound mozzarella cheese,	2 eggs, lightly beaten
sliced thin	1 cup olive oil
8 anchovy filets	

Place a slice of mozzarella and 1 filet of anchovy on each of 8 slices of bread. Sprinkle with pepper and cover with another slice of bread. Dip into plain cold water, roll in flour, dip into beaten egg and fry in olive oil until golden brown on each side. Serve immediately. Serves 2 or 4.

FRIED MOZZARELLA

¾ pound mozzarella
½ cup flour
2 eggs, lightly beaten with

¼ teaspoon salt
1 cup bread crumbs
1 cup olive oil

Cut mozzarella into 4-inch squares, 2 inches thick. Roll in flour, dip into egg, roll in bread crumbs, again into egg and again in bread crumbs. Fry in hot oil just long enough for the bread crumbs to turn golden in color. Serve immediately. Serves 4.

ICED WINTER MELON WITH WINE

1 medium winter melon

1 cup wine, port, sherry or Marsala

Cut a triangle in melon and remove seeds with spoon. Fill with wine, replace triangle and refrigerate 3 hours, taking care that none of the wine spills out. Serves 4.

ITALIAN ANTIPASTO*

4 thin slices Italian salami
4 thin slices prosciutto
4 anchovy filets
2 celery hearts, cut in halves lengthwise
1 small can Italian tuna fish
1 small can imported Italian antipasto (optional)

8 large green olives
2 teaspoons capers
4 artichoke hearts in oil
1 small can pimentos
4 slices tomato
4 vinegar peppers
8 black ripe olives

Use a large oval platter. Place tuna fish and imported antipasto in center of dish and arrange all the other ingredients around, making as pretty a pattern as you can. Serve with crusty Italian bread and butter. Serves 4.

NEAPOLITAN APPETIZERS

4 thin slices bread
8 2 x 4-inch slices mozzarella cheese, 1 inch thick
8 anchovy filets

⅛ teaspoon pepper
¼ cup butter, or 4 tablespoons olive oil
½ teaspoon oregano

Toast bread on one side and cut slices in two. Place 1 slice mozzarella, 1 anchovy filet and a little oregano on toasted side of 4 half slices, sprinkle with a little pepper, and cover with other half slices, toasted side in. Melt butter or heat oil and place little sandwiches in it, frying gently about 4 minutes on each side, or until cheese is melted. Serve immediately. Serves 4.

PIQUANT APPETIZERS

1/4 cup butter
1 tablespoon flour
1 1/2 cups stock or bouillon
8 anchovy filets, chopped
2 tablespoons capers, minced

2 tablespoons minced parsley
1/4 teaspoon pepper
8 thin slices bread
1/2 cup butter

Melt the 1/4 cup butter, blend in flour, add stock, mixing thoroughly, and cook over moderate flame until thick. Add anchovies, capers, parsley and pepper and mix well. Fry bread in 1/2 cup butter, cut slices in half, spread with anchovy mixture and serve. Serves 6 or 8.

PORK LIVER CANAPE

1/2 pound chopped pork liver
1/2 clove garlic, chopped
4 anchovy filets, chopped
2 vinegar peppers, chopped
1 tablespoon olive oil

1/4 teaspoon salt
1/8 teaspoon pepper
1/2 teaspoon marjoram
2 tablespoons water
4 slices bread, cut into triangles
   and fried in butter

Place liver, garlic, anchovies, peppers and olive oil in frying pan and fry 5 minutes. Add marjoram, salt and pepper and continue cooking 5 minutes more or until brown. Add water and cook 5 minutes longer. Remove from fire and spread liver mixture on fried bread triangles. Serves 4.

PROSCIUTTO AND HONEY

1 small jar honey
8 thin slices Italian bread,
   long loaf

8 slices prosciutto (about
   1/4 pound)

Spread each slice of bread lightly with honey and add 1 slice prosciutto. Serves 4.

STUFFED TOMATOES

4 large firm tomatoes
2 hard boiled eggs, diced fine
1 small can tuna fish, grated
1/4 teaspoon pepper

1 teaspoon capers
1 teaspoon chopped parsley
2 tablespoons mayonnaise

Cut tops off tomatoes and remove seeds and liquid. Mix together eggs, tuna, pepper, capers, parsley and mayonnaise. Fill tomatoes with mixture, chill and serve. Serves 4.

TUNNIED VEAL

2 pounds leg of veal without bones	¼ pound Italian tuna fish in olive oil
2 salted anchovies	2 anchovies
¼ onion	2 teaspoons lemon juice
2 cloves	½ teaspoon capers in vinegar
1 bay leaf	¼ to ½ cup olive oil (amount
1 carrot	varies according to oil and
1 stalk celery	liquid contained in other in-
2 sprigs parsley	gredients
1 teaspoon salt	

Remove fat and tendons from veal. Clean 2 salted anchovies, removing heads, tails and backbones, split them and cut into 8 pieces each. Lard the veal with anchovy pieces, and tie meat to hold it in shape. Place enough water to cover meat in large pot, add ¼ onion, into which 2 cloves have been stuck, bay leaf, carrot, celery, parsley and salt and bring water to boiling point. Add meat, cover and cook over low flame 1½ hours.

When veal is done, remove from pan and dry it. Mix together tuna fish, anchovies, lemon juice, capers and add olive oil a little at a time, mixing and blending well until sauce is smooth and fluid and is sufficient in quantity to cover meat. Let meat stand in this marinade 2 or 3 days. Serve veal cold, sliced thin and with sauce poured over slices. Serves 8.

FISH ANTIPASTO

HERRING SALAD

1 herring	1 small onion, chopped
2 teaspoons olive oil	⅛ teaspoon paprika
1 teaspoon vinegar	

Cut fileted herring into small pieces, place in serving dish and sprinkle with oil, vinegar, chopped onion and paprika. Serves 2.

MUSSELS IN PIQUANT SAUCE

2 pounds mussels, with shells	1½ cups dry white wine
2 tablespoons olive oil	1½ cups vinegar
1 clove garlic	1 tablespoon chopped parsley
5 anchovy filets, chopped	dash cayenne pepper

Open mussels, wash in salt water and drain. Brown garlic in oil, remove from oil and add mussels and anchovies. Keep fire low and add wine and vinegar. Simmer until liquid is half the original quantity.

Add parsley and cayenne pepper. Remove mussels and marinade, place in earthen container and allow to marinate 3 days. Serves 4.

OYSTERS VENETIAN STYLE

8 oysters	dash cayenne pepper
2 teaspoons lemon juice	2 teaspoons caviar

Open oysters but keep both shells. Mix lemon juice, cayenne and caviar and spread thinly over each oyster. Close shell and serve on ice. Serves 2.

OYSTERS TARANTO STYLE

8 oysters	2 teaspoons lemon juice
⅛ teaspoon pepper	2 thin slices smoked salmon, cut into 8 pieces

Open oyster, sprinkle with pepper, lemon juice and cover with slice of salmon. Serve on ice. Serves 2.

SHRIMP AND RICE SALAD

½ cup rice	½ teaspoon salt
2 cups water	2 tablespoons olive oil
¼ teaspoon salt	1 teaspoon vinegar
½ pound shrimps	½ teaspoon prepared mustard
4 cups water	

Bring 2 cups water to boil, add ¼ teaspoon salt and rice and boil 15 minutes. Add ½ teaspoon salt to 4 cups water, bring to boiling point, add shrimps and boil 20 minutes. Drain shrimps, shell and remove vein. Mix together rice, shrimps, olive oil, vinegar and mustard. Chill and serve in little mounds on lettuce leaves. Serves 4.

2. Soups

Meat and Chicken Soups

SOUP ALLA PAVESE

8 thin slices French bread
½ cup butter
1 quart broth or bouillon
4 eggs

⅛ teaspoon salt
2 tablespoons grated Parmesan
   cheese

Melt butter in frying pan and fry bread in it until golden on both sides. Bring broth to boiling point. Place 2 slices bread in each soup dish, top with whole egg and sprinkle ½ tablespoon cheese on each egg. Pour ¼ of the boiling broth into each dish, taking care that the egg does not break. Serves 4.

BAVETTE SOUP GENOESE STYLE

1½ pound package bavette
   (fine noodles)
1 quart beef broth or
   bouillon
2 fresh marjoram leaves

1 egg
2 tablespoons grated Parmesan
   cheese
¼ teaspoon salt
⅛ teaspoon pepper

Bring broth to boiling point and add marjoram leaves. Add bavette and cook 8 minutes. Mix egg with 2 tablespoons broth, Parmesan, salt and pepper and add to soup. Boil 1 minute and serve hot. Serves 4.

BEEF BROTH*

1 pound chuck of beef
1 good marrow bone
1 good sponge bone
3 quarts water
3 stalks celery

1 small onion
2 carrots
3 fresh tomatoes, cut into pieces,
   or ½ medium can tomatoes
1 teaspoon salt

Place meat and bones in cold water with salt and bring to a boil. Remove scum that forms on top of water. Add celery, onion, carrots and tomatoes, cover pan and cook about 1¼ hours, or until meat is tender. Remove meat and use as desired. Strain broth. This should make about 2 quarts beef broth. A little water may be added if broth seems too condensed.

9

BRODETTO ROMAN STYLE

1½ quarts lamb broth
6 egg yolks
2 teaspoons lemon juice
¼ teaspoon salt

¼ teaspoon fresh marjoram, crushed
18 thin slices French bread, toasted
6 teaspoons grated Parmesan cheese

Beat eggs with fork in large soup pan 5 minutes; add lemon juice and salt and beat 1 minute longer. Bring lamb broth to boil and pour slowly over eggs, stirring constantly. Place pan over very low flame and continue to stir constantly. Cook soup very slowly 5 minutes, allowing it to become slightly thickened. Do not allow it to boil. Remove from fire. Place 3 slices toasted bread in each soup dish, pour soup over bread, sprinkle with Parmesan and serve. Serves 6.

CAPPELLETTI (Tortellini) IN BROTH

2 quarts chicken broth
1½ cups flour

2 eggs

On a large pastry board make a well of the flour, break eggs into the well and slowly mix flour and eggs. Work dough with hands 20 minutes, adding more flour if necessary. Sprinkle bread board with more flour and roll dough very thin with rolling pin. Cut rolled dough into circles 2½ inches across.

Make stuffing using following ingredients:

3 slices prosciutto, chopped
¼ pound boiled chicken, chopped
⅛ pound roast pork, chopped
1 egg

¼ teaspoon salt
⅛ teaspoon pepper
⅛ teaspoon nutmeg
2 teaspoons grated Parmesan cheese

Mix all the above ingredients together and place 1 teaspoon of this mixture in center of each disc of dough. Fold over dough, closing in stuffing and pressing edges together with fingers to give the shape of little dunce caps. Bring broth to boiling point, add cappelletti and cook 20 minutes. Serves 6.

CHICKEN BROTH*

1 4-pound chicken, cleaned and left whole
1 teaspoon salt
4 stalks celery

2 medium carrots
3 fresh tomatoes, cut into pieces, or ½ medium can tomatoes
3 quarts water

Place cleaned and washed chicken in cold water, add salt and bring to boil. Remove scum that forms on top of water. Add celery, carrots and tomatoes, cover pan and cook from 1½ hours for a tender chicken to 2½ hours for a tough one. Add a little water if soup seems too condensed. Remove chicken whole and serve as you wish. Strain broth. Makes about 2 quarts chicken broth.

PORK HEART SOUP

2 pounds pork heart, cut into small pieces
⅛ pound salt pork rind, cut into pieces
1 tablespoon leaf lard
¼ teaspoon salt
½ teaspoon pepper
½ cup dry red wine
½ teaspoon rosemary
½ bay leaf, broken into small pieces
2 tablespoons tomato paste, diluted in
2 tablespoons warm water
1 quart water
18 thin slices French bread, toasted

Place pork heart, salt pork rind and leaf lard in soup pan and brown well over brisk fire. Add salt and pepper and, when really dark brown, add wine. Let wine evaporate, then add rosemary, bay leaf and diluted tomato paste. Cook 5 minutes. Add 1 quart water, cover pan and cook over slow fire 1¼ hours. Place 3 slices toast in each soup dish and pour soup over it. Serves 6.

RUSTIC MINESTRONE

½ pound sweet Italian sausage
1 pound spareribs
½ medium cabbage, shredded
2 stalks celery, diced
2 medium onions, sliced
4 white turnips, diced
½ teaspoon salt
½ teaspoon pepper
turnip leaves, shredded
½ head chicory, shredded
2 teaspoons chopped parsley
4 stalks Swiss chard, shredded

Mix all vegetables together, divide in half, and place half the quantity in large soup pan. Add enough water to cover, salt and pepper and place sausage and spareribs on vegetables. Cover with remaining vegetables. Cover pan tightly and cook gently 3 hours. Serve sausage, spareribs and vegetables together. Serves 4.

SOUP WITH TINY MEATBALLS*

¼ pound chopped beef
1 tablespoon grated Roman cheese
½ slice bread, soaked in water and squeezed dry
1 egg yolk
dash salt
1 teaspoon parsley

Mix all ingredients together thoroughly and shape into small meatballs, about the size of marbles.

2 cups beef broth (see index)   2 tablespoons grated Parmesan
¾ cup acini di pepe (fine   cheese
   soup pasta)

Bring broth to a boil, add soup pasta and little meatballs and cook
gently about 7 minutes, or until pasta is cooked to your liking. Serve
with grated cheese. Serves 4 or 6.

STRACCIATELLA SOUP

1 quart beef or chicken broth   1½ tablespoons semolina
   or bouillon   2 tablespoons grated Parmesan
2 eggs   cheese
⅛ teaspoon salt

Combine eggs, salt, semolina, cheese and 3 tablespoons cool broth
in mixing bowl and beat with fork 5 minutes. Bring rest of broth to
boiling point and add egg mixture slowly, stirring constantly. Continue
stirring while soup simmers 5 minutes. Serves 4.

TAGLIOLINE BOLOGNA STYLE

4 cups flour (scant)   1½ quarts chicken or beef
2 eggs   broth

Place 3 cups flour on pastry board, make a well of flour and break
eggs into it. Work eggs and flour together until flour has been absorbed
and continue working dough 20 minutes, adding more flour if necessary.
Cut dough into 2 parts and roll very thin with rolling pin. Let 2 sheets
of dough dry ½ hour on floured towels, and when reasonably dry, fold
over and cut into strips ¼ inch wide. Unravel. Bring broth to boiling
point, add taglioline and cook 5 minutes. Serves 6.

FISH SOUPS

CACCIUCCO LEGHORN STYLE (Number 1)

½ cup olive oil   2 tablespoons tomato paste
1 clove garlic, chopped   3 cups water
1 tiny red pepper   ½ teaspoon salt
1½ pound shrimps, shelled and   1 pound cod filet, cut into pieces
   cut into pieces   ½ pound scallops, cut into pieces
½ pound squid, skinned,   ½ pound halibut, cut into pieces
   cleaned and cut into small   4 slices Italian bread, toasted
   pieces   and rubbed with clove of
½ cup dry white wine   garlic

Place oil, garlic and pepper in soup pan and brown garlic lightly. Add shrimps and squid, cover pan and cook 30 minutes, or until squid is tender. Add wine and continue cooking until it evaporates. Add tomato paste, water and salt and cook 5 minutes. Add other fish and cook 15 minutes longer, adding more water if needed. Place 1 slice toasted garlic bread in each soup dish and pour serving of soup over it. Serves 4.

CACCIUCCO LEGHORN STYLE (Number 2)

½ cup olive oil	½ pound halibut, cut into pieces
½ clove garlic	½ pound filet of haddock
1 teaspoon chopped parsley	½ pound scallops, cut into small
½ teaspoon sage	pieces
1 small lobster, cut into	½ teaspoon grated lemon rind
pieces with shell	2 tablespoons dry white wine
½ pound squid, peeled, cleaned	2 tablespoons Marsala or sherry
and cut into small pieces	wine
½ teaspoon salt	4 slices French or Italian bread,
½ teaspoon pepper	toasted and rubbed with
2 tablespoons tomato purée	garlic
½ pound cod filet	

Place olive oil, garlic, parsley and sage in large soup pan and brown lightly. Add lobster, squid, salt and pepper and cook 15 minutes. Add tomato purée and other fish and cook 20 minutes, adding ½ cup water if needed. Add lemon rind, wine and Marsala or sherry and cook 1 minute longer. Place 1 slice toasted garlic bread in each soup dish and pour serving of soup over it. Serves 4.

CLAM SOUP

40 Little Neck clams	1 tablespoon tomato paste
½ cup olive oil	½ cup warm water
1 clove garlic	½ teaspoon salt
3 anchovy filets, chopped	½ teaspoon pepper
1 tablespoon chopped parsley	¼ teaspoon oregano
½ cup dry red wine	8 thin slices Italian bread,
	fried in olive oil

Wash clams and scrub shells well with vegetable brush. Place oil in large saucepan, add garlic, brown and remove. Add anchovies, parsley and wine to oil and cook 5 minutes. Add tomato paste, water, salt and pepper and cook 3 or 4 minutes. Add clams, cover pan and cook no more than 5 minutes, or until all the shells are open. Add oregano and cook 2 minutes longer. Place 2 slices fried bread in each soup dish, pour over them serving of clams and juice. Serves 4.

CREAM OF CLAM SOUP

40 Little Neck clams	4 cups stock or bouillon
1 tablespoon olive oil	1 tablespoon flour
¼ pound mushrooms, sliced thin	3 egg yolks
1 tablespoon butter	¼ cup light cream
3 slices bread, cut into small	2 tablespoons butter, melted
squares	¼ teaspoon salt
¼ cup butter	¼ teaspoon pepper

Wash clams well and place them in frying pan with olive oil. Cover pan and heat clams until they are open. Remove clams from shells, strain juice, keep warm and save. Cook mushrooms with butter 5 minutes and add clams. Fry bread squares in butter. Bring stock to boil, blend in flour and cook until slightly thick. Mix together egg yolks, cream, melted butter, salt and pepper and add to stock, stirring well. Add clams, clam broth and mushrooms and pour over fried bread squares to serve. Serves 4.

CREAM OF LITTLE NECK CLAM SOUP

2 dozen Little Neck clams	2 tablespoons chicken stock
with shells	2 slices white bread, diced and
1 tablespoon olive oil	fried in butter
4½ cups chicken stock	3 egg yolks
1 tablespoon potato flour	2 tablespoons heavy cream
2 tablespoons cold water	2 tablespoons butter, melted
¼ pound mushrooms,	salt to taste (will depend on
sliced thin	saltiness of stock)
1 tablespoon butter	

Scrub clams well and place in skillet with oil. Cover pan and keep over high flame until all clams are open. Remove clams from shells and cut into 2 or 3 pieces each. Set aside until later. Strain clam juice and save.

Bring chicken stock to a boil. Blend potato flour and water, add to chicken stock slowly and continue cooking until slightly thickened, stirring constantly. Add clams and clam juice and keep hot. Cook mushrooms in 1 tablespoon butter and 2 tablespoons stock 3 or 4 minutes and add to soup. Prepare bread. Mix together egg yolks, cream and melted butter and pour into soup tureen. Pour hot soup over this mixture, stirring constantly, salting to taste. Place bread croutons on top and serve. Serves 4.

FISH BRODETTO ANCONA STYLE

2 pounds mixed fish in season (sole, mullet, mackerel, whiting, dogfish or porgy)
½ dozen Little Neck clams, shelled, with juice
1 small eel, cut into pieces (optional)
2 small squid, skinned, cleaned and cut into small pieces (optional)
½ cup olive oil
1 large onion, sliced thin
½ clove garlic
1 tablespoon chopped parsley
1 small can peeled tomatoes, cut into pieces
2 tablespoons tomato sauce
¾ teaspoon salt
½ teaspoon pepper
small dash cayenne pepper (optional)
1 teaspoon wine vinegar
4 slices Italian bread, 1½ inches thick, toasted

Clean fish and cut into pieces. (This dish should be cooked in an earthen pan, but if this is not available an ordinary soup pan will do.) Brown onion and garlic in olive oil, add parsley, tomatoes, tomato sauce, salt, pepper and cayenne and cook 3 minutes. Add fish and bring to boiling point. Add vinegar and cook, without cover, 20 minutes, adding a little warm water, if more liquid is desired. Place 1 slice toasted bread in each soup dish and pour soup over it. Serves 4.

FISH BRODETTO RIMINI STYLE

2½ pounds mixed fish (sole, mullet, mackerel, whiting, dogfish, etc. with heads)
2 tablespoons olive oil
1 large onion, sliced
½ can peeled tomatoes
1 tablespoon chopped parsley
½ teaspoon salt
½ teaspoon pepper
½ teaspoon wine vinegar
1½ quarts water

Cut off fish heads and wash. Cut fish into pieces and set aside until later. Brown onion in olive oil, add tomatoes and cook 5 minutes. Add parsley, fish heads, salt, pepper, vinegar and water, cover pot and simmer 35 minutes. Strain well and save broth.

To prepare fish use the following ingredients:

3 tablespoons olive oil
1 large onion, chopped
3 tablespoons tomato sauce
1 tablespoon chopped parsley
½ teaspoon salt
½ teaspoon pepper
½ teaspoon wine vinegar
8 thin slices Italian whole wheat bread, toasted

Brown onion in olive oil in skillet. Add tomato sauce and cook 3 minutes. Add parsley, salt, pepper, vinegar and fish pieces and cook 20 minutes, or until fish is well cooked, shaking pan often to prevent fish from sticking to skillet. Place toasted bread slices in deep serving dish and pour the fish broth over them. Serve cooked fish and broth at the same time but in separate serving dishes. Serves 4.

FISH SOUP ROMAN STYLE

8 Little Neck clams,
  with juice
4 oysters, cut into pieces,
  with juice
½ cup olive oil
1 clove garlic
1 tablespoon chopped
  parsley
4 anchovy filets, cut into pieces
3 seeds hot pepper, or
1 pinch cayenne pepper
1 cup dry red wine

1 cup canned tomatoes
½ pound cod filet, cut into
  large pieces
1 lobster tail, cut into pieces
1 small lobster, washed and
  cut into pieces with shell
½ pound halibut, cut into pieces
½ pound filet of sole, cut into pieces
½ teaspoon salt
4 slices French or Italian
  bread, toasted

Place clams and oysters in pan and heat until shells open. Cut oysters into pieces and strain juice of oysters and clams, reserving juice. Place olive oil and garlic in large soup pan, add parsley, anchovies and pepper and brown slowly, stirring well. Add wine and cook until it evaporates. Add tomatoes and cook 5 minutes. Add all the fish, clams, oysters, lobster and oyster and clam juice. Add salt and enough water to cover fish and cook 30 minutes, adding more water if necessary, as soup should not be too condensed. Place 1 slice toasted bread in each soup dish and pour serving of soup over it. Serves 4.

MOCK FISH SOUP

½ cup olive oil
2 cloves garlic
¼ pound anchovies
1 tablespoon chopped parsley
2 tablespoons tomato paste

5 cups stock or water
8 slices bread, soaked in water
  and squeezed dry
¼ teaspoon salt
¼ teaspoon pepper

Heat olive oil, add garlic, brown and remove. Wash, bone and chop anchovies and add to the oil. Add parsley, tomato paste and stock or water and boil gently 15 minutes. Pass soaked bread through a sieve and add to the liquid, mixing very well. Boil 3 or 4 minutes longer and serve on toasted bread in soup dish. Serves 4.

MUSSEL SOUP

3 dozen mussels with shells
½ cup olive oil
2 cloves garlic
2 tablespoons tomato sauce
½ teaspoon salt

1 tiny piece red pepper
  (optional)
8 slices long Italian bread,
  1 inch thick
½ teaspoon oregano

Scrub mussels well. Place oil in large pan, add 1 clove garlic and brown. Add tomato sauce, pepper, salt and mussels and cook over

very high flame until all mussels are open. Add oregano and cook 1
minute longer. Toast bread slices and, while hot, rub with 1 clove
garlic. Place 2 slices toast on each plate, pour mussels over toast and
serve. Serves 4.

SALTED CODFISH (Baccalà) SOUP

1½ pounds baccalà,† soaked	1 small can tomatoes
½ cup olive oil	½ cup dry white wine
2 small onions, sliced	3 medium potatoes, sliced
2 cloves garlic	(not too thin)
1 stalk celery, diced	3 cups water
1 bay leaf	½ teaspoon pepper
½ teaspoon thyme	4 slices Italian bread, toasted
1 teaspoon chopped parsley	and rubbed with garlic

If soaked baccalà is not available at market, prepare it by placing
in large pan full of water and soak 12 hours, changing water once. Cut
soaked baccalà into pieces 4 inches square.

Place oil, onion and garlic in large pan and brown gently. Add
celery, bay leaf, thyme and parsley and continue browning. Add tomatoes and cook 5 minutes. Add wine, potatoes and water. Cook 10 minutes. Add baccalà, lower flame, cover pan and cook slowly 40 minutes, or
until potatoes and baccalà are done. Add pepper. Taste for salting
as baccalà is already salty. Pour soup over toasted garlic bread in soup
dishes. Serves 4.

SHRIMP SOUP

1 small onion, sliced	3 tablespoons stock
1 small carrot, chopped	½ cup dry red wine
¼ teaspoon thyme	3 tablespoons rice
1 bay leaf	3 cups stock
1 teaspoon chopped parsley	2 cups stock
1½ tablespoons butter	1 small dash cayenne pepper
1½ pounds small shrimps	1 tablespoon butter

Place onion, carrot, thyme, bay leaf, parsley and butter in skillet and
brown gently. Add shrimps which have been shelled and cleaned, 3
tablespoons stock and cook 15 minutes. Add wine, cover skillet and
cook 15 minutes longer. Remove from fire.

Cook rice in boiling stock 20 minutes until very well done. Pass
rice through sieve. Remove shrimps from gravy and run gravy through
sieve. Mix together shrimps, gravy and strained rice, add 2 cups stock,
dash of cayenne and butter, heat well and serve. Serves 4.

†If soaked baccalà is not available, soak in water 24 hours, changing water every 8 hours.

THRIFTY FISH SOUP

2 pounds whiting, haddock, mullet or other fish in season	1 stalk celery
	1 bay leaf
	1 teaspoon salt
1 medium onion	2½ quarts water

Wash fish well and place in soup pan with onion, celery, bay leaf, salt and water and boil gently 30 minutes. Drain fish and save fish broth. Skin and bone fish and serve with any sauce you prefer, or sprinkle with oil and lemon juice. (A suggested sauce is aromatic sauce, see index).

For the soup use the following ingredients:

2 tablespoons olive oil	½ pound linguine (flat type spaghetti), cut into short pieces
1 clove garlic	
1½ tablespoons tomato sauce	
4 cups leftover fish stock	1 teaspoon anchovy paste
	1 tablespoon chopped parsley

Brown garlic in hot olive oil and remove. Add tomato sauce to oil and cook 2 minutes. Add fish stock and boil 5 minutes. Add linguine and cook 10 minutes, or until tender. Add anchovy paste and parsley and serve. Serves 4.

VEGETABLE SOUPS

BEANS AND MACARONI VENETIAN STYLE

1 cup red beans	½ teaspoon salt
2 tablespoons olive oil	½ teaspoon pepper
1 large onion, chopped	6 cups water
⅛ teaspoon cinnamon	1½ cups medium noodles, cut into short pieces
½ pound fresh pork rind	
1 ham bone	2 tablespoons grated Parmesan cheese
⅛ pound salt pork, chopped	

Choose a soup pot with a good cover. Place all ingredients except noodles and grated cheese in soup pan, cover tightly and boil gently 2½ hours, or until the beans are tender. Add noodles and cook 8 minutes longer. Sprinkle with cheese and serve. Serves 4.

BEAN SOUP ROMAN STYLE

1 tablespoon leaf lard	2 fresh tomatoes, peeled and cut into pieces
⅛ pound salt pork, chopped fine	
	1 teaspoon salt
1 medium onion, chopped fine	½ teaspoon pepper
	1 quart warm water
1 clove garlic, chopped fine	2 cups cooked white beans
1 stalk celery, chopped fine	1 cup elbow macaroni
	2 tablespoons grated Roman cheese

Melt lard in saucepan, add chopped salt pork, onion, garlic, celery and brown well. Add tomatoes, salt, pepper, warm water and beans. Cook 5 minutes. Add elbow macaroni and cook 8 minutes longer. Sprinkle with Roman cheese and serve. Serves 6.

BROCCOLI AND MACARONI SOUP

⅛ pound salt pork, chopped fine
1 tablespoon olive oil
½ clove garlic
1 tablespoon tomato paste, diluted in
3 cups water

¼ teaspoon salt
¼ teaspoon pepper
½ bunch broccoli flowerlets, cleaned and washed
2 cups short macaroni
2 tablespoons grated Roman cheese

Place oil, salt pork and garlic in soup pan and brown. Add tomato paste, diluted in water, salt and pepper and bring to boiling point. Add broccoli, cover pan and cook 5 minutes. Add macaroni and continue cooking 10 minutes. Sprinkle with grated Roman cheese and serve. Makes 4 large or 6 medium servings.

CECI SOUP ROMAN STYLE

½ cup olive oil
½ teaspoon rosemary
1 clove garlic, chopped fine
3 anchovy filets, chopped
1 tablespoon tomato paste, diluted in

4 tablespoons water
1 can ceci (garbanzo beans or chick peas)
¼ teaspoon salt
1 cup elbow macaroni
½ teaspoon pepper

Place oil, rosemary, garlic and anchovies in soup pan and brown well. Add diluted tomato paste and cook over slow fire 20 minutes. Add ceci beans with liquid and add another can full of water. Add salt and bring to boiling point. Add elbow macaroni and cook 8 minutes longer or until macaroni is tender. Add pepper and serve. Serves 4.

MINESTRONE GENOESE STYLE

GARLIC PASTE

3 cloves garlic, chopped
2 tablespoons minced basil leaves
¼ teaspoon salt

2 tablespoons grated Parmesan cheese
2 tablespoons olive oil
1 tablespoon butter

Mix garlic and basil together with salt and chop very fine. Add cheese and olive oil and mix to a paste. When ready to add to soup, add butter and mix in well.

Make soup, using following ingredients:

¼ small cabbage, shredded	1 cup green beans, cut into
2 small potatoes, diced	small pieces
2 zucchini, diced	2 cups cooked dried beans
4 tablespoons shelled	1 stalk celery, diced
fresh peas	2 quarts water

Bring water to a boil and add all the vegetables. Simmer gently 1 hour, then add garlic paste. Mix paste into soup well and cook 5 minutes. Serves 4.

MINESTRONE MILAN STYLE

1 teaspoon olive oil	3 stalks celery, chopped
⅛ pound salt pork, chopped	2 carrots, sliced
½ clove garlic, chopped	2 potatoes, diced
½ medium-sized onion,	2 cups cooked pea beans
chopped	¼ small cabbage, shredded
1 teaspoon chopped	2 zucchini, diced
parsley	1 cup shelled peas
1 teaspoon chopped sage	1½ quarts water or stock
1 teaspoon salt	1 cup elbow macaroni
½ teaspoon pepper	4 tablespoons grated Roman
1 tablespoon tomato paste	cheese

Place olive oil in a large soup pan, add salt pork, garlic, onion, parsley, sage, salt and pepper and brown a little. Add tomato paste diluted in 1 cup water. Cook 5 minutes. Add all vegetables and 1½ quarts water or stock and cook slowly 45 minutes. Add elbow macaroni and cook 10 minutes longer. Sprinkle soup with grated cheese. Serves 6.

MINESTRONE TUSCAN STYLE

½ pound dry white beans	1 zucchini, diced
2 tablespoons olive oil	1 teaspoon chopped parsley
1 clove garlic, chopped fine	1 teaspoon salt
1 small onion, chopped fine	½ teaspoon pepper
1 stalk celery, chopped	1 clove
1 teaspoon rosemary	12 slices French bread,
1 tablespoon tomato paste	toasted
(diluted)	2 tablespoons grated
1 very small cabbage,	Roman cheese
shredded	

Soak beans overnight; then, boil in 3 quarts water 1 hour or until tender. While beans are cooking, place oil, garlic, onion, celery and rosemary in soup pan and brown lightly. Add tomato paste diluted in 2 tablespoons warm water and cook 5 minutes. To this add cabbage, zucchini, parsley, clove, salt, pepper and beans in their liquid. Cook slowly 20 minutes. Place 2 slices toasted bread in each soup dish, add soup and sprinkle with cheese. Serves 6.

MUSHROOM SOUP

1 tablespoon butter	2 cups stock or bouillon
1 teaspoon olive oil	4 eggs
1 medium-sized onion, sliced	1 teaspoon chopped parsley
2 cloves garlic	2 tablespoons grated Parmesan cheese
1 tablespoon tomato paste (diluted)	8 slices French bread, fried in butter
1 pound mushrooms, washed and sliced thin	

Place butter and olive oil in soup pan, add onion and garlic, brown and remove garlic. Add tomato paste, diluted in 1 tablespoon water, and mushrooms and cook 5 minutes. Add stock or bouillon and boil 5 minutes. In mixing bowl beat eggs lightly and add cheese and parsley. Remove soup from fire, add egg mixture and let stand 2 minutes, stirring in egg mixture well. Serve on fried bread. Serves 4.

ONION AND EGG SOUP

1/4 pound butter	4 egg yolks
2 large onions, sliced	6 tablespoons grated Parmesan cheese
2 tablespoons flour	
1 1/2 quarts stock or water	8 slices French bread, toasted
1/2 teaspoon salt	

Melt butter in soup pan, add onion and brown slowly. Add flour and blend well. Add hot stock or water and salt, cover pan and simmer 30 minutes. Beat egg yolks lightly in mixing bowl and add cheese. Remove soup from fire, add egg mixture, stirring well. Serve on toasted bread. Serves 4.

PEAS AND RICE VENETIAN STYLE

3 pounds fresh peas	1 small onion, chopped
3/4 pound rice	2 1/2 cups stock or bouillon
2 tablespoons olive oil	1/4 teaspoon salt
1/2 cup butter	1/8 teaspoon pepper
1 slice bacon, cut into small pieces	2 tablespoons grated Parmesan cheese

Shell peas and wash. Place olive oil, butter, bacon and onion in soup pan and brown lightly. When brown, add peas, cook 5 minutes and add stock. When boiling, add rice and cook about 12 minutes, or until rice is tender. Add salt, pepper and cheese. This makes a very thick soup. Serves 4.

POTATO AND RICE SOUP

½ tablespoon tomato paste diluted in 6 cups water	4 medium potatoes, pared and diced
2 slices bacon, chopped	1 cup rice
½ clove garlic, chopped	½ teaspoon salt
1 teaspoon minced parsley	½ teaspoon pepper

Place bacon, garlic and parsley in soup pan and brown well. Add tomato paste, diluted in water, salt and pepper and bring to boiling point. When water is boiling rapidly, add potatoes and rice and cook 20 minutes. Sprinkle with grated Parmesan cheese, if desired, and serve hot. Serves 4.

POTATO SOUP ITALIAN STYLE

4 large potatoes (about 2 pounds)	½ clove garlic
3 tablespoons butter	2 carrots, diced
1 small onion	1 cup tomato sauce
2 stalks celery, diced	½ teaspoon salt
1 tablespoon chopped parsley	¼ teaspoon pepper
	4 cups warm water
	3 tablespoons grated Parmesan cheese

Boil potatoes until thoroughly cooked, peel and put through sieve. While potatoes are cooking, melt butter in soup pan, add onion, celery, parsley, garlic and carrot and brown gently. Remove garlic, add tomato sauce, salt, pepper, warm water and strained potatoes and simmer 15 minutes. Serve with Parmesan cheese. Serves 4.

RICE AND BEANS ABRUZZI STYLE

2 cups cooked white beans	⅛ teaspoon chopped, red, hot pepper
½ cup rice	1 teaspoon salt
2 tablespoons olive oil	6 cups water
1 medium onion, chopped	2 tablespoons grated Roman cheese
1 stalk celery, cut in small pieces	
2 large fresh tomatoes, peeled and cut in pieces	

Heat oil in soup pan, add onion and celery and brown. Add

tomatoes, red pepper, salt, beans and water and bring to boiling point. Add rice and continue cooking 20 minutes. Sprinkle with Roman cheese and serve. Serves 4.

RICE AND POTATOES HOME STYLE

2 medium potatoes, diced	1 tablespoon chopped parsley
½ cup rice	4 cups warm water
1 tablespoon leaf lard	1 tablespoon tomato paste
1 small onion, sliced	½ teaspoon salt
2 slices prosciutto or	½ teaspoon pepper
lean bacon	3 tablespoons grated Roman
½ clove garlic	cheese

Melt lard, add onion, prosciutto, garlic and parsley and brown gently. Remove garlic, add warm water and tomato paste and bring to a boil. Add potatoes, rice, salt and pepper and cook about 12 minutes, or until rice and potatoes are cooked. Serve with grated cheese. Serves 4.

VEGETABLE SOUP

6 cups water	1 clove
4 small potatoes, cubed	2 tablespoons split green peas
2 medium onions, sliced	½ teaspoon salt
2 carrots, diced	½ cup butter
3 stalks celery, cut in	4 teaspoons grated Parmesan
small pieces	cheese
3 large tomatoes, skinned	
and cut in pieces	

Combine all the ingredients except the butter and cheese in large soup pan, cover pan and boil gently 1½ hours. Remove from fire, add butter and sprinkle with Parmesan cheese. Serves 4.

ZUCCHINI SOUP

8 small zucchini, diced	1 quart water
1 tablespoon leaf lard	4 eggs, lightly beaten
1 teaspoon olive oil	4 tablespoons grated Parmesan
½ teaspoon salt	cheese
½ teaspoon pepper	1 teaspoon chopped parsley
	½ teaspoon chopped sweet basil

Melt leaf lard in soup pan, add oil, zucchini, salt and pepper and brown lightly. Add water, cover pan and cook 20 minutes. Beat eggs lightly in mixing bowl, add cheese, parsley and basil and blend together well. Remove soup from fire, add egg mixture, stirring it in well, and let stand 3 minutes before serving. Serves 4.

3. *Egg Dishes*

EGG CROQUETTES

4 hard cooked eggs, chopped
1 cup thick cream sauce
  (see index)
1 tablespoon grated
  Parmesan cheese
4 slices prosciutto, shredded

¼ teaspoon salt
⅛ teaspoon pepper
½ cup flour
1 egg, lightly beaten
1 cup fine bread crumbs
2 cups oil or leaf lard

Mix together chopped eggs, cream sauce, Parmesan cheese, prosciutto, salt and pepper and let cool thoroughly. When cool, shape into croquettes, flour, dip into beaten egg and roll in bread crumbs. Fry in hot oil or leaf lard until golden in color. Serve hot. Serves 4.

EGGS AND POTATOES

2 medium-size boiled
  potatoes, sliced
4 thin slices mozzarella
  cheese (½ pound)
4 eggs

½ teaspoon salt
½ teaspoon pepper
4 tablespoons grated
  Parmesan cheese
1 tablespoon butter

Place sliced potatoes in greased shallow baking dish, place mozzarella slices over them and break eggs gently over mozzarella. Sprinkle with salt, pepper and Parmesan cheese, dot with butter and bake in hot oven (400°F.) 20 minutes. Serve immediately. Serves 4.

EGGS AU GRATIN

¼ cup butter
1 tablespoon flour
1¼ cups milk
4 eggs
¼ teaspoon salt
⅛ teaspoon pepper

2 tablespoons grated
  Parmesan cheese
2 tablespoons fine bread
  crumbs
1 tablespoon butter,
  melted

Melt butter, blend in flour and cook lightly 1 minute. Add milk and cook until thickened, sirring constantly. Pour sauce into shallow baking dish, break in eggs and sprinkle with salt, pepper, cheese, crumbs and melted butter. Bake in hot oven (400°F.) 15 minutes, or until eggs are set and cheese melted. Serves 4.

24

EGGS BORGHESE

4 hard cooked eggs	1½ cups milk
2 tablespoons butter	½ teaspoon salt
1 medium onion, sliced	½ teaspoon pepper
1 teaspoon flour	⅛ teaspoon nutmeg

Cut eggs in 4 parts each. Place onion in saucepan with butter and brown gently. Blend in flour, add milk, salt, pepper and nutmeg and cook slowly 20 minutes. Add eggs, simmer 2 minutes and serve. Serves 4.

CREAMED EGGS ON TOAST

8 thin slices toast	⅛ teaspoon nutmeg
2 tablespoons butter	⅛ teaspoon salt
½ tube anchovy paste	⅛ teaspoon pepper
4 egg yolks	1 tablespoon butter, melted
½ cup milk	2 tablespoons grated
½ cup stock	Parmesan cheese

Butter toast on both sides and spread anchovy paste on one side. Break egg yolks in a small pan, add milk, stock, nutmeg, salt, pepper and melted butter and cook slowly over very low fire, stirring constantly, until slightly thickened. Take care not to allow mixture to boil. When slightly thick, remove from fire, add Parmesan cheese and pour over prepared toast. Keep warm 5 minutes before serving. Serves 4.

EGGS FLORENTINE STYLE

1 pound spinach, cooked, chopped and strained	8 tart shells, or 8 slices toast
1 tablespoon butter	8 soft fried eggs
⅛ teaspoon salt	½ tube anchovy paste
⅛ teaspoon pepper	2 tablespoons grated Parmesan cheese

Place spinach in small pan with butter, salt and pepper and cook 5 minutes. Line shells, or cover toast, with some spinach, place eggs on top of spinach, squirt anchovy paste over eggs, sprinkle with cheese and place in moderate oven (350°F.) 10 minutes. Serves 4.

FRIED EGGS ITALIAN STYLE

2 tablespoons olive oil	⅛ teaspoon pepper
2 eggs	1 teaspoon grated
¼ teaspoon salt	Parmesan cheese

Heat oil in medium frying pan, break 2 eggs into oil and fry gently. Add salt and pepper and remove from fire. Sprinkle cheese over eggs and place frying pan in hot oven 5 minutes, or until cheese has melted. Serves 2.

FRIED EGGS WITH POLENTA (Cornmeal)

¼ pound polenta (cornmeal)	2 tablespoons olive oil
3 quarts water	1 cup tomato sauce (see index)
1 teaspoon salt	2 tablespoons grated
2 tablespoons butter	Roman cheese
8 eggs	

Cook cornmeal in boiling salted water 30 minutes, or until cornmeal comes away from pan. Stir constantly during cooking. Spread in large dish 1½ inches in height and let cool. When cool, cut into 8 rounds and fry in butter until brown on both sides. Fry each egg separately in olive oil and place each egg on a round of fried polenta. Pour warm tomato sauce over all, sprinkle with cheese and serve. Serves 4.

EGGS GYPSY STYLE

2 tablespoons butter	⅛ teaspoon pepper
½ tablespoon flour	¼ pound mushrooms, sliced
½ teaspoon meat extract, blended in	4 poached eggs
½ cup boiling water	4 slices toast
1 teaspoon tomato paste	1 teaspoon chopped parsley
⅛ teaspoon salt	1 tablespoon grated Parmesan cheese (optional)

Melt 1 tablespoon butter in saucepan, blend in flour, add water in which meat extract has been dissolved, tomato paste, salt and pepper and cook 5 minutes. Sauté mushrooms in 1 tablespoon butter 5 minutes and add to sauce. Place 1 poached egg on each slice of toast in serving dish, pour some of mushrooms and sauce over each egg, sprinkle with cheese, if desired, and serve. Serves 4.

EGGS HUNTER STYLE

4 hard cooked eggs	4 anchovy filets, chopped
½ cup bread crumbs	½ teaspoon meat extract, blended in 2 tablespoons warm water
1 egg, lightly beaten	
3 tablespoons olive oil	
½ cup vinegar	1 tablespoon capers
¼ cup butter	

Roll eggs in bread crumbs, dip into beaten egg and fry in very hot olive oil until golden brown in color. Boil vinegar in small saucepan until reduced ⅔ in quantity. Add butter and anchovies and then the meat extract, blended in water. Mix together well, boil 3 minutes, **add** capers, pour over fried eggs and serve. Serves 4.

EGGS IN ANCHOVY BUTTER

4 eggs	4 thin slices mozzarella
¼ teaspoon salt	cheese (about ¼ pound)
⅛ teaspoon pepper	¼ tube anchovy paste
4 anchovy filets	2 tablespoons butter, melted

Break eggs into shallow baking dish, sprinkle with salt and **pepper** and place 1 anchovy filet and 1 slice mozzarella cheese over each **egg** Blend anchovy paste with melted butter and sprinkle over all. Bake **in** hot oven (400°F.) 15 minutes, or until eggs are set and cheese melted. Serves 4.

EGGS IN TOMATO

8 medium tomatoes,	8 eggs
not too ripe	½ teaspoon oregano
⅛ teaspoon salt	8 slices bread,
⅛ teaspoon pepper	fried in butter
2 tablespoons olive oil	

Cut off tomato tops and remove seeds and juice. Place in shallow greased casserole, sprinkle with oil, salt and pepper and break one **egg** into each tomato. Sprinkle a little more oil, salt, pepper and the oregano on each egg. Place in hot oven (400°F.) for about 20 minutes, or until egg is set and tomato cooked. Remove from oven and serve on **slices** of fried bread. Serves 4 or 8.

EGGS NUN STYLE

4 hard cooked eggs	⅛ teaspoon nutmeg
½ pound ricotta	1 tablespoon flour
1 tablespoon grated	1 egg, lightly beaten
Parmesan cheese	with fork
¼ teaspoon salt	1 cup bread crumbs
⅛ teaspoon pepper	

Cut eggs in half and remove yolks. Mix yolks with ricotta, Parmesan, salt, pepper and nutmeg. Fill egg whites with yolk mixture and shape so that each half looks like a whole egg. Roll in flour, dip into beaten egg, roll in bread crumbs and fry in deep oil until golden brown in color. Serves 4.

EGGS PARMESAN STYLE

4 eggs
¼ teaspoon salt
2 slices prosciutto,
   cut in slivers

2 tablespoons grated
   Parmesan cheese
2 teaspoons butter,
   melted

Break 4 eggs into greased shallow casserole, sprinkle with salt, prosciutto and grated cheese and pour melted butter over all. Bake in hot oven (400°F.) 15 minutes, or until eggs are set and Parmesan cheese melted. Serves 4.

EGGS ROMAN STYLE

2 slices bacon or
   salt pork, chopped
½ small onion
¼ clove garlic
2 tablespoons olive oil
¼ teaspoon salt
¼ teaspoon pepper
1 medium can tomatoes

1 bay leaf
½ teaspoon basil leaves
4 eggs
3 tablespoons grated
   Roman cheese
3 mint leaves, chopped
   (optional)

Place bacon or salt pork in saucepan with onion, garlic, oil, ⅛ teaspoon salt and ⅛ teaspoon pepper and sauté 5 minutes. Add tomatoes, cover and cook 45 minutes. Add bay leaf and basil and cook 5 minutes longer. Beat eggs lightly with a fork, and add rest of salt and pepper. Apportion eggs in 4 equal amounts to make four small omelettes and brown them gently on both sides in a buttered skillet. Cut omelettes into 1-inch strips, place in sauce, sprinkle with cheese, add mint and cook 5 minutes. Serves 4.

EGGS SHEPHERD STYLE

8 slices toast
8 thin slices mozzarella
   cheese
4 thin slices prosciutto

4 eggs
2 tablespoons olive oil
¼ teaspoon salt

Place 1 slice mozzarella and ½ slice prosciutto between 2 slices of toast. Fry each egg in olive oil on one side and place a fried egg on each sandwich. Sprinkle with salt and place all sandwiches on greased baking dish. Bake in hot oven (400°F.) 15 minutes, or until mozzarella has melted. Serves 4.

EGGS SPRING STYLE

4 hard cooked eggs	½ pound spinach, boiled,
1½ tablespoons butter	chopped and strained
1 tablespoon flour	1 tablespoon grated
½ cup milk	Roman cheese
¼ teaspoon salt	1 cup flour
¼ teaspoon pepper	1 egg, slightly beaten
dash nutmeg	2 cups bread crumbs
	1 cup olive oil

Cut eggs in two, remove and mince yolks. Melt butter in saucepan, blend in flour, add milk and cook slowly, stirring constantly, until thick. Add salt, pepper, nutmeg, spinach and minced egg yolks to sauce and mix well. Add cheese, pour into dish and let cool. When mixture is cool and firm, fill egg whites with it. Roll in flour, then in beaten egg, then in bread crumbs and fry in hot oil until golden in color. Serves 4.

STUFFED EGGS

4 hard cooked eggs	½ teaspoon chopped
1 tablespoon butter	parsley
¼ teaspoon salt	1 raw egg yolk
¼ teaspoon pepper	1 tablespoon cream sauce
⅛ teaspoon nutmeg	(see index)
1 teaspoon grated	1 cup tomato sauce
Parmesan cheese	(see index)

Cut eggs in half and remove yolks. Mash yolks and mix with butter, salt, pepper, nutmeg, cheese, parsley, raw egg yolk and cream sauce. Fill egg whites with yolk mixture, place in shallow greased casserole and bake in moderate oven 5 minutes. Serve with tomato sauce. Serves 4.

EGGS WITH CHICKEN LIVERS

4 chicken livers,	4 eggs
diced fine	1 tablespoon butter
2 tablespoons butter	½ teaspoon salt
1 tablespoon Marsala or	½ teaspoon pepper
sherry wine	8 asparagus tips
3 tablespoons warm water	

Brown chicken livers lightly in butter, add Marsala or sherry and cook 5 minutes. Add 3 tablespoons warm water and cook 2 minutes longer. Break eggs into greased shallow baking dish, sprinkle with butter, salt and pepper and cook in hot oven (400°F.) 10 minutes. Pour chicken livers over eggs, garnish with asparagus tips, bake 5 minutes longer and serve. Serves 4.

EGGS WITH PROSCIUTTO

2 cups cream sauce
  (see index)
4 slices prosciutto
4 eggs

2 tablespoons grated
  Parmesan cheese
½ teaspoon salt
½ teaspoon pepper
1 tablespoon butter

Pour cream sauce into shallow baking dish and place prosciutto slices over it. Break 4 eggs gently over prosciutto, sprinkle with cheese, salt and pepper and dot with butter. Bake in hot oven (400°F.) 10 minutes, or until eggs are set. Serves 4.

OMELETTES

ANCHOVY OMELETTE

4 eggs
2 tablespoons grated
  Parmesan cheese
¼ teaspoon pepper

¼ cup butter
2 teaspoons anchovy
  butter

Beat eggs lightly with fork and add Parmesan and pepper. Fry egg mixture in butter in four parts, making 4 small omelettes. Spread each little omelette with a fourth of the anchovy butter and fold. Serve immediately. Serves 4.

CLAM OMELETTE

1 dozen Little Neck
  clams, cleaned
2 tablespoons olive oil
1 clove garlic
2 tablespoons tomato
  sauce

1 tablespoon olive oil
4 eggs, beaten well
¼ teaspoon salt
½ teaspoon pepper
1 tablespoon chopped
  parsley

Wash clams carefully and place in frying pan with olive oil. Cover pan and stir often. The clams will soon open up. Extract clams from shells and leave clams and juice in pan. Add tomato sauce and cook 15 minutes. At same time heat olive oil in large pan and pour in eggs which have been beaten with salt, pepper and parsley. Cook lightly 4 minutes on each side and remove to serving dish. Pour clam mixture over omelette and serve. Serves 4.

COUNTRY STYLE OMELETTE

2 tablespoons olive oil
1 zucchini, diced
1 celery heart, diced
2 fresh tomatoes, skinned
  and cut into pieces
¼ teaspoon salt
⅛ teaspoon pepper

4 eggs, lightly beaten
  with fork
2 tablespoons grated
  Parmesan cheese
1 teaspoon minced basil
2 tablespoons olive oil

Place oil, zucchini and celery in frying pan and brown well. Add tomatoes, salt and pepper and cook for 15 minutes. In a bowl mix together eggs, Parmesan and basil and pour over vegetables. Cook slowly, using additional olive oil, 12 minutes on each side. Serves 4.

KIDNEY OMELETTE

1 teaspoon butter
1 tablespoon olive oil
1 veal kidney, sliced thin
⅛ teaspoon salt
⅛ teaspoon pepper
2 tablespoons Marsala or
  sherry wine

1 teaspoon meat extract,
  blended in 1 tablespoon
  warm water
4 eggs, lightly beaten with
  fork with
  ¼ teaspoon salt
1 tablespoon butter

Place butter and olive oil in frying pan, add kidney slices and cook over high flame 10 minutes, turning often. Add salt and pepper, remove kidney from pan and place in warm dish. Add Marsala or sherry to pan gravy and cook until it evaporates. Add meat extract and water, mix well and let cook 2 minutes. Return kidney to pan and turn until sauce covers all sides. Make 1 large omelette, pour kidney slices and sauce over omelette and serve. Serves 4.

LOBSTER OMELETTE

1 cup cooked lobster meat,
  diced
2 tablespoons tomato sauce
  (see index)
4 eggs, beaten

⅛ teaspoon salt
⅛ teaspoon pepper
¼ cup butter
4 anchovy filets, chopped

Mix lobster meat with tomato sauce and heat but do not cook. Make 1 large omelette of 4 eggs beaten with salt and pepper, cooked 3 minutes on each side. Blend butter with chopped anchovies and spread on omelette. Pour lobster over omelette and fold once. Serves 4.

NEAPOLITAN OMELETTE

3 cups leftover spaghetti with sauce	⅛ teaspoon pepper
4 eggs, lightly beaten with fork	1 tablespoon minced parsley
⅛ teaspoon salt	2 tablespoons grated Parmesan cheese
	2 tablespoons olive oil

Cut up spaghetti, add eggs, salt, pepper, parsley and Parmesan cheese and mix very well. Heat oil in frying pan, pour in spaghetti mixture and cook very slowly but thoroughly on both sides. Allow about 15 minutes cooking time for each side. Serves 4.

RICOTTA OMELETTE

2 tablespoons flour	1 tablespoon warm water
2 tablespoons water	⅛ teaspoon salt
4 eggs	1 tablespoon grated Roman cheese
½ pound ricotta	1 tablespoon leaf lard

Mix flour with water, add eggs and beat with fork 3 minutes. Mix ricotta in a bowl with water, salt and Roman cheese. Heat lard in frying pan and add 1 tablespoon egg mixture. Cook slowly until omelette is hard on under side. Place 1 tablespoon ricotta in center of omelette and cover with 1 tablespoon egg mixture, rolling around until ricotta is closed in. Brown small omelette on both sides, remove and keep warm. Repeat procedure until all the egg mixture is used. These small omelettes may be served plain or with tomato sauce (see index). Serves 4.

OMELETTE SARDINIAN STYLE

1 medium zucchini, chopped	⅛ teaspoon sugar
1 tablespoon bread crumbs, soaked in	½ teaspoon grated lemon peel
½ cup milk	4 eggs
1 tablespoon grated Parmesan cheese	2 tablespoons olive oil
	½ cup bread crumbs

Mix together zucchini, bread crumbs which have been soaked in milk, Parmesan, sugar and lemon peel. Add lightly beaten eggs and mix well. Grease baking dish with olive oil and coat with bread crumbs. Pour egg mixture into casserole and place in hot oven (400°F.) 20 minutes. Serves 4.

SAVOY STYLE OMELETTE

2 tablespoons butter	⅛ teaspoon pepper
2 small potatoes, diced fine	1 tablespoon milk
4 eggs	1 tablespoon grated Parmesan
¼ teaspoon salt	cheese

Melt butter in frying pan, add potatoes and brown. Beat eggs lightly, add salt, pepper, milk and cheese and add to potatoes. Cook over moderate fire 12 minutes on each side and serve. Serves 4.

TUSCAN STYLE OMELETTE

2 artichokes	4 eggs, lightly beaten with fork
2 tablespoons flour	¼ teaspoon salt
3 tablespoons olive oil	⅛ teaspoon pepper

Cut outer leaves off the artichokes, cut in half, remove chokes and slice lengthwise in very thin slices. Flour the artichoke slices and fry in olive oil until crisp. When crisp, add eggs which have been beaten lightly with salt and pepper. Continue frying 12 minutes on each side. Serves 4.

OMELETTE WITH ARTICHOKES

3 artichokes	1 teaspoon chopped marjoram
2 tablespoons olive oil	leaves
¼ teaspoon salt	4 eggs, lightly beaten
⅛ teaspoon pepper	½ clove garlic, chopped
2 slices bread, soaked in	¼ teaspoon salt
water and squeezed dry	⅛ teaspoon pepper
2 tablespoons grated	2 tablespoons olive oil
Parmesan cheese	

Remove outer leaves of artichokes, cut in half, remove chokes and cut hearts into 8 or 10 slivers. Place artichoke slivers in saucepan with oil, salt and pepper, cover pan and cook slowly, stirring often, for 25 minutes or until tender. Mix together thoroughly bread, cheese, marjoram, eggs, garlic, salt and pepper. To this mixture add cooked artichokes and mix well.

Heat oil in frying pan, add egg and artichoke mixture and cook slowly 10 minutes on one side, turn and cook 8 minutes on other side. Serve immediately. Serves 4.

OMELETTE WITH BREAD CUBES

2 slices bread, cubed	½ teaspoon salt
¼ cup butter	½ teaspoon pepper
4 eggs, slightly beaten	¼ pound mozzarella, diced

Fry bread cubes in butter until golden in color. Mix eggs with salt, pepper and diced mozzarella. Pour egg mixture over bread cubes and cook gently 5 minutes on each side. Serves 4.

OMELETTE WITH CHEESE

4 eggs	½ teaspoon salt
2 tablespoons grated Parmesan cheese	¼ teaspoon pepper
	2 tablespoons butter
1 tablespoon Swiss type cheese, cut into very small pieces	

Mix eggs lightly with Parmesan cheese, Swiss cheese, salt and pepper. Melt butter in frying pan and when hot, pour in egg mixture. Cook over low flame 5 minutes on each side. Serves 4.

OMELETTE WITH CREAM

¼ pound mushrooms, sliced	4 eggs, lightly beaten with fork
1 tablespoon butter	
1 cup cooked chicken or veal, diced	½ teaspoon salt
	2 tablespoons butter
1 slice prosciutto, cut into slivers	1 tablespoon grated Parmesan cheese
1 cup cream sauce (see index)	

Cook mushrooms in butter 5 minutes, add diced meat, prosciutto and half the cream sauce, mix well and cook 1 minute longer. Make as many small omelettes as possible, using 2 tablespoonfuls to an omelette. Place 1 tablespoon of meat and mushroom mixture on each omelette and roll. Place omelettes in shallow buttered casserole, add remaining cream sauce and sprinkle with Parmesan cheese. Bake in hot oven 10 minutes. Serves 4.

OMELETTE WITH GREENS

½ small onion, sliced	½ teaspoon oregano
2 tablespoons olive oil	⅛ teaspoon salt
½ cup cooked shelled peas	⅛ teaspoon pepper
1 medium-size green pepper, cut into small pieces	2 tablespoons flour
	½ cup milk
1 small zucchini, diced	4 eggs
1 small tomato, skinned and sliced	¼ teaspoon salt
	⅛ teaspoon pepper

Place onion and oil in small saucepan and sauté lightly. Add peas, green pepper and zucchini and sauté 20 minutes. Add tomato, oregano, salt and pepper and cook 3 minutes longer. Set aside. Mix flour and milk until very smooth, add eggs, salt and pepper and beat well 5 minutes.

Grease a small frying pan, pour into it 1 tablespoon egg mixture and cook slowly until firm. Place 1 tablespoon vegetable mixture in center, cover with another tablespoon egg mixture and cook gently on both sides, turning gently so vegetables do not come out. Repeat procedure until both mixtures are used. Serves 4.

OMELETTE WITH HERBS

4 eggs
1/2 teaspoon salt
1/4 teaspoon pepper
1 tablespoon chopped
   mint leaves

1/2 tablespoon chopped
   sweet basil
2 tablespoons butter

Beat eggs lightly with salt, pepper, mint leaves and basil. Melt butter in frying pan and, when hot, pour in egg mixture. Cook over low flame 5 minutes on each side. Serves 4.

OMELETTE WITH MEAT AND GREENS

2 tablespoons oil
2 tablespoons butter
1 medium onion, sliced
2 fresh tomatoes, peeled
   and cut into pieces
1/2 cup water or stock
1/4 teaspoon salt
1/4 teaspoon pepper
1 teaspoon marjoram leaves

1 1/2 cups leftover meat (beef,
   lamb, veal or chicken), diced
3 medium-size boiled potatoes,
   diced
4 egg yolks, lightly beaten
1/4 teaspoon salt
1/4 teaspoon pepper
4 egg whites, beaten stiff

Brown sliced onion in oil and butter, add tomatoes, water or stock, salt, pepper and marjoram and cook 15 minutes. Add diced meat and potatoes and cook 5 minutes longer. Grease a casserole and place meat and potato mixture in it. Add salt and pepper to egg yolks and fold in beaten egg whites. Pour eggs over meat and potatoes and bake in hot oven (400°F.) 8 minutes, or until eggs are gold color. Serves 4.

OMELETTE WITH RICOTTA

2 tablespoons flour	½ pound ricotta
1 tablespoon milk or water	2 tablespoons warm water
4 eggs, lightly beaten	1 teaspoon grated
with fork	Parmesan cheese
¼ teaspoon salt	⅛ teaspoon salt
2 tablespoons butter	1 cup tomato sauce (optional)

Blend flour with water and mix with beaten eggs and salt. Melt a little butter in small frying pan, add 2 tablespoons egg mixture and cook 3 minutes on each side. Make as many little omelettes as the mixture allows. Mix ricotta with water, Parmesan cheese and salt. Place some of the ricotta mixture on each omelette and roll omelette around it. Serve plain or with tomato sauce (see index). Serves 4.

OMELETTE WITH SWISS CHEESE

4 eggs, lightly beaten	½ cup milk
with fork	2 slices prosciutto, cut
¼ teaspoon salt	into slivers
2 tablespoons olive oil	1 cup milk
1 tablespoon butter	⅛ pound Swiss cheese,
1 tablespoon flour	sliced thin

Add salt to beaten eggs. Heat oil in small frying pan and make as many small omelettes as possible, using 2 tablespoons egg mixture to each omelette. Melt butter, blend in flour, add ½ cup milk, mix well and add prosciutto. Cook 1 minute. Place 1 teaspoon prosciutto mixture on each omelette and roll. Place omelette rolls in shallow casserole, pour 1 cup milk over them and cover with slices of cheese. Bake in hot oven (400°F.) 20 minutes, or until cheese is melted. Serves 4.

OMELETTE WITH TUNA

½ clove garlic	1 teaspoon chopped parsley
4 eggs, lightly beaten	½ teaspoon oregano
with fork	1 medium can grated tuna fish
⅛ teaspoon salt	2 anchovy filets, minced
¼ teaspoon pepper	2 tablespoons olive oil

Rub a bowl with garlic and mix together in the bowl the eggs, salt, pepper, parsley, oregano, tuna fish and anchovies. Mix well. Heat oil in frying pan, add egg mixture and cook on low fire 12 minutes on each side. Serves 4.

PANDORATO ROMAN STYLE

8 slices white bread	2 eggs, lightly beaten with
½ cup lukewarm milk	¼ teaspoon salt
	1 cup butter

Remove crusts from bread and cut slices in half. Sprinkle lightly with milk and dip into egg. Place bread on flat dish, cover and let stand 30 minutes so that the egg will soak through. Fry in hot butter until golden brown. Serves 4.

PREZIOSINI AL TOMATO

½ long loaf French bread	1 tablespoon chopped parsley
4 eggs	1 cup olive oil
3 tablespoons grated	2 cups tomato sauce alla
Parmesan cheese	pizzaiola (see index)
¼ teaspoon salt	2 tablespoons grated
¼ teaspoon pepper	Parmesan cheese

Cut bread into pieces, place in warm water and let stand until thoroughly soaked. Remove, squeeze and mash well. Add eggs, cheese, salt, pepper and parsley and mix very well. Make about 16 little "cushions" and fry in hot olive oil until golden brown on both sides. Serve with tomato sauce and Parmesan cheese. Serves 4.

PROSCIUTTO AND EGGS ITALIAN STYLE

2 tablespoons butter	4 eggs
4 slices prosciutto	salt and pepper to taste

Melt butter in large frying pan, add prosciutto and cook gently until edges begin to curl. Break 1 egg on each slice of prosciutto and fry as long as you like. Sprinkle with salt and pepper and serve hot. Serves 2.

PROSCIUTTO SOUFFLE (Number 1)

4 egg yolks, lightly beaten	¼ pound prosciutto, sliced and
with wooden spoon	cut into thin strips
⅛ teaspoon salt	4 egg whites, beaten stiff
⅛ teaspoon white pepper	½ cup butter, melted
2 tablespoons grated	
Parmesan cheese	

Mix egg yolks with salt, pepper, cheese and prosciutto. Fold in egg whites and melted butter. Grease a casserole and pour in egg mixture. The mixture must not be more than ⅓ the height of the casserole. Bake in moderate oven (350°F.) 20 minutes. Serve immediately. Serves 4.

PROSCIUTTO SOUFFLE (Number 2)

1 tablespoon butter	½ pound prosciutto, minced
1 tablespoon flour	very fine
1 cup milk	¼ cup butter
¼ teaspoon salt	3 egg yolks
	3 egg whites, beaten stiff

Melt 1 tablespoon butter, blend in flour, add milk and salt and simmer until thick and smooth. Cool. Mince and pound prosciutto as fine as possible and cook with butter until thoroughly blended. Add cooled cream sauce. Add 3 egg yolks and mix well. Blend in the stiff egg whites gently. Butter a casserole and pour in the mixture. Bake in moderate oven (375°F.) 25 minutes. Serve immediately. Serves 4.

4. Cheese

LA FONDUA (Melted Cheese Piedmont Style)

¾ pound fontina cheese, diced
milk to cover cheese
1 tablespoon butter
6 egg yolks

¼ teaspoon white pepper
1 white truffle, sliced
paper thin
1 tablespoon butter

Place diced cheese in dish and cover with milk. Let stand for at least 6 hours, overnight if possible. Place butter and egg yolks in upper part of double boiler, add cheese and milk and place over boiling water. Beat with rotary beater. At first the cheese will melt and then will become a little harder. When it becomes harder, remove from over boiling water, add pepper, truffle and butter and mix well. Serve on toast or with rice or polenta (see index). Serves 4.

MOZZARELLA CROQUETTES

½ pound fresh mozzarella
1 tablespoon flour
1 egg

¼ teaspoon salt
½ cup flour
1 cup olive oil

Place mozzarella in bowl and work and squeeze it with your hands until it begins to get soft and malleable. Add 1 tablespoon flour, egg and salt and mix together well. Shape into small croquettes, roll in flour and fry in hot olive oil until golden brown. This will make 12 croquettes. Serves 4.

MOZZARELLA IN CARROZZA (In Carriage)

8 slices white bread,
cut thin
¾ pound mozzarella,
sliced medium thin

½ cup flour
2 eggs, lightly beaten with
¼ teaspoon salt
1 cup lard or oil

Cut off crust from bread and cut slices in halves. On each half slice bread place 1 slice mozzarella, approximately same size as bread. Roll bread and cheese in flour, dip into egg and fry gently on both sides in the lard or oil. Serve very hot. Serves 4.

OLD-FASHIONED CHEESE BALLS

1½ cups fresh bread crumbs	¼ teaspoon pepper
½ pound grated caciocavallo	dash nutmeg
(Parmesan cheese may be	½ tablespoon chopped parsley
substituted)	½ cup flour
3 eggs	1 egg, lightly beaten
¼ teaspoon salt	2 cups olive oil

Mix together bread crumbs, grated cheese, eggs, salt, pepper, nutmeg and parsley. This mixture should be moderately hard. If too hard, add a teaspoonful milk. Shape into small balls, roll in flour, dip into beaten egg and fry briskly in hot olive oil until golden in color. Serve hot. Serves 4.

PILLOWS WITH PROSCIUTTO
(Cuscinetti Filanti Al Prosciutto)

8 thin slices white bread	½ cup milk
½ pound mozzarella, sliced	½ cup flour
thin	1 egg
8 large slices prosciutto,	1 cup lard or oil
sliced thin	

Remove crust from bread. Place one slice of cheese and 2 slices prosciutto on each of 4 slices of bread and cover with other bread slices. Cut sandwiches crosswise, making three-cornered sandwiches. Dip into milk, roll in flour, dip into egg and fry in hot oil or lard until golden brown on both sides. Serves 2 or 4.

RICOTTA PILLOWS

1½ cups flour	¾ pound ricotta
1½ tablespoons butter	1 egg
¼ tablespoon salt	2 tablespoons grated Parmesan
2 tablespoons lukewarm	cheese
water	1½ cups olive oil or leaf lard

Knead together flour, butter, salt and water, adding the latter 1 tablespoon at a time. A little more or less water may be used according to consistency of flour. Make a ball of dough, cover and let stand 1 hour.

Roll dough rather thin and cut in discs the size of a large tumbler. Mix the ricotta with egg and Parmesan cheese. Place ½ tablespoon ricotta mixture on each disc and fold over dough, closing it all around. Take care to close tightly to prevent ricotta mixture from coming out. Fry in hot oil or lard until golden brown and serve plain or with 2 cups spaghetti sauce (see index). Sprinkle with grated Parmesan cheese. Serves 4.

STUFFED BUNDLES (Fagottini Ripieni)

2 cups flour	10 anchovy filets, cut into pieces
1½ cups lukewarm water	1 tablespoon chopped parsley
1 envelope dry yeast	¼ teaspoon salt
½ pound mozzarella cheese, diced	¼ teaspoon pepper
	1½ cups oil or leaf lard

Sift flour. Blend yeast with 2 tablespoons of the lukewarm water. Place flour on pastry board, making a well in center. Place yeast and remaining lukewarm water in well and knead the mixture until smooth and elastic. Cover and let rise in warm place 2 hours.

Place dough on floured board, cut into pieces as large as an egg and stretch each piece with hands to form a thin disc. Place some cheese and anchovies on each disc, add parsley, salt and pepper and fold each disc over once, closing edges as tightly as possible. Heat oil or leaf lard well and fry the little bundles briskly until golden and crisp. Serve hot, either plain or with 2 cups tomato sauce (see index). Makes about 24 bundles. Serves 6.

5. *Fish and Shell Fish*

BURIDDA

BURIDDA GENOA STYLE (Number 1)

1½ pounds greyling (bass or mackerel may be used)
1 small onion, sliced
1 tablespoon chopped parsley
3 tablespoons olive oil
4 anchovy filets, minced
1 tablespoon pine nuts
½ clove garlic
½ teaspoon salt
½ teaspoon pepper
½ cup dry white wine

Cut fish into 2-inch slices, wash and dry. Brown onion and parsley in olive oil in large skillet, add anchovies, pine nuts and garlic and cook a few minutes longer. Place fish slices over ingredients in skillet, sprinkle with salt and pepper and brown gently on both sides. Add wine and place skillet in moderate oven until wine has evaporated completely (about 15 minutes). Serves 4.

BURIDDA GENOA STYLE (Number 2)

1½ pounds mackerel
½ cup olive oil
2 medium onions, sliced thin
1 tablespoon chopped parsley
8 clams, shelled
½ teaspoon salt
½ teaspoon pepper
1 small can tomatoes, drained
½ cup dry white wine

Wash and dry fish and cut into 2-inch slices. Place ¼ cup olive oil in shallow casserole and place half the fish slices in it. Cover fish with half the onions, parsley, clams, salt and pepper. Repeat, using remaining half and cover top layer with tomatoes, remaining oil and wine. Bake in moderate oven (375°F.) 40 minutes, or until all wine has evaporated. Serves 4.

BUTTERFISH

GRILLED BUTTERFISH

3 pounds butterfish
¼ cup olive oil
½ teaspoon salt
½ teaspoon pepper
4 teaspoons lemon juice

Clean, wash and dry fish. Place in dish with oil, salt, pepper and lemon juice and marinate 1 hour. Place on grill and cook 15 minutes on each side, brushing occasionally with marinade. Serves 4.

42

BUTTERFISH IN SKILLET

3 pounds butterfish	½ teaspoon salt
3 tablespoons olive oil	½ teaspoon pepper
1 clove garlic	1 teaspoon chopped **parsley**
	juice of ½ lemon

Place olive oil in skillet and brown garlic in it. Remove garlic, place fish in skillet, add salt, pepper and parsley and cook slowly, first on one side, then on the other, allowing 12 minutes on each side. Remove from fire, sprinkle with lemon juice and serve. Serves 4.

BUTTERFISH IN WHITE WINE

1 large onion, sliced	1 cup dry white wine
¼ pound mushrooms, sliced	2 tablespoons water
3 anchovy filets, chopped	3 pounds butterfish, cleaned
1 tablespoon chopped	2 tablespoons flour
parsley	1 tablespoon butter
¼ cup butter	juice of ½ lemon

Place onion, mushrooms, anchovies, parsley and ¼ cup butter in large skillet and brown gently. Add wine and water and cook 1 minute. Roll fish in flour and place in skillet. Cover skillet and cook slowly 20 minutes. Remove fish to serving dish. Add 1 tablespoon butter and lemon juice to pan gravy and pour over fish. Serves 4.

Cod

COD SPONGE MODERNA

1 pound filet of cod	2 egg whites, lightly beaten
½ teaspoon salt	with fork
½ teaspoon white pepper	2 cups heavy cream

Chop fish fine and strain. Add salt and pepper. Add egg whites, 1 teaspoon at a time, blending in each teaspoonful completely before adding the next. Chill in refrigerator 2 hours. Add cream to fish slowly, mixing with wooden spoon constantly. Pour into well greased tubular mold, place mold in pan of water in moderate oven (375°F.) 45 minutes, or until solid to the touch. Remove from oven and allow mold to stand in water 5 minutes longer. Turn mold upside down on serving dish and unmold. This may be served plain or with aromatic sauce (see index). Serves 4.

FILET OF COD DEVIL STYLE

½ teaspoon powdered mustard	2 teaspoons lemon juice
small dash cayenne pepper	8 small filets of cod
½ teaspoon oregano	½ cup flour
1 tube anchovy paste	1 egg, lightly beaten
½ cup olive oil	1 cup olive oil
	1 lemon, cut in quarters

Mix together well the mustard, pepper, oregano, anchovy paste, olive oil and lemon juice, spread mixture on one side of filets and let stand 1 hour. Roll filets and fasten with toothpicks. Roll in flour, dip in egg and fry gently in olive oil until brown and crisp. Remove toothpicks and serve fish with lemon quarters. Serves 4.

FRIED COD FILETS

1½ pounds filets of cod	½ teaspoon salt and
½ cup flour	½ teaspoon pepper
1 egg, lightly beaten with	½ cup bread crumbs
	1 cup olive oil

Roll filets in flour, dip in egg mixture, roll in crumbs and fry in hot olive oil until golden brown on each side. Serves 4.

FILET OF COD IN WHITE WINE

1 pound filets of cod	2 tablespoons white wine
½ teaspoon salt	2 tablespoons fish stock
½ teaspoon pepper	(see index)
	2 tablespoons butter

Butter skillet and add filets in single layer. Sprinkle with salt and pepper and add wine and fish stock. Cover skillet, place over very low flame and cook 5 minutes. Baste filets and cook 5 minutes longer. Remove to serving dish. Add butter to pan gravy and pour over fish. Serves 4.

FILET OF COD WITH MUSHROOMS

9 small filets of cod	1 tablespoon dry white wine
1 slice white bread, soaked in water and squeezed dry	½ black truffle, sliced thin
1 tablespoon butter	1 tablespoon butter
¼ teaspoon salt	½ tablespoon flour
¼ teaspoon pepper	½ pound mushrooms
½ cup stock	2 tablespoons butter

Chop 1 cod filet and mix together with bread, butter, salt and pepper. Spread mixture over 1 side of each filet. Roll filets and spear through with toothpicks. Place in well-greased baking dish. Add stock and wine, cover baking dish and bake in moderate oven (375°F.) 15 minutes.

Remove fish from baking dish and keep warm. Add truffle, 1 tablespoon butter and flour to pan gravy, mix well and cook until slightly thickened. Fry mushrooms in 2 tablespoons of butter 10 minutes and arrange around fish. Pour sauce over all and serve. Serves 4.

SALTED COD (Baccalà) BOLOGNA STYLE

1½ pounds soaked baccalà†	1 tablespoon chopped parsley
½ cup flour	½ clove garlic, chopped
3 tablespoons olive oil	½ teaspoon pepper
½ cup butter, melted	4 teaspoons lemon juice

Skin fish and cut into 4- by 6-inch strips. Dry well, flour and place in single layer in large skillet with hot olive oil. Brown fish well on both sides. Drain off oil from skillet and add melted butter to fish. Sprinkle with parsley, chopped garlic, pepper and lemon juice, cover skillet and keep over very low flame 10 minutes. Serves 4.

SALTED COD (Baccalà) CROQUETTES

1½ pounds soaked baccalà†	2 slices white bread, soaked in
3 anchovy filets, chopped	water and squeezed dry
1 tablespoon chopped parsley	2 eggs, lightly beaten
½ teaspoon pepper	½ cup flour
1 tablespoon grated	1 egg, lightly beaten
Parmesan cheese	1 cup bread crumbs
	1 cup olive oil

Boil fish in water 30 minutes and cool. Bone, skin and chop fine. Add anchovies, parsley, pepper, cheese, bread and eggs and mix very well. Shape into croquettes, roll in flour, dip into egg, roll in bread crumbs and fry in olive oil until brown all over. Frying time will be about 4 minutes on each side. Serves 4.

SALTED COD (Baccalà) FILETS ROMAN STYLE

1½ pounds soaked baccalà*	1 cup olive oil
1½ cups pastella (see index)	

Skin baccalà and cut into 2- by 6-inch strips. Dip in pastella and fry on both sides in hot olive oil until golden brown and crisp. Serves 4.

† If soaked baccalà is not available, soak in water 24 hours, changing water every 8 hours

SALTED COD (Baccalà) HARLEQUIN STYLE

1½ pounds baccalà† (2
  pounds if already soaked)
¼ cup olive oil
1 tablespoon butter
1 tablespoon flour
1 cup milk

½ teaspoon pepper
¼ teaspoon salt (if required)
dash nutmeg
1 hard cooked egg, chopped
  coarse
1 tablespoon minced parsley
1 vinegar pickle, chopped

Skin dried fish, cut into 3- by 8-inch strips, brush with oil and place in broiler at low heat. Broil 10 minutes on each side and place in serving dish. Meanwhile, blend together in saucepan butter and flour, add milk, salt, pepper and nutmeg and cook until slightly thickened, stirring constantly. Remove from fire, add chopped egg, parsley and pickle, mix well and pour over fish. Serves 4.

SALTED COD (Baccalà) IN TOMATO SAUCE ROMAN STYLE

1½ pounds soaked baccalà†
3 tablespoons olive oil
1 medium onion, sliced
2 tablespoons tomato paste

1 cup water
¾ teaspoon pepper
2 tablespoons shelled pine nuts
2 tablespoons white raisins

Place oil in large skillet, add onion and brown. Add tomato paste, water and pepper and cook 5 minutes. Add fish cut into 4-inch squares, pine nuts and raisins and cook 20 minutes. Taste and add salt, if needed. Serves 4.

SALTED COD (Baccalà) WITH GREEN OLIVES

1½ pounds soaked baccalà†
½ cup flour
3 tablespoons olive oil
1 small onion
2 tablespoons tomato paste
1 cup water

2 small vinegar pickles, chopped
1 tablespoon capers
½ pound green Italian olives,
  pitted
½ teaspoon pepper
1 tablespoon chopped parsley

Skin fish and cut into 4-inch squares. Dry and roll in flour. Heat 2 tablespoons olive oil in large skillet, add fish and brown well on both sides. Remove fish from skillet and keep warm.

Add 1 tablespoon olive oil to oil remaining in skillet, add onion and brown. Add tomato paste and water and cook 3 minutes. Add pickles, capers, olives and pepper and return fish to skillet. Simmer 20 minutes, basting fish occasionally with tomato gravy. Taste and add salt if needed. Add parsley and serve. Serves 4.

† If soaked baccalà is not available, soak in water 24 hours, changing water every 8 hours.

SALTED COD (Baccalà) WITH PEPPERS ROMAN STYLE

1½ pounds baccalà† (2 pounds if already soaked)
4 large or 6 small green peppers
½ cup olive oil
2 medium onions, sliced

1 large can tomatoes, cut in pieces
1 tablespoon chopped parsley
½ teaspoon pepper
¼ teaspoon salt

Skin baccalà and cut into 4-inch squares. Remove stalks and seeds from peppers and cut lengthwise into 2-inch slices. Brown onion in olive oil in large skillet, add tomatoes, parsley, pepper and salt and cook 3 minutes. Add fish and peppers and cook about 20 minutes, or until fish and peppers are well done. Serves 4.

SALTED COD (Baccalà) LEGHORN STYLE

1½ pounds baccalà† (2 pounds if already soaked)
½ cup olive oil
1 clove garlic, sliced

1 cup canned tomatoes
1 tablespoon minced parsley
½ teaspoon pepper

Skin dried cod. Cut into rectangular pieces, 4 by 6 inches, and fry in hot oil with garlic until golden brown on both sides. Frying time will be about 15 minutes on each side. Remove fish, add tomatoes, parsley and pepper to oil in frying pan and cook 5 minutes. Pour over fish and serve. Because of the extreme saltiness of this fish, do not add salt unless especially desired. Serves 4.

SALTED COD (Baccalà) NEAPOLITAN STYLE

1½ pounds soaked baccalà†
½ cup flour
1 cup olive oil
2 cloves garlic, sliced
2 tablespoons tomato sauce

1 tablespoon capers
12 black olives, pitted and cut into pieces
1 cup water
½ teaspoon pepper

Skin baccalà, roll in flour and fry in olive oil until well browned on both sides. Remove from pan and keep hot. Add garlic to oil, brown and remove. Add tomato sauce, capers, olives, water and pepper and cook 5 minutes. Place fish in large well-oiled baking dish and pour sauce over it. Bake in moderate oven (375°F.) 30 minutes. Taste and add salt if needed. Serves 4.

† If soaked baccalà is not available, soak in water 24 hours, changing water every 8 hours.

SALTED COD (Baccalà) WITH SOUR CHERRIES

1½ pounds soaked baccalà†
1 small onion, chopped
½ clove garlic, chopped

½ cup olive oil
1 tablespoon tomato paste
½ teaspoon pepper
1 can sour cherries, pitted

Skin baccalà and cut into small pieces. Brown onion and garlic lightly in oil, add tomato paste and pepper and cook 4 minutes. Add pitted sour cherries and juice from can. Place baccalà on cherries, cover pan and cook slowly 30 minutes. As baccalà is usually very salty, add salt only if especially desired. Serve hot or cold. Serves 4.

SALTED COD (Baccalà) WITH SPINACH

1 package frozen spinach,
  or 1 pound washed spinach
1 pound soaked baccalà*
2 tablespoons olive oil
½ clove garlic
1 tablespoon chopped
  parsley

¼ teaspoon salt
½ teaspoon pepper
dash nutmeg
3 anchovy filets, chopped
1 cup cream sauce (see index)
2 tablespoons bread crumbs
2 tablespoons butter

Cook spinach 5 minutes in own water and drain. Skin fish, cut into pieces 4 inches square and boil in water 20 minutes. In skillet, brown garlic in oil, add parsley, salt, pepper, nutmeg, anchovies and cooked spinach and cook 3 or 4 minutes. Line a greased baking dish with spinach mixture, place fish over spinach and pour cream sauce over fish. Sprinkle with bread crumbs, dot with butter and bake in hot oven (400°F.) 15 minutes. Serves 4.

Eel (Anguilla)

BAKED EEL

½ cup olive oil
2 tablespoons wine vinegar
2 bay leaves
1 teaspoon salt
½ teaspoon pepper

1 tablespoon bread crumbs
2 pounds eel (large variety),
  skinned and cut into
  4-inch pieces
additional bay leaves

Mix together oil, vinegar, bay leaves, salt, pepper and bread crumbs. Marinate eel pieces in this mixture 3 hours, turning frequently. Place eel pieces on skewers, alternating with bay leaves. Place skewers in greased baking dish and bake in moderate oven (375°F.) 30 minutes, turning often. Brush with remaining marinade while cooking. Serves 4.

† If soaked baccalà is not available, soak in water 24 hours, changing water every 8 hours.

EELS GENOA STYLE

2½ pounds eel (large variety), cut into 4-inch pieces
¾ cup olive oil
1 small onion, sliced
8 anchovy filets, chopped
½ pound mushrooms, sliced
1 teaspoon salt
½ teaspoon pepper
1 cup dry white wine
2 cloves garlic, sliced
3 cups fresh shelled peas
1 tablespoon tomato sauce
½ cup water

Place cut eels in ice water for 15 minutes. Place oil and onion in large pan and brown onion lightly. Add anchovies and cook 2 minutes. Add eel and cook until water from eel evaporates. Add mushrooms, salt and pepper and cook 5 minutes. Add wine, garlic and peas, cover pan and cook until wine has evaporated. Add tomato sauce and water and continue cooking 30 minutes, or until done, adding additional water, if needed. Serves 4.

FRIED SMALL EELS

3 pounds eel, cut into 2-inch pieces
1 cup flour
1 cup olive oil
1 lemon, cut into quarters

Roll eels in flour and fry in hot olive oil until brown on both sides. Frying time will be about 15 minutes on each side. Remove, drain on paper towel, sprinkle with a little salt and serve with lemon quarters. Serves 4.

LARGE EEL MARINATED (Capitone)

1½-pound eel
1 clove garlic, sliced
½ teaspoon salt
½ teaspoon pepper
3 bay leaves
1 cup wine vinegar
1 cup olive oil

Place eel like a doughnut in bottom of large pan. Add garlic, salt, pepper, bay leaves, vinegar and oil. Cover pan and cook gently about 40 minutes, or (according to thickness of fish) until fish is done. Remove fish from pan, place in bowl, pour gravy over it and cool. It will keep for a few days. Serves 4.

EELS WITH PEAS ROMAN STYLE

1½ pounds small eels
3 tablespoons olive oil
½ clove garlic, minced
4 scallions, chopped
½ teaspoon salt
½ teaspoon pepper
½ cup dry white wine
1 tablespoon tomato sauce
2 cups fresh shelled peas
2 tablespoons warm water or stock

Remove heads from eels and cut into pieces 3 inches long. Place oil in small saucepan, add garlic and scallions and brown lightly. Add eels, salt and pepper and cook until liquid from eels has evaporated. Add wine, tomato sauce and peas and mix well. Add water and cook 15 minutes, or until peas are tender. Add a little more water during cooking, if necessary. Serves 4.

FLOUNDER

FRIED FILET OF FLOUNDER

1¼ pounds filets of flounder	½ teaspoon salt
½ cup flour	½ teaspoon pepper
2 eggs, lightly beaten	1 cup olive oil

Roll flounder in flour. Mix eggs with salt and pepper, dip filets in mixture and fry in hot olive oil until golden brown on both sides. Serve plain or with caper sauce (see index). Serves 4.

FILET OF FLOUNDER IN BUTTER

1¼ pounds filets of flounder	½ teaspoon salt
½ cup flour	½ teaspoon pepper
½ cup butter	3 teaspoons lemon juice

Roll flounder in flour. Melt butter in skillet. Add floured filets, sprinkle with salt and pepper and cook over low flame 10 minutes on each side. Remove from pan, sprinkle with lemon juice and serve. Serves 4.

FLOUNDER WITH BLACK BUTTER SAUCE

1 medium onion	3 quarts water
½ teaspoon thyme	3 pounds flounder, cleaned
½ bay leaf	and cut into large pieces
1 teaspoon salt	½ cup butter
½ teaspoon peppercorns	2 tablespoons vinegar
½ cup vinegar	¼ teaspoon salt

Place onion, thyme, bay leaf, salt, peppercorns and ½ cup vinegar in water and bring to a boil. Add fish and boil very gently 15 minutes. Remove from fire and drain. Skin and bone fish, place on serving dish and keep warm.

Melt butter, cook slowly until light brown in color and remove from fire. Boil 2 tablespoons vinegar until half the quantity evaporates, add salt and browned butter. Pour this black butter sauce over fish and serve. Serves 4.

FILET OF FLOUNDER WITH MUSHROOMS

1 pound filets of flounder	1 small onion
3 tablespoons bread crumbs	1 carrot
1 tablespoon chopped parsley	1 stalk celery
1 egg yolk	½ teaspoon salt
½ teaspoon salt	¾ pound mushrooms, sliced
½ teaspoon pepper	1 tablespoon butter
1 cup dry white wine	¼ cup butter
2 fish heads	1 tablespoon flour
1 pint water	

Cut filets into 2 pieces each (if filets are very small, leave in 1 piece). Mix together bread crumbs, parsley, egg yolk, salt and pepper and spread some of this mixture on each filet. Roll filets with mixture inside and fasten with toothpicks. Place rolled filets in buttered shallow casserole, add wine and cover fish with buttered brown paper and casserole cover. Bake in hot oven (400°F.) 20 minutes.

Place fish heads in water with onion, carrot, celery and salt and cook 30 minutes. Drain and save broth. Brown mushrooms in 1 tablespoon butter 5 minutes and add to fish broth. Melt ¼ cup butter, blend in flour and add fish broth and mushrooms. Cook until thickened. Pour this sauce over fish rolls and serve. Serves 4.

Frog Legs

FROG LEGS FRICASSEE

12 whole frogs, cleaned	¼ cup dried mushrooms, soaked
2 tablespoons olive oil	in water for half an hour
1 small onion, chopped	2 tablespoons flour
1 clove garlic, chopped	1 tablespoon parsley, chopped
¼ cup white wine	2 egg yolks, lightly beaten
½ teaspoon salt	1 tablespoon lemon juice
½ teaspoon pepper	12 thin slices French bread,
	toasted

Skin frogs and remove legs. Place frog legs in cold water and let stand 2 hours. Brown onion and garlic in oil and add wine. When wine has evaporated, add frog bodies, salt, pepper and dried mushrooms. Add just enough water to cover and simmer for 1 hour, keeping pan covered. This will make a delicious broth. Strain broth.

Flour frog legs and add to broth. Cook slowly about 30 minutes, mixing well occasionally. When legs are tender, add chopped parsley to sauce. Remove pan from fire and add 2 egg yolks and lemon juice. Mix well and serve on toasted bread slices. Serves four.

FRIED FROG LEGS

16 pairs frog legs	½ small onion, sliced
1 cup white wine	dash nutmeg
½ teaspoon salt	1 cup flour
½ teaspoon pepper	2 eggs, lightly beaten
1 teaspoon chopped parsley	1 cup olive oil

Wash and dry frog legs. Make a marinade of wine, salt, pepper, parsley, onion and nutmeg. Let frog legs stand in marinade 1 hour. Remove, dry lightly, roll in flour, dip into egg and fry in hot olive oil until golden brown on both sides. Serves 4.

HALIBUT

BAKED HALIBUT

4 medium potatoes, sliced thin	½ clove garlic, minced
1 small onion, chopped fine	1 tablespoon chopped parsley
¾ teaspoon salt	4 anchovy filets, chopped
½ teaspoon pepper	½ cup olive oil
	4 slices halibut, 1 inch thick

Grease a casserole, place in it half the sliced potatoes, sprinkle with half the onion, salt, pepper, garlic, parsley, anchovies and oil. Place fish slices over potatoes and cover with remaining potatoes and other ingredients. Bake in hot oven (400°F.) 35 minutes. Serve in the casserole. Serves 4.

BAKED HALIBUT OR SWORDFISH

4 medium slices halibut, or	1 scallion, sliced
2 large slices, 1 inch thick	4 peppercorns
½ cup olive oil	½ cup flour
1 sprig parsley	½ teaspoon salt
¼ teaspoon thyme	½ teaspoon pepper
2 bay leaves	½ lemon, cut in wedges

Place fish slices in marinade made of oil, parsley, thyme, bay leaves, scallion and peppercorns and let stand 2 hours, turning fish occasionally. Remove fish from marinade, strain oil and place oil in iron skillet. Roll fish in flour, place in oil in skillet, sprinkle with salt and pepper and brown lightly on both sides. When brown, transfer skillet to moderate oven (375°F.) and cook 30 minutes, basting frequently with oil from bottom of skillet. Serve with lemon wedges. Serves 4.

LOBSTER

LOBSTER ALLA DIAVOLO

2 medium lobsters (boiled)
2 tablespoons olive oil
2 tablespoons butter, melted
½ cup vinegar
½ teaspoon pepper
5 red pepper seeds (optional)

1 teaspoon meat extract,
  dissolved in
  1 cup boiling water
1 teaspoon tomato paste
1 tablespoon butter
1 teaspoon flour
½ tablespoon prepared mustard

Cut lobster in halves lengthwise and place shell side down in baking dish. Sprinkle with oil and butter and bake in hot oven 20 minutes. Serve with sauce made in the following manner:

Place vinegar, pepper and red pepper seeds together in saucepan and simmer until vinegar is reduced to half quantity. Add meat extract in hot water and tomato paste to vinegar and cook 10 minutes. Mix together butter and flour, blending well, and add slowly to sauce. Mix well, add mustard and pour over baked lobsters. Serves 2 or 4.

LOBSTER ARCHDUKE

4 small live lobsters
1 small black truffle,
  sliced thin
½ cup butter
1¼ tablespoons flour
1 cup milk

½ teaspoon salt
¼ teaspoon white pepper
1 tablespoon prepared mustard
1½ tablespoons Marsala or
  sherry wine

Boil lobsters 15 minutes and cool. Drain and cut in halves lengthwise. Remove all meat from bodies and tails and cut into small pieces. Discard parts not wanted from bodies. Mix together thin slices of truffle and lobster meat and fill lobster bodies with mixture.

Melt butter in saucepan, blend in flour, add milk, salt, pepper, mustard and wine and cook slowly until thickened. Pour sauce over lobsters, filling in every bit of the shells and place in hot oven (425°F.) 10 minutes. Serve immediately. Serves 4.

BAKED LOBSTER

2 medium lobsters (boiled)	½ teaspoon salt
½ tablespoon powdered mustard	2 tablespoons olive oil
½ teaspoon pepper	1½ tablespoons butter, melted
1 tablespoon chopped parsley	3 tablespoons bread crumbs
½ teaspoon oregano	2 tablespoons olive oil
	1 lemon, cut in wedges

Split lobsters lengthwise and place in baking dish, shell side down. Mix together mustard, pepper, parsley, oregano and salt, moisten with oil and melted butter and spread this mixture over meat side of lobsters. Sprinkle with bread crumbs and olive oil and bake in hot oven (400°F.) 20 minutes. Serve with lemon wedges. Serves 2 or 4.

BOILED LOBSTER

1 onion	1 teaspoon salt
1 stalk celery	2 tablespoons vinegar
1 carrot	water to cover lobsters
	2 medium live lobsters

Place onion, celery, carrot, salt and vinegar in water and bring to a boil. Immerse live lobsters in boiling water and cook 20 minutes. Let lobsters cool in water in which they were boiled. Split open and serve with any suitable sauce (see index). Serves 2.

LOBSTER LUCULLUS STYLE

2 large lobsters (boiled)	2 teaspoons bread crumbs
3 tablespoons butter, melted	dash powdered mustard
½ teaspoon salt	dash cayenne pepper
12 oysters	½ cup butter, melted
4 anchovy filets, chopped	

Split lobsters in halves and remove parts not wanted. Brush with butter, sprinkle with salt and place under broiler 18 minutes. Place 3 oysters on each half of lobster. Mix together chopped anchovies, bread crumbs, mustard and cayenne pepper and put some of the mixture on each oyster. Brush well with melted butter, return lobsters to hot oven 10 minutes and serve immediately. Serves 4.

LOBSTER WITH CREAM

1 large live lobster	1 very small onion, chopped
3 tablespoons butter	½ cup butter
½ teaspoon salt	3 tablespoons grated Parmesan cheese
½ teaspoon pepper	3 egg yolks
1 cup light cream	¼ cup Marsala or sherry wine
1 cup rice	2 tablespoons butter
4 cups water	small dash cayenne pepper

Boil lobster in water to cover 20 minutes and let cool. Remove meat from claws and tail in whole piece and slice very thin. Place lobster slices in small saucepan with butter, salt and pepper, and brown lightly. Add cream, lower flame and simmer until cream is reduced to half quantity.

At the same time boil rice in slightly salted water until almost tender. Brown onion in butter, add rice and Parmesan cheese, mixing well, and place rice in serving dish, keeping center of dish empty.

Place lobster slices in center of dish, leaving the cream in the pan. Mix together egg yolks and wine, add to cream and cook over low flame, stirring constantly, until slightly thickened. Add butter and cayenne, mix well and pour over lobster slices. Serve immediately. Serves 4.

MACKEREL

BROILED MACKEREL

2 teaspoons olive oil	½ clove garlic, chopped fine
½ teaspoon salt	1 teaspoon chopped parsley
½ teaspoon pepper	½ teaspoon oregano
1½ teaspoons lemon juice	dash cayenne pepper
2 pounds mackerel, split	2 tablespoons olive oil
	1 tablespoon vinegar

Mix together oil, salt, pepper and lemon juice and marinate fish in this mixture 2 hours. Place fish on broiler 15 minutes on each side, basting with marinade. Mix together garlic, parsley, oregano, pepper, olive oil and vinegar and pour over broiled fish. Serves 2.

MACKEREL IN TOMATO SAUCE

2 tablespoons olive oil	2 tablespoons water
1 small onion, sliced	½ teaspoon salt
½ clove garlic, chopped	½ teaspoon pepper
1 tablespoon chopped parsley	3 pounds mackerel, cut
1 small can tomatoes	into 4 pieces

Place olive oil, onion, garlic and parsley in skillet and brown. Add tomatoes, water, salt and pepper and cook 5 minutes. Add fish, cover skillet and cook 5 minutes. Turn fish over and cook 10 minutes longer. Serves 4.

MULLET

MULLET CALABRIAN STYLE

½ cup olive oil
3 pounds mullet, cleaned
and washed

½ teaspoon salt
juice of 1 lemon
1 teaspoon oregano

Oil bottom of large skillet and add fish in single layer. Sprinkle with salt, lemon, oregano and remaining olive oil and cook over high flame 8 minutes on each side. Serve immediately. Serves 4.

GRILLED MULLET ON TOAST

3 pounds mullet, cleaned
and washed
¼ cup olive oil
½ teaspoon salt
8 slices white bread, toasted

2 tablespoons butter
½ tube anchovy paste
½ teaspoon minced parsley
juice of ½ lemon

Place fish in oil and salt for ½ hour. Grill fish 10 minutes on each side. Spread toast with butter, anchovy paste, parsley and lemon juice and on top of each toast square place a piece of grilled fish. Serves 4.

MULLET IN PIQUANT SAUCE

3 tablespoons olive oil
3 pounds mullet, cleaned
and washed
½ teaspoon salt
½ teaspoon pepper

juice of ½ lemon
¼ cup dry white wine
1 tablespoon tomato sauce
1 teaspoon prepared mustard

Place oil in large skillet and add fish in one layer. Sprinkle with salt, pepper, lemon juice and wine. Cover skillet and cook gently 15 minutes. Remove fish from skillet and place on serving dish. Add tomato sauce and mustard to pan gravy, mix well and cook 3 minutes. Pour sauce over fish and serve hot or cold. Serves 4.

MULLET IN SKILLET

¼ cup olive oil
3 pounds mullet, cleaned
and washed
½ teaspoon salt
¼ teaspoon pepper
1 teaspoon oregano

1 tablespoon chopped parsley
½ clove garlic, minced
2 tablespoons fine bread crumbs
2 fresh tomatoes, peeled and
sliced thin
3 tablespoons olive oil
juice of ½ lemon

Pour ¼ cup oil into large baking dish and add mullet in single layer. Sprinkle with salt, pepper, oregano, parsley, garlic and bread crumbs. Place slices of tomato over fish and sprinkle tomatoes with 3 tablespoons olive oil. Bake fish in moderate oven (375°F.) 25 minutes. Remove from oven, sprinkle with lemon juice and serve. Serves 4.

MULLET LEGHORN STYLE

3 pounds mullet, cleaned and washed	½ small onion, minced
½ cup flour	¼ clove garlic, minced
2 tablespoons olive oil	¼ teaspoon thyme
¼ teaspoon salt	1 bay leaf
1 teaspoon minced parsley	⅛ teaspoon pepper
	½ cup tomato sauce

Dry mullet well and flour. Place in large skillet with warm olive oil and cook gently 3 minutes on each side. Add salt, parsley, onion, garlic, thyme, bay leaf and pepper. Pour tomato sauce over all and cook 3 or 4 minutes. Serves 4.

MULLET WITH PROSCIUTTO

3 pounds mullet	¼ teaspoon sage
¼ cup olive oil	½ cup fine bread crumbs
juice of 1 lemon	3 tablespoons olive oil
½ teaspoon salt	8 thin slices prosciutto (or lean
¼ teaspoon pepper	ham or bacon)

Remove fish heads, slit one side and bone. Cut in 8 pieces. Marinate in ¼ cup oil, lemon juice, salt, pepper and sage for 2 hours. Drain and roll in bread crumbs. Pour 3 tablespoons oil into large baking dish and place fish in one layer. Place 1 slice prosciutto in slit in each piece. Sprinkle with marinade liquid and bake in moderate oven (375°F.) 20 minutes. Serves 4.

PERCH

PERCH FILETS MILANESE STYLE

1 pound perch filets	1 cup bread crumbs
1 cup flour	½ cup butter
1 egg, lightly beaten with	1 lemon, cut in quarters
½ teaspoon salt and	
½ teaspoon pepper	

Roll filets in flour, dip into egg mixture, roll in bread crumbs and fry in hot butter until nicely browned on each side (frying time will be about 5 minutes on each side). Serve with lemon quarters. Serves 4.

PERCH HOUSEWIFE STYLE

3 pounds perch	1½ cups cream sauce (see index)
2 quarts water	3 tablespoons heavy cream
1 teaspoon salt	2 tablespoons butter
2 tablespoons vinegar	1 hard cooked egg, minced
	1 teaspoon minced parsley

Clean and wash fish and cook 20 minutes in boiling water to which salt and vinegar have been added. Remove from water, skin and place on serving plate. Heat cream sauce, add cream and butter and mix well. Mix together minced egg and parsley. Cover fish with egg mixture, pour cream sauce over all and serve. Serves 4.

PIKE

PIKE SAILOR STYLE

½ teaspoon salt	¼ teaspoon pepper
1 tablespoon olive oil	3 cups dry red wine
1 large onion, sliced fine	3 pounds pike, cut into
1 clove garlic, chopped	4 or 8 pieces
1 carrot, diced	¼ cup butter
1 tablespoon chopped parsley	1 tablespoon flour

Mix together in a bowl the salt, oil, onion, garlic, carrot, parsley, pepper and wine. Marinate fish in this liquid 2 hours. Transfer fish and marinade to large skillet and cook 18 minutes, turning pike once. Remove fish from gravy. Strain gravy and cook 5 minutes longer. Mix together flour and butter and add to gravy, blending in well. Return fish to skillet and let gravy coat it. Serve hot. Serves 4.

PIKE WITH RAISINS

3 pounds pike	1 medium onion, chopped
4 cups dry white wine	½ teaspoon salt
1 large carrot, diced	1 cup seedless raisins
1 tablespoon minced parsley	1 tablespoon butter
2 bay leaves	

Clean and wash pike. Place in deep skillet, add wine, carrot, parsley, bay leaves, onion and salt and cook 45 minutes. Remove fish, place in serving dish and keep warm. Strain pan gravy, add raisins and boil gently 15 minutes. Add butter, mix well, pour over fish and serve. Serves 4.

PORGY

GRILLED PORGIES

2 tablespoons olive oil	1½ teaspoons lemon juice
½ teaspoon salt	3 pounds porgy
½ teaspoon pepper	½ lemon, cut into wedges

Mix together oil, salt, pepper and lemon juice, add fish, turning until well covered with mixture and let stand 40 minutes. Place porgy on grill and cook 15 minutes on each side, brushing occasionally with oil mixture. Serve with lemon wedges. Serves 4.

MARINATED PORGIES

3 pounds porgy	1 tablespoon white vinegar
½ cup olive oil	1 tablespoon dry white wine
1 small onion, sliced thin	¼ teaspoon salt
2 cloves garlic, sliced	½ teaspoon pepper
½ cup olive oil	1 teaspoon sage

Clean and wash porgy and fry in ½ cup olive oil. Remove from pan and drain on paper. Brown onion and garlic in ½ cup olive oil and add vinegar, wine, salt, pepper and sage. Place fried fish in casserole, pour marinade over them and let stand 24 hours. Serve cold. Serves 4.

PORGY WITH PEAS ROMAN STYLE

1 small onion, sliced	½ teaspoon pepper
2 tablespoons olive oil	1 package frozen peas, or
1 teaspoon chopped parsley	2 pounds fresh peas, shelled
1 tablespoon tomato sauce	3 pounds porgy, cut into
½ teaspoon salt	2-inch slices

Brown onion in olive oil, add parsley, tomato sauce, salt, pepper, peas and enough water to cover peas and cook gently 15 minutes, or until peas are almost done. Add fish and cook slowly 15 minutes longer. Serves 4.

PORGY WITH RICE

1 large fish head	1 clove
1½ quarts water	1 carrot
½ teaspoon salt	1 stalk celery
1 small onion	1 sprig parsley

Place fish head in water, add salt, onion, clove, carrot, celery and parsley and boil 30 minutes. Strain and save the stock.

1 medium onion, sliced	1 cup fish stock
1 carrot, diced fine	4 anchovy filets, chopped
½ cup butter	½ pound mushrooms, sliced
½ clove garlic, chopped	2 tablespoons olive oil
1 tablespoon chopped parsley	2 tablespoons flour
1 bay leaf	3 pounds porgy
¼ teaspoon thyme	2 tablespoons olive oil
½ teaspoon salt	1 cup rice
½ teaspoon pepper	2 cups fish stock
½ cup dry white wine	1 cup dry white wine
	1 tablespoon butter

Place onion, carrot and butter in saucepan and brown a little. Add garlic, parsley, bay leaf, thyme, salt and pepper and cook 5 minutes. Add ½ cup wine and cook until wine evaporates. Add 1 cup fish stock, anchovies and mushrooms and cook 10 minutes.

Heat 2 tablespoons olive oil in frying pan, flour the fish and fry in oil on both sides. Drain on paper, place in prepared gravy, cover pan and cook 6 minutes. Remove from fire and keep warm.

Place 2 tablespoons oil in another saucepan, heat and add rice. Cook rice in oil 3 or 4 minutes, stirring well, add 2 cups fish stock and 1 cup wine, cover pan and place in heated oven (400°F.) 18 minutes. The rice will then be cooked and dry. Add butter to rice, place on serving dish and place fish and gravy over it. Serves 4.

SALMON

FRESH SALMON CHEF STYLE

2 pounds salmon steak, cut into pieces	1 medium onion, sliced
3 quarts water	2 tablespoons wine vinegar
½ teaspoon salt	4 tablespoons olive oil
8 peppercorns	1 teaspoon chopped parsley
½ cup vinegar	1 tablespoon capers
	3 tiny sour pickles, sliced

Boil fish in water with salt, peppercorns, vinegar and onion 20 minutes, or until tender. Remove from fire and drain. Mix together vinegar, oil, parsley, capers and pickles and pour over boiled fish. Serves 4.

SARDINES

FRESH SARDINES AND ARTICHOKES

2 pounds fresh sardines	¼ cup olive oil
4 artichokes	1 tablespoon chopped parsley
2 tablespoons olive oil	2 tablespoons fine bread crumbs
½ teaspoon salt	juice of 1 lemon

Clean sardines and remove heads. Split on one side, bone and close again. Remove tough outer leaves of artichokes, cut off stems and tips, slice in half and remove chokes. Cut into thin slices lengthwise.

Oil well a large baking dish. Place in baking dish 1 layer artichokes, sprinkle with a little salt and olive oil, cover with 1 layer sardines, sprinkle with salt, oil and parsley and repeat layers until all fish and artichokes are used, ending with layer of fish. Sprinkle with bread crumbs, oil and salt and bake in moderate oven (375°F.) 50 minutes. Remove from oven, sprinkle with lemon juice and serve. Serves 4.

FRESH SARDINE CROQUETTES

1½ pounds fresh sardines, heads removed, cleaned, boned and chopped	½ teaspoon pepper dash nutmeg 1 teaspoon minced parsley
¼ cup butter	1 tablespoon seedless raisins
2 slices white bread, soaked in water and squeezed dry	½ cup flour 1 cup olive oil
½ teaspoon salt	2 cups tomato sauce (see index)

Mix together chopped sardines, butter, bread, salt, pepper, nutmeg, parsley and raisins and shape into small croquettes. Roll in flour and fry in hot olive oil 4 minutes on each side. Heat tomato sauce, place croquettes in sauce and cook gently 5 minutes. Serves 4.

GRILLED FRESH SARDINES

1½ pounds fresh sardines	1 tablespoon olive oil
½ teaspoon salt	1 lemon, cut into wedges
½ teaspoon pepper	

Clean sardines and remove heads. Sprinkle with salt, pepper and olive oil, place on grill and cook 5 minutes on each side, brushing with oil frequently. Serve with lemon wedges. Serves 4.

FRESH SARDINES IN BAKING DISH

1½ pounds fresh sardines	¼ cup olive oil
½ teaspoon salt	½ teaspoon rosemary
½ teaspoon pepper	½ cup fine bread crumbs

Clean sardines and remove heads. Place in dish with salt, pepper, olive oil and rosemary and marinate 1½ hours. Roll sardines in bread crumbs, place in well-oiled baking dish, pour marinade liquid over sardines and bake in hot oven (400°F.) 15 minutes. Serves 4.

FRESH SARDINES IN PIQUANT SAUCE

1½ pounds fresh sardines	½ teaspoon oregano
1 teaspoon powdered mustard	3 tablespoons olive oil
½ teaspoon pepper	juice of ½ lemon
10 anchovy filets, chopped	1 cup flour
1 tablespoon chopped parsley	1 egg, lightly beaten
	1 cup olive oil

Clean sardines and remove heads. Split on one side and bone. Wash and dry. Mix together mustard, pepper, anchovies, parsley, oregano, olive oil and lemon juice and let sardines stand in this marinade 1 hour. Remove from marinade, flour, dip into egg and fry in hot olive oil. Serve with lemon wedges. Serves 4.

FRESH SARDINES LIGURIAN STYLE

16 fresh sardines	¼ clove garlic, chopped
4 slices bread, soaked in water and squeezed dry	¼ teaspoon marjoram
	½ teaspoon oregano
2 eggs	½ teaspoon salt
1 tablespoon Parmesan cheese	½ teaspoon pepper
	½ cup flour
¼ pound mushrooms, sliced and cooked in butter	1 egg, lightly beaten
	1 cup olive oil

Remove heads from sardines, slit on one side and remove bones. Mix together well bread, eggs, cheese, mushrooms, garlic, marjoram, oregano, salt and pepper. Open sardines, spread with this mixture and do not close fish again. The sardines should somewhat resemble cutlets. Roll in flour, dip into egg and fry in hot oil until golden brown on each side. Serves 4.

FRESH SARDINES MARITATE

24 fresh sardines	4 egg yolks
4 tablespoons olive oil	1 tablespoon water
½ teaspoon salt	½ tablespoon vinegar
½ teaspoon pepper	2 tablespoons butter
1 tablespoon minced parsley	¼ teaspoon salt
juice of ½ lemon	¼ teaspoon pepper
8 slices bread, toasted and	small dash nutmeg
buttered	1 tablespoon prepared mustard

Clean sardines, remove heads, split on one side and bone. Place in oiled baking dish, sprinkle with salt, pepper, parsley, remaining oil and lemon juice and bake in moderate oven (375°F.) 15 minutes. Place 3 cooked sardines on each slice buttered toast and keep warm.

Mix together egg yolks, water and vinegar in saucepan, add butter, salt, pepper, nutmeg and mustard and cook over low flame, stirring constantly, until slightly thickened. Pour sauce over fish and toast and serve immediately. Serves 4.

FRESH SARDINES NEAPOLITAN STYLE

1½ pounds fresh sardines,	1 tablespoon minced parsley
heads removed and cleaned	½ teaspoon oregano
½ cup olive oil	1 small can tomatoes, drained
½ teaspoon salt	and broken in small pieces
½ teaspoon pepper	

Place sardines in well-oiled skillet, sprinkle with salt, pepper, parsley and oregano. Add tomatoes, pour remaining oil over fish and cook over high flame 3 minutes. Turn sardines carefully and cook 5 minutes longer. Serves 4.

FRESH SARDINES PALERMO STYLE

16 fresh sardines	½ teaspoon salt
½ cup olive oil	½ teaspoon pepper
4 tablespoons fine bread	dash nutmeg
crumbs	1 tablespoon chopped parsley
2 tablespoons white raisins	10 anchovy filets, chopped
1 tablespoon shelled	3 bay leaves
pine nuts	3 tablespoons olive oil
½ teaspoon sugar	juice 1 lemon

Remove heads from sardines, slit on one side and bone. Mix together very well ½ cup olive oil, bread crumbs, raisins, pine nuts, sugar, salt, pepper, nutmeg, parsley and anchovies. Stuff sardines with this mixture and close. Place in well-oiled baking dish, dot with bay leaves, sprinkle with 3 tablespoons olive oil and if any of the stuffing is left sprinkle it over fish. Bake in hot oven (400°F.) 20 minutes. Remove from oven, sprinkle with lemon juice and serve. Serves 4.

FRESH SARDINE PIE

1 cup bread crumbs	½ clove garlic, chopped
½ teaspoon salt	1 tablespoon water
½ teaspoon pepper	16 fresh sardines, boned and
1 tablespoon chopped parsley	with heads removed
½ cup olive oil	juice of 1 lemon

Mix together well bread crumbs, salt, pepper, parsley, olive oil, garlic and water. Place 1 layer fish in well-oiled casserole, top with some of the bread mixture and repeat layers, ending with bread mixture. Sprinkle with a little more oil and bake in moderate oven (375°F.) 40 minutes. Remove from oven, sprinkle with lemon juice and serve. Serves 4.

FRESH SARDINES TONGUE STYLE

1½ pounds fresh sardines	½ cup flour
½ cup vinegar	1 cup olive oil
½ teaspoon salt	

Cut heads off sardines, split open on one side and bone. Marinate in vinegar and salt 24 hours. Dry, flour and fry in hot olive oil. Serves 4.

FRESH SARDINES WITH FENNEL

16 fresh sardines	½ teaspoon salt
1 large onion, sliced	½ teaspoon pepper
2 tablespoons olive oil	2 tablespoons fine bread crumbs
½ glass dry white wine	1 tablespoon fennel seeds,
1 medium can tomatoes	chopped
	2 tablespoons olive oil

Remove heads from sardines, bone fish and wash well. Brown onion gently in 2 tablespoons olive oil, add wine and cook 10 minutes. Add tomatoes and mix well. Pour this sauce in baking dish and place sardines over it in one layer. Sprinkle with salt, pepper, bread crumbs and fennel seeds. Pour 2 tablespoons oil over bread crumbs and bake in moderate oven (375°F.) 30 minutes. Serves 4.

SCUNGILLI

SCUNGILLI MARINARA*

½ pounds of scungilli (pulp
   of conch), thinly sliced
3 tablespoons olive oil
2 cloves garlic
1 small onion, sliced thin
1 stalk celery, minced
2 cups canned tomatoes

2 tablespoons tomato sauce
½ teaspoon salt
½ teaspoon oregano
½ teaspoon basil, crushed
2 bay leaves
¼ teaspoon hot pepper seeds

Boil scungilli about 15 minutes and drain. Place oil, scungilli, garlic, onion and celery in large skillet and brown well. Remove garlic, add tomatoes, tomato sauce and salt, cover and cook slowly until scungilli seems well cooked. Add oregano, basil, bay leaves and hot pepper seeds and cook 5 minutes longer. Hot pepper may be omitted or a smaller quantity used, if so desired. Serve hot. Serves 4.

BASS

SEA BASS IN WHITE WINE

3 pounds sea bass, each
   fish cut in two
2 tablespoons flour
¼ cup olive oil
2 tablespoons olive oil
3 scallions, chopped

2 anchovy filets
1 teaspoon chopped parsley
1 cup dry white wine
¼ cup stock or water
¼ teaspoon salt
½ teaspoon pepper

Flour fish and fry in ¼ cup oil in skillet. In small frying pan place 2 tablespoons oil, scallions, anchovies and parsley and brown gently. Add wine, let wine evaporate and add stock or water, salt and pepper. Pour this sauce over fish and cook 1 minute. Serves 4.

SHRIMP

BOILED SHRIMP

1 pound shrimp
1 quart water
½ teaspoon salt
1 tablespoon vinegar

4 peppercorns
1 stalk celery
1 small onion

Wash shrimp. Bring water to boil, add salt, vinegar, peppercorns, celery, onion and shrimp and cook 10 minutes. Shell shrimp, remove black vein and serve with any sauce that pleases you (see index). Serves 2.

SHRIMP BUONGUSTO

2 pounds shrimp, shelled
and veined
½ cup flour
½ cup olive oil
½ cup dry white wine
½ tablespoon tomato paste
4 tablespoons warm water

½ teaspoon salt
½ teaspoon pepper
small dash cayenne pepper
1 tablespoon chopped parsley
1 small scallion, chopped
½ black truffle, sliced thin
(optional)
2 teaspoons lemon juice

Wash and dry shrimp and roll in flour. Brown in hot oil on both sides in large skillet. Remove oil from skillet and save. Add wine to shrimp and cook until wine has evaporated. Place oil in small saucepan, add tomato paste, water, salt, pepper and cayenne and cook 3 or 4 minutes. Pour over shrimp, add parsley, scallion and truffle and cook 4 minutes. Remove from pan, add lemon juice and serve. Serves 4 or 6.

FRIED JUMBO SHRIMP

16 very large shrimp, shelled
and veined
½ cup flour
1 egg, lightly beaten

¼ teaspoon salt
¼ teaspoon pepper
1 cup olive oil
½ lemon, cut into 4 wedges

Wash shrimp in ice water, dry and roll in flour. Dip into egg, to which salt and pepper have been added, and fry in hot olive oil until golden brown on all sides. Frying time will be about 8 minutes. Serve with lemon wedges. Serves 2.

GRILLED SHRIMP

16 large shrimp, shelled
and veined
½ cup cognac
16 thin slices fatty prosciutto
or ham

16 fresh sage leaves or bay leaves
2 tablespoons bread crumbs
½ teaspoon salt
½ teaspoon pepper
2 teaspoons lemon juice

Wash shrimp and marinate in cognac 1 hour. Drain and wrap each shrimp in slice of prosciutto. Place shrimp on skewers alternately with sage or bay leaves. Place in broiler and cook until ham fat begins to sizzle. Roll skewers in bread crumbs, sprinkle with salt and pepper and return to broiler until golden brown in color. Sprinkle with lemon juice and serve very hot. Serves 2.

SHRIMP WITH CREAM

1 pound shrimp	1 tablespoon chopped parsley
1 cup light cream	½ teaspoon salt
½ cup butter	½ teaspoon white pepper

Shell shrimp, remove vein, wash and dry. Place in saucepan, add cream, butter, parsley, salt and pepper and simmer 20 minutes. Serve hot. Serves 2.

SNAILS

LAND SNAILS ROMAN STYLE

4 pounds land snails, alive	1 cup vinegar
4 slices bread, soaked in water	2 tablespoons salt

Put snails in a large vessel with the soaked bread broken into pieces. Leave snails in the pan for two days, covering pan so that they may breathe freely but not escape. After 2 days, make a bath of water, vinegar and salt and place snails in it. Mix well with hands. This will make a lot of foam. Repeat, changing water, salt and vinegar a few times until there is no more foam. Rinse thoroughly in fresh water. Place snails in large pan, with enough water to cover, over slow fire. When snails begin to push heads out of shells, turn fire high and boil about 10 minutes.

Then take:

3 tablespoons olive oil	1 large can tomatoes
2 cloves garlic, sliced	1 sprig fresh mint
6 anchovy filets, chopped	1 pinch red pepper

Brown garlic in olive oil, add anchovies and brown. Add tomatoes and salt and cook about 15 minutes. Add mint, red pepper and snails (drained). Simmer for about half an hour and serve. (Use small oyster fork or nut pick to extract snail.) Serves 6.

SOLE

FILET OF SOLE CARDINALE

2 tablespoons dry white wine	¼ cup butter
2 cups clam broth	1 tablespoon flour
½ teaspoon salt	½ truffle, sliced thin
½ teaspoon pepper	½ pound shrimps, boiled,
1 pound filet of sole	shelled and sliced

Butter well a large baking dish. Add wine, 2 tablespoons clam broth, salt and pepper and place filets in dish. Cover with greased paper, then with baking dish cover and bake in moderate oven (375°F.) 15 minutes.

Blend butter with flour, add remaining clam broth, truffle and shrimp and cook a few minutes until slightly thickened. Pour over filet of sole and serve. Serves 4.

FRIED FILET OF SOLE ITALIAN STYLE

4 medium filets	salt
½ cup flour	1 lemon, cut into 4 wedges
1 cup olive oil	

Flour the sole and fry in hot olive oil 8 minutes on each side. Drain on paper, sprinkle with salt and lemon juice and serve. Serves 4.

GOLDEN FRIED FILET OF SOLE

4 medium filets	½ teaspoon salt
½ cup flour	½ teaspoon pepper
1 egg, lightly beaten	1 cup olive oil

Roll filets in flour, dip into egg which has been beaten lightly with salt and pepper, and fry in hot olive oil until golden brown on both sides. Frying time will be about 8 minutes to a side. Serves 4.

FILET OF SOLE IN WHITE WINE

1 tablespoon butter	1 tablespoon chopped parsley
1½ pounds filet of sole	½ teaspoon thyme
½ teaspoon salt	2 bay leaves, crushed
½ teaspoon pepper	1 tablespoon butter
1 scallion, chopped	1½ teaspoons flour
¼ cup butter, melted	2 tablespoons light cream
½ cup dry white wine	

Butter well a large baking dish that has a cover. Place filets in baking dish in single layer and sprinkle with salt, pepper, scallion, melted butter, wine, parsley, thyme and bay leaves. Cover baking dish with greased paper, then with dish cover and bake in medium oven (375°F.) 20 minutes. Remove filets from baking dish. Pour baking dish gravy into small saucepan, add butter and let melt. Blend in flour, add cream and cook 2 minutes. Pour over fish and serve. Serves 4.

FILET OF SOLE MARGHERITA

8 shrimp	1½ pounds filet of sole
12 mussels, scrubbed clean	1 tablespoon butter
5 tablespoons dry white wine	2 tablespoons butter
1 cup clam broth	1½ teaspoons flour
¼ teaspoon salt	2 egg yolks, slightly beaten
¼ teaspoon thyme	1 tablespoon heavy cream
1 bay leaf	¼ cup butter
juice of ½ lemon	

Boil shrimp 10 minutes and shell. Place mussels in small pan with 1 tablespoon wine and cook until all mussels are open. Strain juice from mussels, mix with clam broth, add 2 tablespoons wine, salt, thyme, bay leaf and lemon juice and boil gently 20 minutes. Strain and save liquid. Place sole in well-greased baking dish, add just enough clam liquid to cover dish. Add 2 tablespoons wine. Dot with butter, cover with greased paper and bake in moderate oven (375°F.) 12 minutes. Remove from oven and keep warm.

Blend together 2 tablespoons butter and flour, add remaining clam liquid and gravy from baking dish and mix well. Add egg yolks and cream and mix with rotary beater until smooth. Place over very low flame and continue mixing until slightly thick. Add ¼ cup butter, a little at a time, mixing constantly. Place mussels and shrimp around filets, pour sauce over all and place in hot oven (400°F.) 3 minutes. Serves 4.

FILET OF SOLE PREZIOSA

1 scallion, sliced	small dash cayenne pepper
2 tablespoons butter	1 tablespoon chopped parsley
1 large can tomatoes,	1 pound filet of sole
cut into small pieces	6 raw oysters, shelled
½ pound mushrooms, sliced	½ cup bread crumbs
½ cup stock	¼ cup butter, melted
½ teaspoon salt	

Brown scallion lightly in 2 tablespoons butter, add tomatoes and mushrooms and cook 5 minutes. Add stock, salt, pepper and parsley and cook 15 minutes, or until gravy has thickened a little. Transfer some of gravy to baking dish, add fish and pour remaining gravy over it. Place oysters over fish and gravy, sprinkle with bread crumbs and pour ¼ cup melted butter over all. Bake in hot oven (400°F.) 30 minutes, or until fish is done. Serves 4.

SOLE MANFREDI

2 pounds sole	1 cup bread crumbs, mixed with
1 small onion, chopped	1 tablespoon chopped cooked
½ teaspoon salt	ham
2 tablespoons dry white wine	¼ cup butter, melted
1 egg, lightly beaten	2 anchovy filets, chopped
	2 tablespoons butter, melted

Clean and wash fish, place in greased baking dish and sprinkle with onion, salt and wine. Cover dish with greased paper and place in hot oven (400°F.) 4 minutes. Remove from oven and cool. Dip fish into egg, roll in bread crumb and ham mixture and return to baking dish. Sprinkle ¼ cup melted butter over fish and bake in hot oven (400°F.) 30 minutes, or until fish is done. Add chopped anchovies and 2 tablespoons butter to pan gravy, mix well and serve with fish. Serves 4.

SOLE MOLINARA

3 pounds sole, cleaned	1 lemon, cut into wedges
and washed	1 teaspoon chopped parsley
1 cup flour	2 tablespoons butter, melted
½ cup butter	and browned

Clean and wash sole, roll in flour and fry in ½ cup hot butter, browning well on both sides. Remove from pan, drain on absorbent paper and place on serving dish with lemon wedges. Sprinkle parsley, a little lemon juice and the brown butter over the sole and serve. Serves 4.

SQUID

GRILLED SQUID

2 pounds squid	½ teaspoon salt
2 tablespoons olive oil	½ teaspoon pepper

Skin squid, remove head and insides, and cut into several pieces. Place in dish with oil, salt and pepper and let stand 1 hour, turning occasionally. Remove, drain and place on medium hot grill (400°F.) and cook 20 minutes on each side, brushing occasionally with oil. Serves 4.

SQUID IN MUSHROOM SAUCE

2 pounds small squid
½ cup olive oil
3 anchovy filets, chopped
½ clove garlic, chopped
1 teaspoon minced parsley
2 tablespoons dry white wine

1½ tablespoons tomato sauce
¼ teaspoon salt
½ teaspoon pepper
½ cup water
2 tablespoons dry mushrooms,
    well washed and cut into pieces

Skin squid, remove head and insides, cut into small pieces and wash well. Heat oil in saucepan, add anchovies, garlic, parsley and wine and cook 5 minutes. Add tomato sauce, squid, salt, pepper and ½ cup water, cover pan and cook 20 minutes. Add mushrooms and cook over low flame 40 minutes longer, adding water occasionally if needed. Serves 4.

LARGE SQUID LUCIANO STYLE

1½ pounds squid
1 teaspoon salt
½ teaspoon pepper, or
    red pepper seeds

2 sprigs parsley
2 fresh tomatoes, cut into pices
½ cup olive oil
juice of ½ lemon

Skin squid, remove insides and eyes, and wash well. Place in soup pan, add salt, pepper, parsley, tomatoes and olive oil and place a piece of brown paper over the top. Tie brown paper around top of pan with string and place lid over it. Place pan on very low flame and cook 2 hours. Do not remove cover during cooking and keep flame as low as possible. Sprinkle with lemon juice and serve either hot or cold. Serves 2.

SMALL SQUID GENOA STYLE

1½ pounds squid
3 tablespoons olive oil
1 onion, chopped
1 tablespoon chopped
    parsley

1 clove garlic
½ teaspoon rosemary
¼ pound mushrooms, sliced
2 tablespoons tomato sauce
½ cup water

Skin squid, remove insides and cut into small pieces. Brown onion in olive oil, add parsley, garlic, rosemary and mushrooms and cook 5 minutes. Add tomato sauce, water and squid, cover pan and cook slowly about 40 minutes, or until squid is tender (cooking time will depend on size of squid). Serves 4.

SMALL SQUID MARCHE STYLE

1½ pounds small squid	2 anchovy filets, chopped
½ cup olive oil	1 tiny piece hot red pepper
1 clove garlic, sliced	1 cup dry white wine
1 tablespoon parsley	½ cup stock or water
½ teaspoon salt	

Skin squid, remove insides, wash well and cut into pieces. Brown garlic in olive oil, add squid, parsley, salt, anchovies and red pepper and cook until the liquid from squid has evaporated. Add wine and cook until it evaporates. Add stock or water and cook over very low flame 20 minutes, or until squid are thoroughly cooked. Serves 4.

SMALL SQUID NEAPOLITAN STYLE

1½ pounds small squid	1 tablespoon pine nuts
3 tablespoons olive oil	10 ripe black olives, pitted and
1 clove garlic, sliced	chopped
1 medium can peeled	1 tablespoon seedless raisins
tomatoes	½ cup water
½ teaspoon salt	4 thin slices Italian bread,
½ teaspoon pepper	toasted

Clean squid, cut off heads and wash well. Brown garlic in olive oil. Remove garlic from pan and add tomatoes, salt, pepper and squid to the oil. Cook 10 minutes and add pine nuts, olives, raisins and water, cover pan and cook about 20 minutes, or until squid are tender (cooking time will vary according to size of squid). Place 1 slice toast in each dish, pour squid and gravy over toast and serve. Serves 4.

SMALL SQUID PIQUANT

1½ pounds very small	1 very small hot pepper
squid	1 tablespoon bread crumbs
½ cup olive oil	1 tablespoon butter
2 cloves garlic	1 tablespoon chopped parsley
½ teaspoon salt	1 lemon, cut into wedges

Skin squid, remove insides and wash thoroughly. Brown garlic in olive oil, add squid, salt and hot pepper and cook over high flame until squid are tender. Remove garlic and red pepper. Add bread crumbs, butter and parsley and keep on fire 2 minutes longer, stirring well. Serve with lemon wedges. Serves 4.

SMALL SQUID WITH CHARD

1 bunch Swiss chard	½ cup dry white wine
1 pound small squid	3 tablespoons tomato sauce
3 tablespoons olive oil	1 tiny hot red pepper
½ teaspoon salt	1 tablespoon chopped parsley
½ teaspoon pepper	2 teaspoons lemon juice

Parboil chard 5 minutes and drain well. Peel squid, remove inner tubes, slice squid in 1-inch rings and cut tentacles into small pieces. Brown lightly in oil 5 minutes, with salt and pepper added. Add chard and wine and cook 10 minutes. Add tomato sauce, red pepper and parsley and cook 25 minutes. Remove from fire, add lemon juice and serve. Serves 4.

STUFFED SQUID (Number 1)

2 pounds squid	1 very small tomato, minced
1 clove garlic	1 anchovy filet, chopped
2 sprigs minced parsley	1 tablespoon olive oil
½ teaspoon salt	2 tablespoons bread crumbs
½ teaspoon pepper	½ cup olive oil
1 tablespoon uncooked rice	

Peel squid and remove insides, keeping body whole. Cut off tentacles and heads, remove eyes and put heads and tentacles through meat chopper. Add parsley, salt, pepper, rice, tomato, anchovy and 1 tablespoon oil and mix well.

Stuff squid bodies with this mixture, place in oiled baking dish, prinkle with bread crumbs and pour oil over all. Bake in hot oven (400°F.) 35 minutes. Slice and serve. Serves 4.

STUFFED SQUID (Number 2)

8 small squid	2 slices white bread, crumbled
½ clove garlic, chopped	½ teaspoon salt
¼ pound mushrooms, chopped	½ teaspoon pepper
¼ teaspoon oregano	½ cup olive oil
½ tablespoon chopped parsley	1 lemon, cut into wedges

Skin squid, remove insides and sever tentacles and heads from bodies. Remove eyes and chop tentacles and heads very fine. Mix together chopped tentacles and heads with garlic, mushrooms, oregano, parsley, bread, salt, pepper and half the olive oil.

Stuff squid bodies with this mixture and sew tops closed. Place stuffed squid in oiled casserole, sprinkle with a little salt and pepper and the remaining oil and bake in moderate oven (375°F.) 45 minutes. Serve with lemon wedges. Serves 4.

SQUID WITH ARTICHOKES

2 pounds squid	½ teaspoon pepper
4 tablespoons olive oil	½ cup water
1 clove garlic	4 artichoke hearts
½ teaspoon salt	

Skin squid, remove insides, wash well and cut into thin slices. Brown garlic in oil and remove from skillet. Add squid, salt and pepper to oil and cook 5 minutes. Add ½ cup water, cover skillet and cook slowly 20 minutes.

Clean artichokes of outside leaves, cut off tips and stalks, cut into thin slivers and add to squid. Cook slowly 30 minutes, or until artichokes and squid are tender, adding a little water, if needed. Serves 4.

STOCKFISH

STOCKFISH ANCONA STYLE

1½ pounds soaked stockfish	¼ teaspoon marjoram
1 cup olive oil	½ teaspoon salt
2 large onions, sliced	½ teaspoon pepper
1 carrot, diced	4 anchovy filets, chopped
1 stalk celery, cut in	1 small can tomato sauce
tiny pieces	½ cup milk
1 tablespoon chopped parsley	

If soaked stockfish is not available, buy it dry and soak in fresh water 4 days, changing water every 6 hours. Split stockfish in half, remove center bone and cut into large pieces. Heat ½ cup olive oil, add onions, carrot, celery, parsley, marjoram, salt and pepper and brown well. Add anchovies and tomato sauce and cook 3 minutes.

Place some of sauce in bottom of Dutch oven, add fish, cover with more sauce and more fish. Top with ½ cup olive oil and milk, cover Dutch oven and cook slowly 2 hours, shaking pan from time to time to prevent scorching. Do not stir. Serve with boiled potatoes. Serves 4.

STOCKFISH MESSINA STYLE (Sicilian)

1½ pounds soaked stockfish	2 tablespoons capers
½ cup olive oil	12 black olives, pitted and diced
1 medium onion, sliced	2 large, or 4 small, potatoes,
1 large can peeled tomatoes	sliced thin
1½ tablespoons pine nuts	¼ teaspoon salt
1½ tablespoons seedless	¾ teaspoon pepper
raisins	1 cup dry white wine

If soaked stockfish is not available, buy it dry and soak in fresh water 4 days, changing water every 6 hours. Split fish, remove center bone and cut into medium pieces. Brown onion in olive oil in large skillet and add tomatoes. Add fish, pine nuts, raisins, capers, olives, potatoes, salt and pepper. Pour wine over all, cover skillet and bake in moderate oven (375°F.) 1 hour. Serves 4.

POTACCHIO MARCHE STYLE

1½ pounds soaked stockfish	½ cup dry white wine
¾ cup olive oil	¼ teaspoon salt
1½ cloves garlic, chopped	¾ teaspoon pepper
2 teaspoons rosemary	3 tablespoons butter
1 large can peeled tomatoes	

If soaked stockfish is not available, buy it dry and soak in fresh water 4 days, changing water every 6 hours. Split fish, remove center bone and cut into several pieces. Place fish in pottery casserole. Brown garlic and rosemary in oil, add tomatoes, wine, salt and pepper, mixing well, and pour over fish. Cover casserole and cook on top of stove over very low flame 1 hour. Add butter, remove to moderate oven (375°F.) and bake 1 hour. Serves 4.

STOCKFISH VENETIAN STYLE

1½ pounds soaked stockfish	½ teaspoon pepper
1 clove garlic	½ cup light cream
½ cup olive oil	dash nutmeg
1 cup milk	

If soaked stockfish is not available, buy it dry and soak in fresh water 4 days, changing water every 6 hours. Cut into pieces and boil in water 20 minutes, or until very tender.

Drain, remove skin and center bones and flake. Rub a large saucepan with garlic and add flaked fish. Heat fish, add a little of the oil and mix well. Add a little of the milk and continue cooking, adding oil and milk a little at a time until all is used, stirring constantly. Add pepper, cream and nutmeg and serve on toast. Serves 4.

STOCKFISH VICENZA STYLE

1½ pounds soaked stockfish	1 cup olive oil
½ cup flour	1 very small onion, sliced
¼ teaspoon salt	½ clove garlic, chopped
½ teaspoon pepper	2 anchovy filets, diced
dash nutmeg	1 tablespoon chopped parsley
3 tablespoons grated	2 cups dry white wine
Parmesan cheese	3 cups milk
	2 tablespoons butter

If soaked stockfish is not available, buy it dry and soak it in fresh water 4 days, changing water every 6 hours. Split, remove center bone and cut into large pieces. Mix together flour, salt, pepper and nutmeg. Roll fish in flour, place in casserole and sprinkle with Parmesan cheese.

Place oil in saucepan, add onion and garlic and brown lightly. Add anchovies and parsley and mix well. Add wine and cook until wine has evaporated. Add milk and butter, blending together well and pour this sauce over fish in casserole. Cover casserole and bake in moderate oven 1½ hours, or until liquid has all been absorbed. Serve with slices of cooked polenta (see index). Serves 4.

SWORDFISH

FRIED SWORDFISH

¼ cup olive oil	1½ pounds swordfish, cut
½ teaspoon salt	into 1-inch slices
½ teaspoon pepper	½ cup flour
1 tablespoon chopped	1 egg, lightly beaten
parsley	½ cup olive oil
2 teaspoons lemon juice	½ lemon, cut into wedges

Mix together olive oil, salt, pepper, parsley and lemon juice and marinate fish in this mixture 2 hours. Remove, dry, roll in flour, dip in egg and fry in hot olive oil until golden brown on both sides. Serve with lemon wedges. Serves 4.

SWORDFISH PUDDING

1½ cups rice	1 clove garlic
1 small onion, sliced	2 tablespoons tomato sauce
2 tablespoons olive oil	1½ pounds swordfish, diced
2 tablespoons tomato sauce	¼ pound mushrooms, sliced
½ teaspoon salt	1 cup bread crumbs
½ teaspoon pepper	1 egg, lightly beaten
1 egg, lightly beaten	2 tablespoons butter
2 tablespoons olive oil	

Wash and drain rice. Brown onion in olive oil, add 2 tablespoons tomato sauce, rice, salt, pepper and enough water to cover and cook until rice is almost done, adding a little water if needed. Remove from fire, add beaten egg and let cool.

Brown garlic in oil and remove garlic. Add 2 tablespoons tomato sauce and diced fish and cook 10 minutes. Add mushrooms and cook 3 minutes. Cool. Grease well a 2-quart pudding mold and sprinkle all over with bread crumbs. Brush with beaten egg and sprinkle again with bread crumbs. Line mold with partly cooked rice, leaving a large well in center. Fill the well with fish, cover with additional bread crumbs and dot with butter. Bake in moderate oven (375°F.) 45 minutes. Let cool 5 minutes before turning out on serving dish. Serves 6.

TROUT

BLUE BROOK TROUT

3 pounds brook trout	½ cup vinegar
water to cover fish	½ cup butter, melted
2 teaspoons salt	1 tablespoon minced parsley
	¼ teaspoon pepper

Clean and wash trout. Bring water to a boil, add salt, vinegar and trout and cook gently 12 minutes. Remove trout from pan and place on serving dish. Mix melted butter with parsley and pepper and serve with fish. Serves 4.

TROUT SAVOY STYLE

2 pounds trout	¼ teaspoon salt
¼ teaspoon salt	¼ teaspoon pepper
½ teaspoon pepper	1 teaspoon minced parsley
½ cup flour	1½ tablespoons fine bread
½ cup butter	crumbs
1 tablespoon olive oil	2 tablespoons butter, melted
1 tablespoon butter	¼ cup butter
½ pound mushrooms, sliced	1 scallion, minced

Clean and wash trout and sprinkle with salt and pepper. Roll in flour and fry in ½ cup butter slowly 10 minutes on each side, or until well done. Fry mushrooms in 1 tablespoon butter and oil 10 minutes and add salt, pepper and parsley. Spread mushrooms in baking dish and place trout over them. Sprinkle with butter in which trout was fried and with bread crumbs. Sprinkle with 2 tablespoons melted butter and bake in moderate oven (375°F.) 5 minutes. Heat ¼ cup butter, add minced scallion and simmer 1 minute. Pour over fish and serve. Serves 2.

STEAMED TROUT

2 pounds trout (or	¼ teaspoon thyme
any other good fish)	½ bay leaf, minced
½ teaspoon salt	2 cups extra dry red wine
½ teaspoon pepper	(Barolo), heated
¼ cup butter	2 tablespoons butter
1 small onion, chopped fine	½ tablespoon flour
1 small carrot, chopped fine	½ cup light cream
1 stalk celery, chopped fine	¼ cup butter
1 teaspoon minced parsley	

Clean trout, wash and sprinkle with salt and pepper, inside and out. Butter thoroughly roasting pan that has a cover. Place in the roasting pan the onion, carrot, celery, parsley, thyme and bay leaf and place fish over this. Add a little more butter, cover fish with greased paper, then with pan cover, and place in moderate oven (350°F.) 15 minutes. Remove cover, add hot wine, cover again and continue cooking 40 minutes, basting occasionally. Remove from oven, place fish on serving dish, strain pan liquid and save.

Blend 2 tablespoons butter with flour, add pan gravy and cream, stirring constantly until gravy thickens. Add ¼ cup butter, a little at a time, beating well until smooth. Pour over trout and serve. Serves 2.

Tuna

BRAISED FRESH TUNA

1½ pounds fresh tuna,	1 small onion, sliced
in one piece	½ teaspoon salt
3 tablespoons olive oil	½ teaspoon pepper

Wash tuna in ice water. Place onion in olive oil in large pan and brown lightly. Add fish and brown on all sides. Browning time will be about 30 minutes. Add salt, pepper and enough water to cover fish, cover pan and cook slowly 1 hour. Slice fish and serve with pan gravy. Use leftover gravy as sauce for spaghetti or rice. Serves 4.

CANNED TUNA WITH PEAS

2 tablespoons olive oil	2 medium cans tuna fish
1 medium onion, sliced	in oil
1 tablespoon chopped parsley	½ teaspoon pepper
1 tablespoon tomato sauce	¼ teaspoon salt
2 cups shelled fresh peas	¼ teaspoon oregano

Heat oil in large pan, add onion and parsley and brown. Add tomato sauce, peas and enough water to cover and cook 10 minutes, or until peas are tender. Slice tuna, add to mixture and cook 5 minutes over low flame. Add pepper, salt and oregano, cook 5 minutes longer and serve. Serves 4.

COLD PUREE OF TUNA

3 large potatoes	1/4 teaspoon salt
1 cup milk	1/4 teaspoon pepper
1 large can tuna fish, grated	1 cup mayonnaise sauce

Boil potatoes thoroughly, peel and mash. Add milk and mix well. Add tuna, salt and pepper and mix well. Mold in fish shape or any shape you desire, and chill. Serve with mayonnaise sauce. Serves 4.

FRESH TUNA IN TOMATO

1½ pounds fresh tuna, sliced 1-inch thick	1 tablespoon chopped parsley
½ teaspoon salt	½ cup dry white wine
½ cup flour	3 tablespoons tomato paste
3 tablespoons olive oil	1 cup warm water
1 clove garlic	1 bay leaf
½ medium onion, sliced	½ teaspoon basil
2 anchovy filets, chopped	½ teaspoon oregano

Sprinkle slices of tuna with salt, roll in flour and fry in 2 table spoons oil until lightly browned. Brown onion and garlic in 1 tablespoon oil and remove garlic. Add anchovies and parsley and cook 1 minute. Add wine and cook until it evaporates. Add tomato paste, water, bay leaf, basil and oregano and cook 15 minutes. Pour sauce over fish and cook 10 minutes. Serves 4.

FRESH TUNA RAGOUT SICILIAN STYLE

1½ pounds fresh tuna, in one piece	3 tablespoons olive oil
10 mint leaves	2 large onions, sliced
½ teaspoon salt	½ clove garlic, chopped
½ teaspoon pepper	4 tablespoons tomato paste
2 tablespoons flour	1 cup water

Make slits in tuna with point of knife and insert mint leaves. Sprinkle with salt and pepper, roll in flour and brown on all sides in olive oil. Remove tuna and brown onions and garlic in oil. Return fish to pan and continue browning. Add tomato paste and water, cover pan and cook slowly 30 minutes. Slice tuna and serve with pan gravy. Serves 4.

FRESH TUNA SARDINIAN STYLE

1½ pounds fresh tuna
½ cup vinegar
½ cup olive oil
1 small onion, sliced
1 carrot, diced
½ stalk celery, diced
1 tablespoon butter
1 tablespoon dried
  mushrooms, soaked in
  water and minced, or
  ¼ pound fresh mush-
  rooms, sliced

1 bay leaf
½ teaspoon thyme
4 anchovy filets, chopped
2 tablespoons tomato sauce
½ teaspoon salt
½ teaspoon pepper
1 cup dry white wine
½ teaspoon meat extract,
  dissolved in
  ½ cup warm water
2 egg yolks, lightly beaten
2 teaspoons lemon juice

Place tuna in cold water to cover, add vinegar and let stand 2 hours. Heat oil in large pan, add onion, carrot, celery, butter, mushrooms, bay leaf and thyme and brown lightly. Add anchovies. Dry tuna and add, browning on all sides. Add tomato sauce, salt and pepper and cook 3 minutes. Add wine and water in which meat extract has been dissolved and cook 20 minutes. Remove fish from pan and strain gravy. Add egg yolks and lemon juice to gravy, pour over fish and serve. Serves 4.

SKEWERS OF FRESH TUNA

1 pound fresh tuna
1 long loaf French bread
bay leaves
fresh sage leaves

¼ cup butter, melted
½ teaspoon salt
½ teaspoon pepper
2 tablespoons olive oil
4 teaspoons lemon juice

Soak tuna in ice water 1 hour, dry and slice into 1- by 3-inch pieces. Cut bread into thin slices. Place 1 slice of fish on skewer, a bay leaf, a slice of bread, a sage leaf and repeat procedure until all fish is used, using as many skewers as needed. Dip skewers into melted butter, sprinkle with salt and pepper and place under broiler, keeping heat at 375°F. Turn skewers often and brush with olive oil each time. Cook 30 minutes. Remove from broiler, sprinkle with lemon juice and serve. Serves 4.

WHITEBAIT

FRIED WHITEBAIT (Pesciolini Fritti)*

1 pound whitebait
1 cup flour
1½ cups olive oil

salt to taste
½ lemon, cut into wedges

The whitebait are so small that many people do not bother to remove the heads or to eviscerate them. Do as you wish about this. Wash carefully, dry and flour well. Fry in deep oil until crisp, sprinkle with salt and serve with lemon wedges. Serves 2.

WHITING

BAKED WHITING

2 pounds whiting	1 tablespoon chopped parsley
6 anchovy filets, chopped	½ cup olive oil
½ teaspoon pepper	2 tablespoons bread crumbs
	4 teaspoons lemon juice

Clean and wash fish and remove heads. Mix together anchovies, pepper, parsley and 2 tablespoons olive oil. Spread this mixture over fish evenly, roll in bread crumbs and place in well-oiled baking dish. Sprinkle with remaining oil and bake in moderate oven (375°F.) 20 minutes, turning once. Remove from oven, sprinkle with lemon juice and serve. Serves 2.

BOILED WHITING

1 onion	¼ teaspoon pepper
1 stalk celery	¼ cup olive oil
1 teaspoon salt	juice of 1 lemon
2 quarts water	½ teaspoon minced parsley
3 pounds whiting, cleaned	

Place onion, celery and salt in water and bring to a boil. Add fish and boil gently 15 minutes. Drain fish and remove skin and bones. Place in serving dish, sprinkle with pepper, oil, lemon juice and parsley and serve hot or cold. Serves 4.

WHITING IN BAKING DISH

4 pounds whiting	2 tablespoons bread crumbs
1 small onion, sliced fine	1 tablespoon grated Parmesan
½ pound mushrooms,	cheese
sliced thin	2 tablespoons dry white wine
½ teaspoon salt	½ cup butter, melted
½ teaspoon pepper	1 lemon, quartered

Clean and split fish. Grease a large baking dish. Place sliced onions in bottom of baking dish, cover with mushrooms and place fish on mushrooms, skin side up. Sprinkle with salt, pepper, bread crumbs, cheese, wine and melted butter and bake in hot oven (400°F.) 18 minutes. Serve garnished with lemon quarters. Serves 6.

OVEN-STEAMED WHITING

3 pounds whiting, cleaned	1 tablespoon butter
2 tablespoons butter	2 tablespoons stock
1 cup stock	½ teaspoon salt
1 cup dry white wine	¼ teaspoon pepper
½ tablespoon flour	

Grease fish with butter and sprinkle with salt and pepper. Place stock and wine in roasting pan and place fish in it. Cover fish tightly with greased paper first and then with pan cover. Bake in moderate oven (375°F.) 40 minutes, basting occasionally. Remove fish from pan. Add flour to pan gravy and blend in well. Add butter, stock, salt and pepper and cook on top of stove 3 minutes. Pour over fish and serve Serves 4.

Fish Miscellany

BAKED FISH SICILIAN STYLE*

1½ pounds swordfish or halibut	½ teaspoon salt
	½ teaspoon pepper
1 large onion, chopped	1 tablespoon flour
2 tablespoons olive oil	1 tablespoon water
1 medium can peeled tomatoes	12 green olives, pitted and cut into pieces
½ cup water	1 tablespoon chopped parsley
3 cloves	2 tablespoons capers
	1 stalk celery, minced

Wash and dry fish. Brown onion in olive oil, add tomatoes, water, cloves, salt and pepper, cover pan and simmer 20 minutes. Blend to smooth paste the flour and 1 tablespoon water, stir into tomato mixture and cook 5 minutes. Add olives, parsley, capers and celery.

Place fish in greased baking dish, pour the tomato sauce over it and bake in moderate oven (375°F.) 35 minutes, basting occasionally. Serve hot with sauce. Serves 4.

EXQUISITE FISH FILETS

1¼ cups leftover fish or plain boiled fish	2 cups milk
	1 tablespoon grated Parmesan cheese
2 tablespoons flour	
1 tablespoon Cream of Wheat	½ cup flour
2 egg yolks	1 egg, lightly beaten
½ teaspoon salt	1 cup bread crumbs
½ teaspoon pepper	1 cup olive oil
dash nutmeg	1 lemon, cut into wedges

Bone fish and chop. Mix together flour, Cream of Wheat, egg yolks, salt, pepper, nutmeg and milk. Place on fire and cook until thickened, stirring constanly. Add fish and Parmesan cheese and mix well. Pour over well-floured board and spread 1 inch thick. Cut into slices 2 inches wide and 4 inches long. Flour slices well, dip into egg, roll in bread crumbs and fry in hot oil until golden brown on both sides. Serve with lemon wedges. Serves 4.

FISH IN SHELLS

2 cups leftover fish, or canned fish	1 egg yolk
¼ cup butter	1½ tablespoons grated Parmesan cheese
1 tablespoon flour	4 pastry shells
1½ cups milk	½ cup bread crumbs
½ teaspoon salt	2 tablespoons butter

Bone fish and shred. Melt butter in saucepan, blend in flour and cook 2 minutes. Add milk and salt and cook until slightly thickened, stirring constantly. Add egg yolk, mix well and add cheese, continuing to mix well.

Butter 4 large shells, pour 1 tablespoon sauce into each and fill with shredded fish. Pour remaining sauce over fish, sprinkle with bread crumbs and dot with butter. Bake in hot oven (400°F.) 10 minutes. Serve immediately. Serves 4.

FISH TURNOVERS

4 medium slices halibut, cod or tuna (about 2 pounds)	¼ teaspoon salt
3 tablespoons olive oil	½ cup butter
½ teaspoon salt	1 egg
¼ teaspoon pepper	1 egg, lightly beaten
2 cups flour	1 cup plain tomato sauce (see index)

Fry fish in hot oil until well done, add salt and pepper and cool, draining off oil. Sift together flour and salt, cut in butter, add egg and work dough until smooth. Let dough stand 15 minutes, divide into 4 parts and roll out to ⅛-inch thickness, or until you have 4 pieces large enough for turnovers.

Place 1 slice of fish on each piece of dough, fold over and press edges together, sealing with beaten egg. Brush tops of turnovers with beaten egg and place on greased baking dish. Bake in hot oven (400°F.) 40 minutes, or until turnovers are golden brown. Serve plain or with tomato sauce. Serves 4.

FRIED FISH SICILIAN STYLE

½ cup olive oil
1 teaspoon salt

2 pounds fish (porgy, bass,
   trout, butterfish)
½ lemon, cut into wedges

Heat olive oil in frying pan, add salt and let oil become very hot. Add fish, cover pan and cook 15 minutes on each side. Serve with lemon wedges. Serves 2.

GRILLED FISH ADRIATIC STYLE

1½ pounds whiting
1½ pounds mullet
1 pound halibut
½ cup olive oil

1 teaspoon salt
1 teaspoon pepper
4 teaspoons lemon juice
½ teaspoon rosemary

This dish is best if it can be broiled over charcoal but it can be broiled in gas or electric broiler as well. Clean and wash fish. Marinate all fish in oil, salt, pepper, lemon juice and rosemary 2 hours. Place on grill and cook 20 minutes on each side, or until fish skin is crisp. Brush with marinade occasionally during broiling. Serve with additional lemon juice. Serves 4.

RICE AND FISH IN SHELLS

4 pastry shells
1 cup cooked rice
2 tablespoons butter
2 tablespoons grated Parmesan
   cheese

1 cup leftover fish, lobster,
   or shrimp, shredded
½ cup cream sauce
1 egg, lightly beaten
2 tablespoons grated Parmesan
   cheese

Butter 4 large shells. Mix hot rice with butter and Parmesan cheese and partly fill each shell with this mixture. Place shredded fish on rice, cover with cream sauce mixed with egg, sprinkle with Parmesan cheese and bake in hot oven (400°F.) 10 minutes. Serves 4.

Other recipes containing fish will be found in Chapters 1, 2 and 9.

6. *Meat*

BEEF

BAKED FILET OF BEEF IN CASSEROLE

1 tablespoon butter
2 pounds filet of beef
   in 1 piece
¼ teaspoon salt
⅛ teaspoon pepper
1 large onion, sliced
2 carrots, sliced thin
1 stalk celery, chopped

4 medium tomatoes, peeled
   and cut into pieces
1 bay leaf
¼ teaspoon thyme
½ cup dry white wine
1 jigger cognac
¼ cup Marsala or sherry wine
½ cup stock

Melt butter in frying pan, add meat and braise quickly on all sides over high flame for about 5 minutes. Remove meat from frying pan and place in large casserole or baking pan with tight-fitting cover. Sprinkle meat with salt and pepper and place onion, carrots, celery and tomatoes around meat. Sprinkle with bay leaf and thyme and pour wine, cognac, Marsala or sherry and stock over all. Cover tightly and place casserole in pan of hot water in moderate oven 3 hours. Do not uncover casserole until ready to serve. Serves 6.

BEEF ALLA CERTOSINA

2½ pounds eye of the
   round of beef
1 tablespoon olive oil
1 tablespoon butter
1 slice bacon, chopped
salt and pepper to taste

⅛ teaspoon nutmeg
3 or 4 anchovy filets,
   chopped fine
2 teaspoons chopped parsley
1 cup stock or water

Put meat in large saucepan with oil, butter, chopped bacon, pepper, salt, nutmeg, and brown slowly but thoroughly. When meat is well browned add the chopped anchovies, parsley and the stock or water. Reduce heat, cover the pan, and cook slowly about 1¼ hours, or until the meat is tender. Slice and serve covered with gravy. Add a little water to the gravy if necessary. Serves 6.

BEEF GRANATINE

1½ pounds chopped lean
   beef
2 slices bread soaked in
   water or milk, squeezed dry
1 egg
¼ teaspoon salt
⅛ teaspoon pepper

⅛ teaspoon nutmeg
1 tablespoon grated Parmesan
   cheese
1 tablespoon flour
1 egg, beaten
1 cup bread crumbs
2 tablespoons butter

Mix thoroughly the chopped beef, bread, the whole egg, salt, pepper, nutmeg and grated cheese. Divide into 6 portions, shape like cutlets, flour lightly, dip into beaten egg, then into bread crumbs. Fry in butter over low fire so that the meat is thoroughly cooked. When golden brown in color, turn gently and fry on the other side. Serves 6.

BEEF RAGOUT WITH GRAVY

2 slices bacon	⅓ cup sauterne wine
1 clove garlic, chopped	2 small onions
¼ teaspoon marjoram	1 large carrot
salt and pepper	2 stalks celery
2-pound piece of the eye of the round of beef	¼ teaspoon chopped parsley
	1 tablespoon butter
4 tablespoons butter, or 2 tablespoons olive oil	2 8-ounce cans tomato sauce

Cut bacon into small pieces and sprinkle with a mixture of garlic, marjoram, salt and pepper. Make small slits in the meat and insert the pieces of bacon until the mixture is all used. Then tie the meat to keep it in shape during cooking. Place meat in large saucepan with butter or olive oil, and let brown slowly on all sides. When meat is well browned, add salt, pepper and sauterne and continue cooking until wine has evaporated. Remove meat from the pan, and keep warm on the stove.

Chop together onions, carrot, celery, and parsley, place in the saucepan with tablespoon of butter and cook slowly until golden in color, adding a little water occasionally. Return meat to pan and continue browning for 10 minutes longer. Add tomato sauce and enough water to cover meat. Cover pan tightly, reduce heat, and simmer over low heat for about 2 hours. If the gravy should be too fat, allow it to cool and remove the fat that will form on top. Slice meat and use gravy for rice, spaghetti or other macaroni. Serves 4.

BEEF SLICES ALLA PIZZAIOLA (Number 1)

4 medium slices top round steak, ½ inch thick (about ½ pound)	1 clove garlic, sliced
	½ large can tomatoes
2 tablespoons olive oil	½ teaspoon oregano
	salt and pepper

Sauté meat in 1 tablespoon olive oil 2 minutes on each side. In separate pan brown garlic in 1 tablespoon olive oil, add tomatoes, oregano, salt and pepper and cook over high flame 10 minutes. Pour sauce over meat slices and serve. Serves 4.

BEEFSTEAK ALLA PIZZAIOLA (Number 2)

1 tablespoon olive oil	⅛ teaspoon pepper
1 medium-sized porterhouse	2 cloves garlic, chopped
steak, 1½ inches thick	1 medium can tomatoes
¼ teaspoon salt	2 teaspoons oregano

Heat olive oil in frying pan. Place steak in it and brown well on both sides on hot fire. Sprinkle with salt and pepper, remove from pan and keep warm on platter. Place garlic and tomatoes in frying pan in which meat was cooked, and cook for 2 or 3 minutes at high heat. Place the steak back in frying pan, add oregano, and cook for about 1 minute longer. Place steak on serving plate and cover with sauce. Serves 2.

BEEFSTEAK CACCIATORA (Hunter Style)

1 tablespoon olive oil	2 tablespoons Marsala or
1 porterhouse steak,	sherry wine
1½ inches thick	½ cup dry red wine
½ teaspoon salt	½ clove garlic, minced
½ teaspoon pepper	½ teaspoon fennel seeds
	1 tablespoon tomato puree

Heat oil in frying pan, add steak, cook on both sides until done to your taste, add salt and pepper, remove from pan and keep warm. Add Marsala or sherry to pan gravy and cook slowly, scraping bottom of pan with wooden spoon, until wine has almost evaporated. Add garlic, fennel seeds and tomato purée, mix together well with pan gravy and cook 1 minute longer. Pour over steak and serve. Serves 2.

BEEFSTEAK FLORENTINE STYLE

1 porterhouse steak,	½ teaspoon salt
2 inches thick	½ teaspoon pepper
1 tablespoon olive oil	1 teaspoon lemon juice
	½ lemon, cut into wedges

Place steak on dish with olive oil, salt and pepper and let stand 1 hour, turning occasionally. Grill over charcoal about 8 minutes on each side. Do not overcook. Remove from grill, return to dish with oil, add lemon juice and garnish with lemon wedges. Serves 2.

BEEF STEW WITH FENNEL

2 slices bacon, chopped
1 stalk celery, chopped
1 onion, chopped
1 tablespoon olive oil
1 tablespoon butter
2½ pounds beef for stew,
  cut into small chunks

salt and pepper to taste
½ cup dry wine
½ tablespoon flour
1 small can tomato sauce
1 clove garlic, chopped
1 tablespoon chopped parsley
½ teaspoon fennel seeds

Brown the chopped bacon, celery and onion in olive oil and butter. Add the beef, salt and pepper, and let meat brown slowly. When meat is brown, baste with wine and cook until the wine has almost completely evaporated. Sprinkle the meat with flour, add the tomato sauce and enough water to cover meat and cook for about 40 minutes. When meat is cooked, add the chopped garlic, parsley and fennel seeds; cook 10 minutes longer, then serve. Serves 6.

BEEF STEW WITH RED WINE

3 pounds lean beef for
  stew, cut into large cubes
¼ teaspoon nutmeg
¼ teaspoon thyme
2 bay leaves
1 clove garlic, sliced
2 cups dry red wine

¼ teaspoon salt
⅛ teaspoon pepper
1 onion, diced
2 cloves garlic, chopped
1 tablespoon lard
½ cup water

Combine all ingredients except onion, garlic, lard and water, and marinate 4 hours or, if possible, overnight. When ready to cook, brown slowly the onion and two cloves of garlic, chopped, in 1 tablespoon lard in stew pot. Add the marinated meat, reserving marinade, and let it brown slowly and thoroughly. Strain the marinade and add to the meat ¼ cup at a time, letting this evaporate before adding the next liquid, until all is used. Then add water, cover and cook about 1 hour or until the meat is tender to the fork. Serves 6.

BEEF TONGUE IN PIQUANT SAUCE

1 tablespoon butter
1 tablespoon olive oil
1 medium onion, sliced
⅓ clove garlic
8 anchovy filets,
  cut into pieces
1 tablespoon capers
2 tablespoons wine vinegar

1 cup water
½ teaspoon meat extract
1 medium beef tongue,
  cooked, skinned and sliced
½ teaspoon pepper
½ teaspoon prepared mustard
2 teaspoons chopped parsley
3 sweet gherkins, sliced

Place butter and oil in saucepan, add onion and brown lightly. Add garlic and brown 1 minute longer. Add anchovies, capers, vinegar and water, mix well and boil 1 minute. Add meat extract and blend well. Add tongue slices and cook over very low fire 10 minutes. Remove tongue from pan and place in serving dish. Add to the sauce the pepper, mustard, parsley and gherkins, mix well and pour over tongue. Serves 8.

BEEF TONGUE IN SWEET-SOUR SAUCE

3½ pounds tongue	1 cup stock or water
½ cup olive oil	3 tablespoons sugar
½ onion, chopped	1 clove garlic
1 carrot, chopped	1 bay leaf
1 stalk celery, chopped	⅓ cup vinegar
1 slice salt pork, ¼ inch thick, cut very fine	2 tablespoons bitter chocolate, grated
½ clove garlic, chopped	1 tablespoon flour
2 teaspoons chopped parsley	½ cup pine nuts
salt	1 tablespoon chopped orange peel
pepper	¼ teaspoon salt
1¼ cups wine	

Place tongue in large pan with oil, chopped onion, carrot, celery, salt pork, chopped garlic and parsley. Add salt and pepper and brown well over moderate heat. When tongue and herbs are well browned, add wine and continue cooking until wine has evaporated. Add stock or water, cover pan and cook about 2 hours, until tongue is well done. When tongue is cooked, remove with a spoon some of the fat that forms on top of the gravy. Remove tongue from pan, strain gravy and keep both warm while preparing sweet-sour sauce.

Place sugar, garlic and bay leaf in a small pan, and let sugar melt over low flame. Mix frequently (do not add water) and when sugar is light brown in color, add vinegar. Mix well, scraping bottom of pan, and keep over moderate flame. Add grated chocolate. Add this sauce to strained gravy and if too thin, thicken with flour. Add pine nuts, orange peel and salt. Slice tongue and serve with sauce. Serves 8.

BOILED BEEF IN RUSTIC SAUCE

5 fresh tomatoes, peeled and cut into pieces, or 1 large can tomatoes	1 teaspoon salt
	1 teaspoon freshly ground pepper
2 cloves garlic, chopped fine	1 tablespoon wine vinegar
2 teaspoons chopped parsley	½ teaspoon grated lemon rind
2 tablespoons chopped basil	1 pound leftover cold boiled beef
½ cup olive oil	

This sauce should be made the day before serving. Mix together well all the ingredients except meat and let stand, covered, in an earthen bowl. When ready to serve, slice beef and pour sauce over it. Serves 4.

BOILED BEEF PIZZAIOLA

1 large can tomatoes, drained	salt and pepper
1 clove garlic, chopped	1 pound sliced boiled beef
2 teaspoons parsley, chopped	3 tablespoons olive oil
1 teaspoon oregano	2 tablespoons water

Grease shallow baking dish with oil. Line with half the total quantity of tomatoes, garlic, parsley, oregano and salt and pepper. Place the sliced beef over this and cover with the rest of the ingredients. Sprinkle with olive oil. Add water and bake in moderate oven for 30 minutes. Serves 4.

BOILED BEEF WITH VEGETABLES

8 small new potatoes	⅛ pound salt pork or bacon, cut into very small pieces
2 tablespoons butter	
4 carrots	3 tablespoons butter
2 cups shelled fresh peas	1 teaspoon flour, mixed with
1½ cups dried mushrooms, soaked in fresh water for 30 minutes	¼ cup white wine
	2 cups broth or water
	1 teaspoon meat extract
1 tablespoon olive oil	1 tablespoon olive oil
4 small onions	1½ pounds cold boiled beef, sliced thin
1 small bunch celery	
3 or 4 fresh tomatoes	¼ cup grated Parmesan cheese

Slice the potatoes and brown gently in 2 tablespoons butter until golden brown. Boil the carrots and slice. Cook fresh peas slightly in salted water. Sauté mushrooms in olive oil. Boil onions and celery together for 15 minutes. Peel tomatoes and cut into thin slices. Put salt pork or bacon in frying pan, add butter and let it all brown. Add flour thoroughly mixed with wine and cook until wine evaporates. Add broth or water and meat extract and cook for 5 minutes. When slightly thickened, remove from fire.

Grease a casserole with the olive oil and put in a layer of sliced beef, then a layer of the vegetables. Sprinkle each layer with Parmesan and repeat until all the meat and vegetables are used, ending with a layer of vegetables and Parmesan. Pour the gravy over all. Cover and bake in a moderate oven (375°F.) for 15 minutes. Serves 8.

BRAISED BEEF ALLA BRESCIANA

2½ pounds top round of
  beef, tied to keep shape
¼ pound butter
½ teaspoon salt
¼ teaspoon pepper

½ clove garlic
½ medium onion, sliced
½ pound salt pork, chopped
2 cups dry red wine
½ cup stock

Place meat in large pan with butter, salt, pepper, garlic, onion and salt pork and brown slowly but thoroughly over moderate flame, turning frequently until meat is well browned on all sides. When browned, cover pan and continue cooking slowly ½ hour, turning often. Add wine and stock, cover pan and cook slowly 1 hour and 15 minutes, or until meat is tender. Slice meat and serve with gravy. Serves 6.

BRAISED BEEF GENOESE STYLE

2 tablespoons dried mushrooms
1 slice bacon
1 small onion
1 stalk celery
1 teaspoon chopped parsley
1 small carrot

4 pounds eye of the round
  of beef
1 tablespoon lard
1 cup dry red wine
salt and pepper to taste
2 cups stock or water

Soak mushrooms in cold water for 30 minutes. Chop bacon and vegetables fine. Place meat in large saucepan with lard and chopped ingredients, mushrooms and ¾ of the wine and cook slowly until the wine has evaporated. Add the rest of the wine, salt and pepper to taste, cover the saucepan and continue to cook slowly until the wine has evaporated and the meat and vegetables are well browned. Add the stock or water, cover pan tightly, and cook for 2 hours or until the meat is tender to the fork. Slice the meat and serve with the gravy. Fresh ham may be substituted for beef. Serves 8.

FALSE LEAN ALLA SICILIANA

4 slices bread
½ pound chopped lean beef
2 eggs
2 egg yolks
2 tablespoons Roman
  cheese, grated
salt and pepper to taste
1 pinch nutmeg
2 teaspoons chopped parsley
2 slices lean bacon
4 hard boiled eggs
3 slices Italian salami, cut

¼ inch thick
⅛ pound fresh provolone cheese
1 large slice of bottom
  round of beef, ¼ inch
  thick and about 1 pound
  in weight
2 tablespoons lard
1 onion
½ cup dry red wine
2 small cans tomato sauce
2 pounds fresh peas, shelled

Soak bread in water and squeeze dry; add to chopped meat. Add eggs, egg yolks, grated cheese, salt, pepper, nutmeg and parsley. Mix thoroughly until well blended. Cut bacon into pieces about 1 inch wide. Slice hard boiled eggs, salami and provolone into 1-inch slivers. Pound the large slice of beef and coat it with the chopped mixture. Place the other ingredients on chopped mixture and roll the whole thing until it resembles a large salami. Tie firmly all around and place in large pan with the lard and onion. Brown thoroughly.

Add the wine, cooking slowly until it evaporates, and continue browning for a few minutes longer. Add salt and pepper and the two small cans of tomato sauce. Add enough water to cover meat, cover the pan, and let the meat cook slowly about 1 hour, until the meat is almost tender. Then, add the fresh peas and cook about 15 minutes, until the peas and meat are done. After having removed the strings, slice the roll and serve surrounded by peas and gravy. If there should be too much gravy, save some for rice or macaroni. Serves 4.

FILET OF BEEF IN SAUCEPAN

1½ pounds filet of beef in 1 piece	½ stalk celery, minced
3 slices lean bacon, cut into small pieces	½ teaspoon chopped parsley
	1 tablespoon butter
½ small truffle, diced (optional)	1 medium onion, chopped
	1 carrot, diced
1 cup Marsala wine	½ stalk celery, minced
1 jigger cognac	1 teaspoon chopped parsley
¼ teaspoon salt	½ cup stock
⅛ teaspoon pepper	1 teaspoon butter
	½ teaspoon flour

Lard filet by making cuts in meat with thin, sharp knife and inserting in each cut 1 piece bacon and 1 piece truffle. Tie meat with string to hold in shape. Place meat in deep dish and pour over it Marsala and cognac. Add salt, pepper, celery and parsley and let stand 2 hours, turning often. At end of 2 hours remove meat from marinade, reserving the marinade.

Place meat in saucepan with butter, onion, carrot, celery and parsley and brown thoroughly on all sides. When brown, add marinade and cook 20 minutes. Filet must be red inside when cooking is finished. Remove meat from pan. Add 1 teaspoon butter and 1 tablespoon flour to liquid in pan, mix well and cook slowly until slightly thickened, stirring constantly. Remove string from meat, slice and serve with gravy. Serves 4.

GARMUGIA LUCCA STYLE

4 small onions	2 cups shelled fresh peas
1 clove garlic	3 or 4 artichokes
2 teaspoons parsley	salt and pepper to taste
2 tablespoons olive oil	1/8 teaspoon sugar
2 pounds beef, diced	1/2 cup stock or water

Chop onions, garlic and parsley, and place in pan with olive oil. Brown lightly and add the diced beef. Continue to brown. When the meat is thoroughly browned, add the peas and the artichokes, the latter cut into eight sections after the removal of the outer leaves and chokes. Add the salt, pepper, sugar and water or stock. Cover the pan and cook slowly for about 30 minutes, or until meat is well done. Serve in a deep dish on layer of toasted or fried bread slices. Serves 6.

LARGE MEATBALL HOME STYLE

1¼ pounds chopped beef	1 teaspoon chopped sweet basil
1/8 pound prosciutto or	1/4 teaspoon salt
lean bacon, chopped	8 cups water
4 slices bread, soaked in	1 onion
water and squeezed dry	1 stalk celery
1 egg	1 carrot
2 tablespoons grated	1 fresh tomato, cut into pieces
Parmesan cheese	1 teaspoon chopped parsley
1 teaspoon chopped parsley	1/4 teaspoon salt

Mix the chopped beef, bacon or prosciutto, bread, egg, Parmesan, parsley, basil and salt together thoroughly, and shape into a large meatball. In a soup pan, put the water, onion, celery, carrot, tomato, parsley and salt and bring to a boil. When the liquid is boiling, immerse the large meatball and lower heat to a simmer. Simmer for 2 hours. Do not boil at high speed because the meatball would come apart.

After simmering for 2 hours, take the meatball out of the liquid and place on a platter, covering it with another platter so as to press it a little. When cold, slice and serve with mayonnaise sauce. Save the liquid for a tasty soup. Serves 4.

LITTLE BEEFSTEAK SURPRISE

8 slices filets of beef, ½ inch thick	1 cup bread crumbs
¼ pound prosciutto, sliced	¼ cup butter
8 slices white truffles (if available)	1 tablespoon flour
	1 cup stock or water
¼ pound mozzarella cheese, thinly sliced	salt and pepper
	1 teaspoon meat extract
½ cup flour	1 tablespoon grated Parmesan cheese
1 egg, beaten with fork for one minute	½ tablespoon chopped parsley

Slit each slice of beef, leaving one end closed, as a bun. In the slit place one slice prosciutto, one slice truffle and one slice mozzarella cheese. Press the filled slices closed with your hand. Roll in flour, dip into beaten egg, roll in bread crumbs, and fry gently in butter until golden brown.

Place 1 tablespoon butter in a saucepan, melt and add 1 tablespoon flour; blend thoroughly and add 1 cup stock or water, salt and pepper to taste. Cook for a few minutes, add the meat extract and mix thoroughly. Remove from fire, add Parmesan cheese and chopped parsley. Place the little beefsteaks on serving dish and pour the sauce over them. Serves 4.

OXTAIL ROMAN STYLE

4 pounds oxtail, cut into pieces	1 teaspoon chopped parsley
1 tablespoon leaf lard	½ teaspoon salt
2 slices bacon, cut into small pieces	½ teaspoon pepper
	1¼ cups dry red wine
1 small onion, sliced	3 tablespoons tomato paste
½ clove garlic	6 celery stalks, cut into large pieces
1 carrot, diced	

Place oxtail in large pan with lard, bacon, onion, garlic, carrot and parsley and brown very well. Add salt and pepper. Add wine and cook slowly until wine evaporates. Add tomato paste with enough water to cover meat, lower fire, cover pan and simmer slowly 4½ hours. Add celery pieces and cook 20 minutes longer. Serves 4.

PICKLED BOILED BEEF

3 tablespoons olive oil	1/8 teaspoon salt
2 onions, sliced fine	1/2 teaspoon pepper
1/2 cup vinegar	1 cup white wine
1 teaspoon sugar	2 cups stock or water
2 cloves garlic	1 pound sliced cold beef
1 bay leaf	4 small pickles
2 teaspoons parsley,	8 green olives
chopped	8 small vinegar peppers
1/8 teaspoon rosemary	8 small mushrooms in oil
2 sage leaves	4 small artichokes in oil

Place 1 teaspoon olive oil in saucepan, add the onions, and brown. Add vinegar, sugar, garlic, bay leaf, parsley, rosemary, sage, salt and pepper. Let simmer until vinegar is nearly evaporated. Add the wine, stock or water, and boil 5 minutes.

Place the sliced beef in a casserole and pour the marinade over it. Place the casserole in a cold place and let stand for about 12 hours. When ready to serve, remove the meat from the marinade, place on serving dish surrounded by pickles, olives, peppers, mushrooms and artichokes and sprinkle all with remaining olive oil. Serves 4.

RAGOUT BOLOGNA STYLE

3/4 pound chopped beef	1 teaspoon tomato paste
1/4 pound pork, chopped	1/4 teaspoon salt
1/4 pound veal, chopped	1/8 teaspoon pepper
1/4 pound salt pork, chopped	1/4 pound mushrooms, cut into
1 medium onion, sliced	pieces
1 carrot, sliced	2 chicken livers, cut into pieces
1 stalk celery, cut into	1/2 cup heavy cream
small pieces	1 small truffle, sliced thin
1 clove	(optional)
1 1/4 cups stock or water	

Place meats, onion, carrot, celery and clove in saucepan and brown slowly but thoroughly. Add stock or water and continue cooking slowly until it evaporates. Add tomato paste, salt, pepper and enough water to cover meat, cover pan and cook slowly 1 hour. Add mushrooms and chicken livers and cook 15 minutes longer. Just before serving add cream and truffle. The gravy may be used on rice, ravioli, spaghetti or noodles. Serves 6.

RAGOUT OF BEEF WITH TOMATO SAUCE

3 pounds eye of the round
  of beef
2 slices bacon, cut into small
  pieces
2 cloves of garlic, cut into
  small pieces
1 teaspoon marjoram leaves
¼ teaspoon salt
⅛ teaspoon pepper
2 tablespoons olive oil
1 tablespoon butter
1 teaspoon chopped parsley
2 small onions, or 1 large
  onion, sliced

1 carrot, diced fine
1 stalk celery, cut into small
  pieces
¼ teaspoon salt
⅛ teaspoon pepper
½ cup dry red wine
1 large can tomatoes
1 small can tomato paste,
  dissolved in
  3 cups warm water
1 tablespoon butter
2 bay leaves

Lard meat by making cuts in it and inserting in each cut 1 piece bacon, 1 piece garlic, a little marjoram, salt and pepper. Press cuts together to close and tie meat with string to hold it in shape. Place larded meat in large saucepan with oil, butter, parsley, onion, carrot, celery, salt and pepper and brown slowly over low flame, turning often, until it is well browned on all sides. Add wine and continue cooking slowly until wine evaporates.

Add tomatoes and tomato paste, dissolved in warm water, cover pan and simmer 2 hours, or until meat is tender, adding a little more water if need. Five minutes before removing from fire add 1 tablespoon butter and bay leaves. Slice meat before serving. Gravy may be used for rice, spaghetti, ravioli or noodles. Serves 6.

RIB OF BEEF AL BAROLO

1 bottle of Barolo wine, or
  any other dry red wine
1 onion, chopped
1 carrot, sliced
1 stalk celery, cut into
  small pieces

1 bay leaf
4 peppercorns
4 pounds rib roast of beef
2 tablespoons butter
2 slices bacon, chopped
⅛ teaspoon salt

This dish should be started the day before the actual serving.

Mix wine, chopped onion, carrot, celery, bay leaf and peppercorns (no salt). In this mixture, place the beef and marinate for 24 hours, turning the meat once or twice. When ready to cook, remove meat from liquid, dry thoroughly and tie to keep in shape. Place in large pan with butter and chopped bacon and brown well on all sides. Strain wine marinade and place in a small saucepan. Boil until reduced to half. Add salt to the meat. Add wine sauce. Cover pan and simmer for about 2 hours.

The meat must be so well cooked that it will not be necessary to cut it with a knife, but just "spoon it." Pour gravy over meat and serve. Serves 8.

STEW ROMAN STYLE

1 tablespoon lard	salt and pepper
1 onion, chopped	⅛ teaspoon marjoram
⅛ pound salt pork, chopped	1 cup red wine
½ clove garlic, chopped	1 small can tomatoes, or 3
2 pounds stew beef, cut	large fresh tomatoes, peeled
into small pieces	and sliced

Place lard, chopped onion, salt pork and garlic in a stew pan and brown slightly; add meat, salt, pepper and marjoram and let the meat brown slowly. When meat is well browned, pour the wine over it and continue cooking until the wine is absorbed. Add the tomatoes and enough hot water to cover meat. Cover the pan and cook for about 2 hours or until the meat is tender. If gravy should be too thick, add a little water. The gravy will be dark and very tasty. Serves 4.

TONGUE FAMILY STYLE

1 4-pound tongue, skinned	½ teaspoon chopped parsley
2 quarts water	½ tablespoon flour
salt and pepper	¼ teaspoon salt
1 teaspoon butter	⅛ teaspoon pepper
1 onion, chopped	½ cup vinegar
1 carrot, chopped	1 cup broth
1 slice fat bacon or salt	2 tablespoons powdered sugar
pork, cut into very small	1 bay leaf
pieces	2 teaspoons pine nuts
½ clove garlic	2 teaspoons raisins

Place tongue in soup pan, add water, salt and pepper and let boil, covered, about 2 hours. This will give a delicious broth that can be used to make an excellent soup. Place butter, onion, carrot, bacon, garlic and parsley in large frying pan and brown gently over moderate flame. Add tongue, cut into slices ½ inch thick, and brown lightly.

When lightly browned, sprinkle with flour, add salt and pepper, turn slices and add vinegar and broth. Keep flame low, add sugar, bay leaf, pine nuts and raisins, and continue cooking gently for 10 minutes until tongue is savory and sauce is not too thin. Taste sauce.

If you prefer it sweeter, add more sugar; if you prefer it very tart, add 1 teaspoon vinegar. Place tongue on serving dish and pour sauce over it. Serves 8.

UPSIDE DOWN MEAT CROQUETTES

1 pound chopped beef	4 tablespoons grated Parmesan
4 slices bread, soaked in	cheese
water and squeezed dry	1 egg, lightly beaten
1/8 pound butter	1/8 teaspoon salt
1/2 teaspoon salt	1/8 teaspoon pepper
1/4 teaspoon pepper	1 cup bread crumbs
1/2 cup boiled rice	1/2 cup oil
1/4 pound butter	

Mix together well the meat, bread, butter, salt and pepper, shape into a roll and cut into 8 pieces, pressing each piece down to make a thin patty like a hamburger. Mix together the rice, butter and cheese, divide into 8 equal parts and shape into 8 little balls. Wrap each rice ball with a meat patty, pressing meat around carefully so that all the rice is covered. Add salt and pepper to beaten egg, dip each croquette into the egg, roll in bread crumbs and fry gently in oil until golden brown on each side. Serves 4.

VEAL

BELLA VISTA VEAL

4-pound leg of veal, tied	3/4 cup Marsala or dry white
to hold shape	wine
1/8 pound butter	1 tablespoon butter
1 medium onion, sliced	1 teaspoon flour
1 teaspoon chopped parsley	3 cups mashed potatoes
1 stalk celery, diced	4 tablespoons melted butter
1 carrot, diced	2 tablespoons grated Parmesan
2 cups stock	cheese

Place veal in large Dutch oven with butter, onion, parsley, celery and carrot; brown slowly, turning meat often, until brown on all sides. Add wine and continue cooking slowly until wine evaporates. Add stock, cover pan and cook slowly 2 hours, or until meat is tender. Remove from pan, slice and keep warm. Strain pan gravy, add butter and flour, blending well, place over low fire and cook slowly, stirring constantly, until thickened. Add a little more stock if gravy is too thick.

Place veal slices on oven platter, pour over them a little gravy, make a border of potatoes, pour on melted butter and sprinkle with grated cheese. Place in hot oven 5 minutes. Serve with remaining gravy. Serves 8.

FRITTURA PICCATA (Veal with Prosciutto)

1 pound veal cutlet, cut very thin (Italian style) into 3-inch pieces
¼ cup butter
2 tablespoons flour
½ teaspoon salt
½ teaspoon pepper

⅛ pound prosciutto, sliced and slivered
2 tablespoons stock
1 tablespoon butter
1 teaspoon chopped parsley
2 teaspoons lemon juice

Heat butter in frying pan. Dredge meat in flour, salt and pepper, place in frying pan and cook over high flame 2 minutes on each side. Remove meat. Place prosciutto in frying pan, cook 3 minutes, remove from pan and place over veal. Add stock, butter and parsley to pan gravy, scrape pan well, cook 2 minutes and add lemon juice. Pour sauce over meat and serve immediately. Serves 4.

VEAL CUTLETS PARMESAN

1 pound veal cutlets
½ cup butter
¼ cup grated Parmesan cheese
½ pound Mozzarella cheese
1 cup dry breadcrumbs

2 eggs, beaten
1 can tomato sauce
¼ teaspoon salt
dash of pepper

Dip cutlets in beaten eggs combined with seasoning, then in mixture of Parmesan cheese and breadcrumbs. Fry in butter until brown (about 8 minutes). Then place cutlets in baking dish, pour tomato sauce over them and add slices of Mozzarella cheese. Bake in moderate oven 10-15 minutes. Serves 4.

LITTLE QUAILS OF VEAL

1 pound veal cutlet, cut very thin (Italian style)
2 tablespoons lemon juice pepper and salt
¼ pound prosciutto or ham, thinly sliced

½ pound bacon, thinly sliced
¼ medium size loaf French bread, sliced in ½-inch slices
4 leaves fresh sage
2 teaspoons drippings or butter

Cut veal into pieces about 6 inches square. Sprinkle salt, pepper and a few drops of lemon juice on each piece. Place 1 slice prosciutto or ham on each piece of veal and roll up. Wrap roll with bacon. On metal or wooden skewers place a slice of bread, a leaf of sage and a veal roll, then sage, bread and veal until skewers are full. Brush with melted drippings or butter and place in moderate oven for about 30 minutes, turning once. If you have a charcoal grill, you can broil them and they will turn out even better. Serves 4.

OSSOBUCO (Hollowbone) MILANESE STYLE

1 tablespoon butter	1 cup water
4 veal shin bones, 4 inches long, with meat	1 teaspoon chopped parsley
	½ clove garlic, chopped
2 tablespoons flour	4 strips lemon peel, 1 inch long
½ teaspoon salt	1 anchovy filet, chopped
½ teaspoon pepper	1 tablespoon stock
½ cup dry white wine	1 tablespoon butter

Grease a deep skillet with butter. Roll bones in flour, place in skillet, add salt and pepper and cook until well browned, turning bones over occasionally during browning process. Add wine and continue cooking until wine evaporates. Add cup of water, cover skillet and cook 1 hour, adding more water if necessary.

Five minutes before serving add parsley, garlic, lemon peel and anchovy and cook 2 minutes longer, turning bones over once. Place bones on serving dish. Add 1 tablespoon stock to pan gravy, add butter, mix well and pour over bones. Serves 4.

ROAST VEAL IN CASSEROLE

5 pounds shoulder or leg of veal	¼ cup butter
	salt and pepper to taste
2 onions, in pieces	4 tablespoons stock or water
2 stalks celery, in pieces	1 tablespoon potato flour
3 sprigs parsley, chopped	⅛ cup Marsala or sherry wine
1 cup olive oil	

Have butcher tie meat. The meat from the leg is preferable, but for economical reasons, the shoulder will do as well. Put onions, celery, and parsley in roasting pan with oil and butter, and place meat on top. Sprinkle salt and pepper over meat and cover entirely with a piece of well greased brown paper, making a little slit in the center of paper. Place cover on pan, leaving it open just a trifle. Put pan on top of stove and cook over high fire until fat makes sound of frying. Place pan in moderate oven (375°F.) and cook for about 2 hours. Turn the meat over 2 or 3 times while roasting, being careful to cover it again. If meat should become dry, add a small amount of water.

When meat is cooked, remove from pan and keep warm. Skim off fat from pan liquid and add stock or water to the vegetables. Place on top of stove and cook slowly for 10 minutes, scraping bottom and sides of pan. Pour gravy through sieve into small saucepan, and add potato flour, mixed with Marsala or sherry.

Replace meat in pan and return to warm oven for about 15 minutes, basting with half the gravy. This will give the meat a shiny, gelatinous crust. Slice meat and serve with rest of gravy. Serves 8.

TINY VEAL ROASTS

4 loin veal chops, 2 inches thick
1 tablespoon flour
3 tablespoons butter
salt and pepper
1 cup dry white wine
1 pint stock or water

1 tablespoon chopped parsley
1 carrot, chopped
1 onion, chopped
1 stalk celery, chopped
½ teaspoon rosemary
¼ clove garlic, chopped

Dust chops with flour. Melt butter in frying pan, season chops with salt and pepper and brown slowly on both sides. Add wine and continue cooking until evaporated, turning chops occasionally. Add stock or water a little at a time and cook slowly for about 15 minutes. Add all the chopped vegetables and seasonings and cook about 20 minutes longer.

Remove chops from pan and place in serving dish. Strain the remaining sauce from vegetables and spoon over chops. Serves 4.

SALTIMBOCCA

2 pounds veal cutlets, sliced very thin (Italian style)
1 teaspoon sage
¼ pound prosciutto or ham, sliced thin

3 tablespoons butter
salt and pepper
2 tablespoons water

Cut veal cutlets into pieces about 5 inches square. On each piece sprinkle a little of the sage and place a slice of prosciutto or ham on top. Keep the prosciutto or ham in place on veal with a toothpick. Melt 2 tablespoons butter in frying pan and place meat in it. Sprinkle with salt and pepper. Cook over a high fire for a few minutes on each side until the veal is well browned.

Place the slices of cooked meat on serving dish with prosciutto or ham facing up. Add water to contents of frying pan and scrape bottom well. Add rest of butter and mix well over low fire. Pour gravy over meat. Serves 6.

SCALOPPINE AL MARSALA

1½ pounds veal cutlets, sliced   2 tablespoons butter
   thin (Italian style)   ½ cup Marsala wine
salt and pepper   2 tablespoons stock or water
1 tablespoon flour

Have butcher pound cutlets very thin. Cut veal into pieces about
6 inches square. Sprinkle with salt and pepper and flour lightly. Melt
butter in large frying pan, and when hot, put in veal and brown thoroughly on both sides over high heat. When well browned, add the
Marsala and, keeping the flame high, let meat cook 1 minute longer.
Place meat in serving dish. Add stock or water to pan, scraping bottom
and sides, and pour over meat. Serves 4.

VEAL SCALOPPINE WITH TRIMMINGS

¾ pound boiled potatoes,   1 teaspoon butter
   mashed   4 tomatoes, cut in half
1 egg yolk   2 tablespoons bread crumbs
⅛ pound butter   1 tablespoon parsley, minced
   dash of nutmeg   2 tablespoons olive oil
salt and pepper   salt and pepper
1 cup flour   1 pound veal cutlets, cut
1 egg, lightly beaten   thin in Italian style
1 pound mushrooms, sliced   2 tablespoons flour
1 tablespoon olive oil   salt and pepper
salt and pepper   2 tablespoons butter, melted
4 anchovy filets, chopped   stock

Mix mashed potatoes with egg yolk, butter, nutmeg, salt and pepper,
shape like eggs and flatten out. Roll each potato cake in flour, then in
beaten egg and place on greased baking dish.

Place mushrooms in small frying pan with oil, salt and pepper, and
sauté 10 minutes. Add chopped anchovies and butter, cook 1 minute
longer and remove from fire.

Sprinkle tomato halves with bread crumbs, parsley, oil, salt and
pepper and place on greased baking dish with potatoes. Bake potato
cakes and tomatoes in moderate oven (375°F.) 20 minutes until golden
brown, turning potato cakes once in order to brown on both sides.

Dredge veal cutlets with flour, salt and pepper, place in frying pan
with melted butter and cook over high flame 5 minutes on each side.
Remove cutlets from frying pan. Add a little stock to pan gravy, cook
2 minutes and pour over meat. Serve veal in center of platter with
tomatoes, potato cakes and mushrooms arranged attractively around it.
Serves 4.

STUFFED PILLOWS

12 small slices veal cutlet,
  cut very thin
12 small slices prosciutto or
  ham, thinly sliced
¾ pound mozzarella cheese,
  thinly sliced

½ cup butter
½ cup Marsala or sherry wine
1 teaspoon butter
⅛ teaspoon salt
⅛ teaspoon pepper

Flatten out veal cutlets with a mallet or ask butcher to do it. Place one slice of prosciutto or ham and a thin slice of mozzarella cheese on each cutlet, and fold together like an envelope, using toothpicks to hold together. Melt butter in frying pan. Brown pillows well on one side, then turn gently, and brown on other side. They should be cooked in a short time.

Remove meat from the pan, pour the Marsala or sherry into it, scraping bottom and sides of pan well. Add 1 teaspoon butter, salt and pepper and pour sauce over pillows on serving dish. Serves 4.

VEAL BIRD STYLE

1 tablespoon butter
1 tablespoon olive oil
1 clove garlic
1 bay leaf
1 pound veal cutlets, sliced
  very thin (Italian style),
  cut into 4-inch pieces

salt and pepper
2 teaspoons lemon juice
½ teaspoon water
1½ tablespoons butter
½ pound mushrooms, sliced

Heat butter and oil with garlic and bay leaf in frying pan, add veal seasoned with salt and pepper, and cook over high flame 3 minutes, turning meat twice during cooking. Remove veal and place in serving dish. Remove garlic and bay leaf from pan, add lemon juice and water to pan gravy and pour over veal.

Place 1½ tablespoons butter in same frying pan, add mushrooms and cook 2 minutes. Pour mushrooms over veal and serve. Serves 4.

VEAL BIRDS HUNTER STYLE

10 chicken livers
1 tablespoon butter
2 slices prosciutto (or lean
  bacon)
1 teaspoon parsley
2 sage leaves
salt and pepper to taste

1½ pounds veal cutlets, sliced
  thin (Italian style), cut
  into 12 pieces
1 tablespoon butter
1 teaspoon flour
1 cup Marsala wine (or dry
  sherry)
12 slices French bread, toasted
2 tablespoons stock or water

Sauté the chicken livers in butter, and when cooked, chop fine with the prosciutto, parsley and sage leaves. Add salt and pepper to taste. On each slice of veal, spread some of the above mixture until all is used. Roll each slice individually and fasten each roll with one or two toothpicks. Put rolls in a large frying pan with second tablespoon of butter and cook until well browned. Sprinkle 1 teaspoon flour over birds, add Marsala or sherry, and cook until the wine is nearly evaporated.

Toast the French bread and place on serving platter. Remove the birds from the pan and place them on the slices of toast. Add water or stock to the pan gravy, mix well and pour over veal birds and toast. Serves 6.

VEAL BREAST GRATELLA

2 pounds veal breast	⅛ teaspoon nutmeg
3 quarts water	1 tablespoon chopped parsley
2 teaspoons salt	2 tablespoons olive oil
2 stalks celery	2 teaspoons lemon juice
1 carrot	1 tablespoon melted butter
1 medium onion	2 eggs, lightly beaten
⅛ teaspoon pepper	1 cup bread crumbs

Place veal in salted water and bring to boiling point. Add celery, carrot and onion and boil gently 1 hour. Remove meat and reserve broth for soups or other cooking purposes. Cool meat and cut into 1-inch strips. Make a marinade of pepper, nutmeg, parsley, oil and lemon juice, add meat and let stand 2 hours, turning occasionally.

Remove meat from marinade and dry with paper towel. Add melted butter to lightly beaten eggs and beat 1 minute. Dip meat into egg mixture, roll in bread crumbs and place in greased baking dish in moderate oven (375°F.). Bake 15 minutes on each side until golden brown. Serve plain or with hot piquant sauce (see index). Serves 6.

VEAL CHOPS ALLA MODENESE

½ teaspoon salt	3 tablespoons butter
⅛ teaspoon pepper	4 thin slices prosciutto
1 egg	4 thin slices Swiss cheese or
4 loin veal chops, cut thin	mozzarella
3 tablespoons bread crumbs	

Add salt and pepper to egg and beat for 1 minute with fork. Dip chops into egg, roll in bread crumbs, and fry slowly in butter until well browned on both sides. Place in shallow baking dish. Place a slice of prosciutto, then a slice of cheese on each chop and bake in moderate oven (375°F.) until cheese is melted. Serve immediately. Serves 4.

VEAL CHOPS IN CASSEROLE

6 veal chops	1½ pounds mushrooms, sliced
2 tablespoons flour	1 large potato, sliced and fried
salt and pepper	in butter
2 tablespoons butter	1 tablespoon chopped parsley
2 tablespoons olive oil	½ teaspoon chopped chives

Dust chops with flour, salt and pepper. Place in frying pan with butter and 1 tablespoon olive oil and brown thoroughly and slowly on both sides. Grease casserole well with remaining oil, leaving a little oil on the bottom. Place a layer of sliced mushrooms in casserole and put the chops over them. Add a layer of the fried potatoes and finish with a layer of mushrooms. Sprinkle parsley and chives over top layer, cover casserole and cook in hot oven (425°F.) 15 minutes. Serves 6.

VEAL CHOPS MILANESE

4 large veal chops, ½ inch	1 egg, well beaten with fork
thick	1 cup bread crumbs
½ teaspoon salt	4 tablespoons butter
½ teaspoon pepper	1 lemon, cut into wedges

Sprinkle veal chops with salt and pepper, dip into beaten egg and roll in bread crumbs. Melt butter in frying pan, add chops and fry slowly 10 minutes on each side. The meat must cook well but slowly. Remove chops to platter, pour butter from pan over them, and serve garnished with lemon wedges. Serves 4.

VEAL CHOPS MILANESE WITH GRAVY

4 veal chops, ½ inch thick	1 cup bread crumbs
1 egg, beaten lightly with fork	1½ cups pizzaiola sauce
½ teaspoon salt	(see index)
½ teaspoon pepper	

Cook chops as in recipe for Veal Chops Milanese, place in serving dish and add pizzaiola sauce. Serves 4.

VEAL CHOPS MOSAIC

6 veal chops	1 black truffle, sliced thin (if
2 tablespoons flour	available)
salt and pepper	2 slices prosciutto
4 tablespoons butter, melted	⅛ pound Swiss cheese, sliced
1 cup dry white wine	very thin
1 teaspoon meat extract,	6 tablespoons canned tomatoes,
dissolved in	mashed
½ cup stock or water	2 tablespoons butter

Dust chops with flour, salt and pepper and place in shallow roasting pan with melted butter. Brown on both sides, on top of stove, over low flame. Add wine and cook until evaporated. Dissolve meat extract in stock or water and add to chops. Lower heat and cook slowly until the sauce will barely cover the chops with a shiny, tasty coat.

Cut truffle, prosciutto and cheese into thin strips. Place a bit of tomato, truffle, prosciutto and cheese on each cutlet and dot with a little butter. Cook in moderate oven (375°F.) about 12 minutes and serve immediately. Serves 6.

VEAL CHOPS PETRONIUS

¼ cup butter	2 tablespoons stock
4 large veal chops, ½ inch thick	1 truffle, sliced thin
2 tablespoons flour	4 tablespoons grated Parmesan cheese
½ teaspoon salt	2 tablespoons stock
½ cup Marsala or sherry wine	

Melt butter in large, heavy frying pan. Dredge chops in flour and place in melted butter in frying pan. Cook over high flame 10 minutes on each side. Add salt and Marsala or sherry and continue cooking until wine evaporates. Push chops to one side of frying pan, add stock and scrape bottom of frying pan. Place chops back in center of pan and cover each chop with slice of truffle and Parmesan cheese. Add 2 more tablespoons stock, cover pan and cook over low fire until cheese has melted. Serves 4.

SAVORY VEAL CHOPS

4 large green peppers	2 anchovy filets, chopped
3 tablespoons olive oil	½ clove garlic, chopped
1 onion, chopped	1 tablespoon flour
salt	4 loin veal chops
6 green olives, chopped	1 tablespoon butter
1 tablespoon capers	salt and pepper
1 small can tomatoes, drained	2 tablespoons stock or water

Slice peppers thin, removing seeds, and fry in 1 tablespoon olive oil with onion and a little salt. When peppers are almost tender, add olives, capers and tomatoes. Cook about 20 minutes, until peppers are thoroughly done. Remove from fire. In another small frying pan, pour 1 tablespoon olive oil, add anchovies and garlic and brown lightly. Pour over peppers and keep the mixture warm.

Flour chops lightly and place in frying pan with melted butter and remaining olive oil. Brown well on both sides and continue cooking slowly for about 20 minutes, until meat is done. Sprinkle with salt and pepper and remove chops from pan. Pour stock or water into pan, scrape bottom well and pour over chops. Over and around chops, place the pepper mixture and serve. Serves 4.

VEAL ROLLS WITH ANCHOVIES

1 pound veal cutlets, sliced thin (Italian style)	¼ cup butter
¼ pound mozzarella cheese	salt and pepper to taste
1 can anchovy filets	½ cup stock or water
pepper	1 sprig parsley, chopped

Cut the veal into pieces no larger than 4 by 6 inches. On each slice place a small piece of mozzarella cheese, one filet of anchovy and a little pepper. Roll the little slices and tie with heavy thread. Melt half the butter in frying pan, add rolls and brown well on both sides. Add salt and pepper, a little water, if necessary, and cook about 15 minutes. Remove rolls and place on serving plate, removing threads.

Pour stock or water in frying pan over low fire and scrape bottom and sides of pan. Cook for a few minutes, remove pan from fire and add rest of butter. Mix well, add chopped parsley and pour over rolls. Serves 4.

VEAL ROLL WITH SAUCE

2½ pounds breast of veal in 1 piece	1 stalk celery
salt and pepper	½ teaspoon salt
2 slices bacon or prosciutto	¼ teaspoon pepper
1 medium onion	½ cup butter
1 clove garlic	1 tablespoon flour
1 carrot	1 cup stock
3 sprigs parsley	2 egg yolks
	1½ tablespoons lemon juice

Have butcher remove bones from breast of veal. Sprinkle meat with salt and pepper and place the bacon or prosciutto on the inner side of the meat. Roll the meat so that it forms a large sausage. Tie with string to keep shape. Choose a large pot which will just hold the veal roll. Half fill it with water and add onion, garlic, carrot, parsley and celery. Add salt and pepper and place over high heat. When water is boiling immerse the veal in it. The water should just cover the meat. Cover and cook gently for about an hour or until the meat is tender to the fork. If water cooks off too much, add a little occasionally. When meat is tender, remove from pan and set aside to keep warm. Strain the broth.

Melt butter in saucepan, add flour and blend thoroughly. Add 1 cup of stock and cook for 5 minutes, stirring constantly. Add more stock if the sauce is too thick. Mix the egg yolks with a little broth and add to sauce, stirring constantly. Remove from fire and return to the large pan with the meat. Warm, but do not boil, over low fire for 15 minutes. Serve meat sliced. Add lemon juice and chopped parsley to the sauce and serve poured over meat. Serves 6.

VEAL STEW WITH TOMATOES

½ cup olive oil	1 bay leaf
2 cloves garlic	½ teaspoon marjoram
1½ pounds boned shoulder of veal, cut into large cubes	1 teaspoon salt
	½ teaspoon pepper
1 tablespoon chopped parsley	1 cup dry white wine
	1 small can tomatoes

Place oil in large stew pan, add garlic and brown gently. Remove garlic, add meat and brown thoroughly on all sides. Add parsley, bay leaf, marjoram, salt and pepper. When meat is well browned, add wine and cook slowly until wine evaporates. Add tomatoes and enough warm water to cover meat. Cover pan, lower flame and cook slowly 1½ hours, or until meat is well done. More water may be added during cooking if necessary. Serves 4.

LAMB

BRAISED KID OR LAMB

1 small leg of lamb or kid	2 teaspoons chopped parsley
1 tablespoon butter	1 teaspoon salt
1 tablespoon olive oil	½ teaspoon pepper
1 large onion, sliced	1 cup dry white wine
1 large carrot, diced	1 cup stock or water
2 stalks celery, diced	1 tablespoon butter
	1 tablespoon water

Place leg of lamb or kid in Dutch oven with butter and oil; brown slowly but thoroughly on all sides. When brown, remove to a dish and keep warm.

Place onion, carrot, celery and parsley in the Dutch oven and brown well without burning, adding a little water if necessary. When vegetables are brown, return meat to pot and pour over it any juices that drained from it while standing. Add salt, pepper and wine and cook until wine evaporates. Add stock, cover pot and cook slowly 2 hours or until meat is tender.

Turn meat often during cooking. Remove meat to serving dish. Strain pan gravy, add butter and water and cook 1 minute, scraping bottom of pan and mixing well. Serve gravy with meat. Serves 6.

LAMB BRODETTATO

1½ pounds lamb for stew, cut into pieces	2 tablespoons flour
2 slices prosciutto or lean bacon, minced	¼ cup dry white wine
	water to cover meat
1 very small onion, chopped	2 egg yolks
1 tablespoon leaf lard	1 tablespoon lemon juice
½ teaspoon salt	1 tablespoon chopped parsley
½ teaspoon pepper	½ teaspoon marjoram

Place lamb, prosciutto or bacon, onion and leaf lard in frying pan and brown thoroughly over slow fire. Add salt and pepper, sprinkle with flour and blend in well. Add wine, cook until wine evaporates, add enough water to cover meat and cook 45 minutes or until meat is tender, adding more water if needed.

Beat the egg yolks and lemon juice together lightly with fork, and when mixed well, add parsley and marjoram, mixing well. Lower flame as much as possible under meat, pour egg mixture over meat, mix well, shut off flame and let stand on stove 5 minutes before serving. Serves 4.

LAMB CHOPS IN PIQUANT SAUCE

1 tablespoon olive oil	4 anchovy filets, chopped
½ teaspoon salt	½ clove garlic
½ teaspoon pepper	½ teaspoon oregano
½ teaspoon oregano	¼ teaspoon salt
½ clove garlic, chopped	⅛ teaspoon pepper
8 loin lamb chops, ½ inch thick	2 teaspoons lemon juice
	1 tablespoon prepared mustard

Make a marinade of oil, salt, pepper, oregano and garlic and let chops stand in this marinade at least 2 hours. Make a sauce by mixing together well the anchovies, garlic, oregano, salt, pepper, lemon juice and mustard. Set broiler at high heat (500°F.), remove chops from marinade, dip into anchovy sauce and broil 10 minutes on one side. Dip chops into sauce and broil on other side 10 minutes. Serve sauce over chops if desired. Serves 4.

LAMB COUNTRY STYLE

1½ pounds lean lamb
shoulder, boned and cut
into large cubes
2 tablespoons olive oil
¼ cup butter
6 anchovy filets, chopped
1 clove garlic, chopped

1 tablespoon fennel seeds
½ teaspoon lemon peel
2 tablespoons wine vinegar
1 teaspoon salt
½ teaspoon pepper
1 tablespoon flour
1 cup stock or water

Brown meat slowly in large frying pan with oil and butter. Mix together anchovies, garlic, fennel seeds, lemon peel and vinegar. When meat is well browned, pour off some of the fat, add salt and pepper and pour anchovy mixture over meat. Mix well and cook until vinegar is almost all evaporated. Sprinkle flour over meat, blending in well, and add stock or water. Cook ½ hour longer, stirring frequently. Serves 4.

LAMB HUNTER STYLE (Roman)

1½ pounds lamb for stew
(lean), cut into pieces
1 tablespoon leaf lard
½ teaspoon salt
¾ teaspoon freshly ground
pepper
½ clove garlic

½ teaspoon rosemary
1 sage leaf, chopped
1½ teaspoons flour
½ cup wine vinegar
½ cup water
2 anchovy filets, chopped

Place lamb in large skillet with leaf lard, and brown well on all sides over high flame. Add salt, pepper, garlic, rosemary and sage and continue browning a little longer. Sprinkle meat with flour and press in flour well with wooden spoon. Add vinegar and water, mix all together well, scraping bottom of pan. Lower flame and cook slowly 45 minutes until meat is almost done. If gravy becomes too dry, add a little water from time to time during cooking. Mix anchovies with 1 teaspoon water, add to meat, and cook 1 minute. Serves 4.

LAMB IN ANCHOVY SAUCE

1 small leg of young lamb
2 tablespoons butter
½ medium onion, sliced
1 teaspoon salt
½ teaspoon pepper
1 tablespoon flour

1 cup dry white wine
1¼ cups stock
4 anchovy filets, chopped
1 tablespoon chopped parsley
½ clove garlic, chopped
½ teaspoon grated lemon peel

Place meat, butter and onion in Dutch oven, add salt and pepper; brown meat slowly but thoroughly, turning often to prevent burning. When brown, sprinkle with flour, turning over several times to spread flour evenly, add wine and cook slowly until wine evaporates. Add stock, cover pot and cook slowly 1½ hours, or until meat is tender. Add anchovies, parsley, garlic and lemon peel, stirring into gravy; cook 1 minute, turning meat once. Serve meat with gravy. Serves 6.

LEG OF LAMB CHIETI STYLE

½ cup olive oil	1 teaspoon pepper
¼ pound salt pork, chopped	2 cloves garlic, sliced
1 small leg of lamb	2 cups dry white wine
1 small onion, sliced	1 small can tomato paste
1 stalk celery, diced	1 tablespoon chopped parsley
2 carrots, diced	¼ teaspoon oregano
1 teaspoon salt	1 cup stock or water

Heat oil and salt pork in Dutch oven, add meat, onion, celery, carrots, salt and pepper and cook over moderate flame, turning often, until meat begins to brown. Add garlic and continue cooking until meat is well browned. Add wine and continue cooking until wine evaporates. Add tomato paste, parsley and oregano and cook 5 minutes. Add stock or water, cover pot and cook 1½ hours, turning often. When meat is done, remove from pot, strain gravy and serve over meat. Serves 6.

LEG OF LAMB HOME STYLE

1 small leg of young lamb	¼ cup butter
1 medium onion	1 tablespoon flour
2 teaspoons salt	2 cups lamb broth
1 clove	⅛ teaspoon pepper
1 stalk celery	dash nutmeg
2 sprigs parsley	1 egg yolk, lightly beaten
1 carrot	2 teaspoons lemon juice

Place meat in Dutch oven with just enough cold water to cover and bring to a boil. Remove scum, add onion, salt, clove, celery, parsley and carrot, cover pot and boil 1½ hours over moderate flame. Melt butter in a saucepan, blend in flour, add broth and cook slowly until sauce thickens. Add pepper and nutmeg, remove from fire and add egg yolk and lemon juice, mixing well. Slice meat and serve with sauce. Serves 6.

LEG OF LAMB IN GALANTINE

1 small tender leg of lamb, boned	1 black truffle, diced (optional)
1¼ cups Marsala or sherry wine	2 tablespoons Marsala or sherry wine
¼ pound tongue, diced	½ pound lean veal, chopped
¼ pound prosciutto, diced	½ pound lean pork, chopped
1 tablespoon shelled pistachio nuts	½ pound salt pork, chopped
	½ teaspoon pepper
	½ teaspoon salt

Place leg of lamb in earthen bowl with wine and let stand overnight. Mix together diced tongue, prosciutto, pistachio nuts and truffle. Soak in 2 tablespoons Marsala or sherry wine for 3 hours. Add chopped veal, pork, salt pork and pepper and mix together well.

With this stuffing fill the leg of lamb in opening left by removal of bone and close together. Wrap leg in towel and tie around as for roast beef. Place in large Dutch oven and add enough water to cover meat. Add 1 teaspoon salt to water, cover pot and simmer gently 2 hours.

Remove meat from pot and let stand 10 minutes. Remove string and towel and rinse towel in cold water. Again wrap lamb in rinsed towel and tie again with string, this time more tightly. Put dish over meat and put something heavy over the dish to press meat down. Let stand until following day. Remove string and towel, slice and serve. Serves 8 to 10.

MUTTON

GRILLED MUTTON CHOPS

4 teaspoons lemon juice	½ small onion, chopped
½ teaspoon salt	1 teaspoon chopped parsley
½ teaspoon pepper	4 mutton chops, 1 inch thick

Mix together lemon juice, salt, pepper, chopped onion and parsley and marinate chops in this mixture at least 2 hours, turning often. Place chops on broiler and broil at high speed 5 minutes on each side. Lower heat and continue broiling 10 minutes on each side. During broiling baste chops frequently with marinade liquid. Serves 4.

LEG OF MUTTON PARSLEY STYLE

1 medium leg of mutton (or lamb)	3 tablespoons olive oil
	1 cup bread crumbs
1 tablespoon salt	2 tablespoons chopped parsley
2 teaspoons pepper	2 lemons, quartered

Have mutton or lamb trimmed and prepared well by butcher. Place in roasting pan, sprinkle with salt and pepper and pour oil over meat. Bake in hot oven (400°F.) 1½ hours. Remove from oven, sprinkle with bread crumbs and parsley, baste well with fat from pan and return to oven for 20 minutes longer, basting frequently. Serve with lemon wedges. Serves 8.

PORK

ARISTA

4 pounds loin of pork	3 cloves garlic, cut into small
2 teaspoons rosemary	slivers
	salt and pepper to taste

Make little slits in meat and insert a little rosemary and a small piece of garlic in each slit. Dust with salt and pepper and cook on a spit or in a hot oven (450°F.) about 1 hour and 45 minutes, until meat is well done. Let meat cool; then slice. Serves 6.

BOILED HAM WITH MARSALA SAUCE

¼ cup butter	4 medium slices boiled
1 tablespoon flour	ham, 1 inch thick
⅓ cup Marsala or sherry wine	

Brown butter without burning. Blend flour in Marsala and add to brown butter. Place over a slow flame and mix well until slightly thickened. Place ham in large shallow casserole. Pour gravy over it and cook in medium oven (375°F.) for 15 minutes. Serve ham slices with gravy poured over. Serves 4.

FRESH HAM AL MARSALA

3-pound slice fresh ham	2 teaspoons minced parsley
1¾ cups Marsala or	¼ teaspoon salt
dry sherry wine	⅛ teaspoon pepper
2 tablespoons olive oil	½ cup stock or bouillon
2 medium onions, chopped	1 teaspoon flour
2 carrots, chopped	1 tablespoon butter, melted
1 stalk celery, chopped	

Place ham in casserole about the same size as the slice. Pour 1 cup wine over it. Let it stand about 6 hours, turning meat occasionally.

Place the oil and chopped vegetables in a large frying pan. Remove meat from wine sauce, drain well and place in frying pan. Add salt and pepper and brown meat slowly on both sides, taking care that the vegetables do not burn. When meat is brown, add the wine in which the meat was marinated 1 tablespoon at a time, browning after each addition. Add ¼ cup stock or bouillon and cook slowly for about an hour, turning meat often.

Place meat on serving dish, slicing it as you wish. Remove some of the fat from the pan gravy, add flour and mix thoroughly. Place on fire

and when gravy starts to thicken remove from fire and add remaining
Marsala or sherry, ¼ cup stock or bouillon and butter. Mix well and
serve on meat. Serves 6.

FRESH HAM WITH CAPERS

½ teaspoon salt	1 teaspoon chopped parsley
½ teaspoon pepper	2 cups dry red wine
½ medium onion, chopped	2 pounds fresh ham
½ carrot, sliced	¼ cup butter
½ clove garlic, chopped	½ tablespoon flour
½ bay leaf	2 cups stock or water
½ teaspoon thyme	2 tablespoons capers

Make a marinade of salt, pepper, onion, carrot, garlic, bay leaf,
thyme, parsley and wine and let meat stand in this bath 10 hours,
turning occasionally.

When ready to cook, melt butter in large pan, remove meat from
marinade, dry it and brown thoroughly in hot butter. Remove meat
from pan when brown, add flour to fat in pan, blend in well and add
strained marinade liquid. Bring to boiling point, stirring well. Return meat to pan, add stock or water, cover pan, lower flame and cook
2 hours. Add capers just before serving. Slice meat and serve with
gravy. Serves 6.

HAM SOUFFLE

⅛ pound butter	2 tablespoons grated Parmesan
2 tablespoons flour	cheese
2 cups milk	3 egg yolks, lightly beaten
2 cups cooked ham, diced	with fork
fine	3 egg whites, beaten stiff

Melt butter in saucepan, blend in flour until smooth, add milk and
cook slowly, stirring constantly, until thickened. Remove from fire.
Add ham, cheese and egg yolks and fold in egg whites. Grease a 1-quart
casserole, pour into it the soufflé mixture, smooth with knife and bake
in moderate oven (350°F.) 20 minutes. Serve immediately. Serves 4.

HOT HAM BREAD

¼ cup butter	2 eggs
4 tablespoons flour	2 tablespoons grated Parmesan
1 cup milk	cheese
⅛ teaspoon pepper	¾ pound boiled or baked
⅛ teaspoon nutmeg	ham, chopped

Melt butter in saucepan and blend in flour. Add milk, stirring constantly, and cook over low heat until thickened. Add pepper and nutmeg. (Do not add salt.) Remove sauce from fire and cool. When cold, add eggs, slightly beaten, Parmesan and ham. Mix well. Grease and flour a mold and pour in the mixture. Place mold in pan with 1½ inches water in it and bake in moderate oven (350°F.) for 1 hour. When done let pan rest for a little while, then unmold onto serving dish. Serves 4.

PIG'S FEET WITH BROCCOLI

4 pig's feet	½ teaspoon pepper
1 bunch broccoli	½ pound mozzarella cheese, cut
½ pound Italian sausage,	into very thin slices
cut into 1-inch lengths	4 tablespoons grated Roman
1 tablespoon olive oil	cheese
1 tablespoon leaf lard	2 eggs

Cook pig's feet in boiling water 1½ hours, or until tender. Remove from fire and reserve the broth. Clean broccoli, cut into small pieces, and boil in slightly salted water 10 minutes. Fry sausage in oil and leaf lard, adding 1 or 2 tablespoons water, if necessary, until sausage is tender.

In a casserole place 3 tablespoons broth obtained from boiling pig's feet, add 2 pig's feet cut into pieces, half the broccoli, half the pepper and cover with half the mozzarella and half the grated Roman cheese. Repeat the procedure and pour over it another 2 tablespoons broth. Break eggs into bowl, add 1 tablespoon grated cheese and beat with fork 5 minutes. Pour egg and cheese mixture over broccoli and pig's feet and bake in moderate oven (350°F.) 45 minutes. Serves 4.

PORK CHOPS AL FINOCCHIO (with Fennel)

4 pork loin chops, medium	½ cup dry red wine
thick	½ cup Marsala or sherry wine
1½ teaspoons butter	⅓ clove garlic
½ teaspoon salt	½ teaspoon fennel seeds
½ teaspoon pepper	1 tablespoon tomato sauce

Place pork chops in skillet with butter, add salt and pepper and brown well on both sides (about 20 minutes on each side). Remove from skillet and place on serving dish in warm place. Pour red wine and Marsala into skillet, add garlic, fennel seeds and tomato sauce, stir well and cook over high flame 5 minutes. Pour sauce over chops and serve immediately. Serves 4.

PORK CHOPS IN PIQUANT SAUCE

4 pork loin chops, ½ inch
    thick
1 tablespoon melted butter
½ teaspoon salt
½ teaspoon pepper
2 tablespoons olive oil
1 tablespoon chopped
    parsley

⅓ clove garlic, chopped
1 tablespoon tomato sauce
2 tablespoons water
5 vinegar peppers, chopped
4 anchovy filets, chopped
½ teaspoon freshly ground
    pepper

Spread pork chops with melted butter and broil in hot broiler (450°F.) 20 minutes on each side. Sprinkle with salt and pepper. Heat oil, parsley and garlic together in small saucepan, add tomato sauce and water and cook 10 minutes. Remove from fire, add peppers, anchovies and pepper, mix well and serve over chops. Serves 4.

PORK CHOPS IN TOMATO SAUCE

6 pork chops, cut very thick
salt and pepper
1 tablespoon olive oil

1 cup dry white wine
6 tablespoons tomato paste
1 cup stock or water

Dust chops with salt and pepper and place in a large frying pan with oil. Brown well on both sides, keeping pan covered so that they will not get too dry. When properly browned, pour off the fat and add the wine. Cover pan and simmer, turning chops occasionally. When the wine is nearly evaporated, add tomato paste and stock or water, well mixed, and cook another half hour or until chops are well done. If gravy is too thick, add a little water. Place chops on serving dish and pour the sauce over. This sauce is very good on macaroni or rice. Serves 6.

PORK CHOPS MODENA STYLE

4 pork chops
2 teaspoons rosemary
2 teaspoons chopped sage

½ clove garlic, chopped
⅛ teaspoon salt
⅛ teaspoon pepper
½ cup dry white wine

Leave all the fat around the chops. Mix rosemary, sage, garlic, salt and pepper. Sprinkle this mixture on both sides of chops and place them in a buttered shallow pan. Pour enough water into pan to cover chops. Cover pan and cook over slow fire for about 1 hour. When water has evaporated, the chops will begin to brown. Turn them occasionally until thoroughly browned. Do not add any more fat as the fat on the meat will be sufficient.

When chops are well browned, add wine, increase heat slightly, turn chops and cook 1 minute. Place on serving dish and pour gravy over them. Serves 4.

PORK CHOPS NEAPOLITAN STYLE

2 sweet peppers	6 loin pork chops
1 pound fresh mushrooms	salt and pepper
2 tablespoons olive oil	3 tablespoons tomato purée
1 clove garlic	1 tablespoon stock or water

Roast the peppers in hot oven, peel and cut into strips. Slice mushrooms thin. Put olive oil in skillet and brown garlic in it. Remove garlic and place chops in skillet. Brown slowly on both sides, adding salt and pepper to taste. Remove chops from pan and keep warm.

Pour tomato purée into pan, add water or stock, peppers, mushrooms and chops. Cover skillet and cook slowly for about half an hour or until chops are well done. Serves 6.

STUFFED PORK CHOPS

4 pork loin chops, 1 inch thick	1/8 teaspoon nutmeg
	1/8 teaspoon salt
1/8 pound mozzarella cheese, sliced thin	1/8 teaspoon pepper
	1 egg, lightly beaten with fork
4 slices prosciutto, cut into strips	1/2 cup bread crumbs
	3 tablespoons frying oil

Have butcher cut a pocket in each chop. Place 1 slice mozzarella, some prosciutto, nutmeg and a little salt and pepper in each pocket and close. Dip chops into egg, roll in bread crumbs and fry in oil 20 minutes on each side. Serves 4.

PORK CHOPS WITH MUSTARD

4 pork loin chops, 1/2 inch thick	1/2 cup stock
	1/2 teaspoon prepared mustard
1 tablespoon butter	1 teaspoon capers
1 small onion, chopped	1/2 teaspoon salt
1 tablespoon flour	1/8 teaspoon pepper
1/2 cup dry white wine	

Braise pork chops in skillet with butter, browning nicely about 20 minutes on each side. Remove chops from skillet. Place onion in skillet, brown slowly, blend in flour, add white wine and stock and boil gently until mixture is slightly thickened. Return chops to skillet and simmer 10 minutes. Add mustard, capers, salt and pepper, mix well and serve. Serves 4.

PORK CUTLETS WITH CAPERS

8 small pork cutlets
3 tablespoons flour
¼ teaspoon salt
⅛ teaspoon pepper
1 egg, lightly beaten
½ cup bread crumbs
3 tablespoons oil
1 small onion, chopped
1 tablespoon butter

2 anchovy filets, cut into
    small pieces
2 tablespoons capers, chopped
1 tablespoon chopped parsley
¼ teaspoon flour
2 tablespoons vinegar
½ cup stock or water
½ tablespoon butter

Dredge cutlets in flour, sprinkle with salt and pepper, dip into egg, roll in crumbs and fry in oil 15 minutes on each side or until well browned. Place onion in saucepan with butter, and brown. Add anchovies, capers, parsley and flour and cook 2 minutes, stirring well. Add vinegar and stock and cook 10 minutes longer. Add butter. Pour sauce over cutlets and serve. Serves 4.

LOIN OF PORK WITH MILK

4 pounds boned loin of
    pork
salt and pepper

2 tablespoons butter
1 quart milk
1 small white truffle (optional)

Have pork boned and trim off excess fat. Dust with salt and pepper and let stand a few hours. Place meat in Dutch oven and brown in butter on top of stove until meat is golden brown on all sides. Add milk, cover pan, and cook slowly over moderate fire about 1 hour and 45 minutes until meat is thoroughly done. The milk sauce will be creamy and thick and slightly brown in color.

Remove meat from pan, slice and place in serving dish. If you desire, add thinly sliced truffle to milk sauce and cook a few minutes. Pour sauce over meat. Serves 6.

SKEWERED PORK FILET

1 pound filet of pork, cut
    into 2-inch slices
½ loaf French bread, sliced
    thin
8 bay leaves

6 slices prosciutto, cut into
    halves
2 tablespoons olive oil
½ teaspoon salt
½ teaspoon pepper

On skewers place 1 piece of pork filet, 1 slice bread, 1 bay leaf and 1 slice prosciutto, repeat until you have filled 4 skewers, ending with bread. Sprinkle with oil, salt and pepper and cook in moderate oven (375°F.) 20 minutes on each side. Serve immediately. Serves 4.

PORK SWEET-SOUR

1 pound pork filet slices, 1/3 inch thick	1 tablespoon cocoa
1 tablespoon olive oil	1½ tablespoon wine vinegar
1/8 teaspoon salt	1 tablespoon pine nuts
1/8 teaspoon pepper	1 tablespoon raisins
1 tablespoon sugar	1 teaspoon diced candied orange peel

Place pork filets in skillet with olive oil, salt and pepper and cook over brisk flame 20 minutes on each side. Remove meat.

Add 2 tablespoons water to pan gravy, scrape bottom of pan and blend in well sugar, cocoa and vinegar. Add pine nuts, raisins and orange peel and boil 2 minutes. Serve sauce over meat. Serves 4.

PORK IN WATER

2 pounds fresh ham	½ teaspoon pepper
3/4 cup water	1¼ cups milk
½ teaspoon salt	water to cover meat

Have butcher tie meat to hold shape. Place meat in pan just large enough to fit it. Add 3/4 cup water and cook slowly until water has evaporated. Brown meat in fat left in pan, adding salt and pepper.

When well browned, add milk, scraping bottom of pan. Add enough water to cover meat, lower flame, cover pan and cook 1 hour, or until meat seems done. Remove from pan, slice and serve with gravy. Serves 6.

VARIETY MEATS

BEANS AND LUNGS

2 tablespoons olive oil	1/4 cup dry red wine
1 tablespoon leaf lard	4 fresh medium tomatoes, skinned and cut into small
1 small onion, sliced	pieces (or 1 small can tomatoes)
1/8 pound salt pork	
½ clove garlic, chopped	1/4 teaspoon salt
1 sprig parsley, minced	1/8 teaspoon pepper
1 stalk celery, chopped	1 large can cooked kidney
1 pound veal lung, cut into cubes	beans
	½ teaspoon chopped sweet basil

Place oil and leaf lard in frying pan, add onion, salt pork, garlic, parsley and celery and brown thoroughly. Add lung and brown well, adding 1 or 2 tablespoons water, if necessary. Add wine and continue cooking until wine evaporates. Add fresh (or canned) tomatoes, salt and pepper and cook slowly 20 minutes. Add beans with liquid from can, cover and cook slowly 1 hour, adding a little water from time to time, if necessary. Before serving add sweet basil. Serves 4.

BREADED CALF'S OR BEEF BRAINS*

1½ pound calf's (or beef) brains	½ teaspoon parsley
2 eggs, lightly beaten	¼ teaspoon salt
2 teaspoons cold water	¼ teaspoon pepper
½ teaspoon grated Roman cheese	½ cup bread crumbs
	½ cup olive oil
	1 lemon, cut into wedges

Wash brains well and parboil 5 minutes. Drain, peel off outer skin and cut into 2- or 3-inch pieces. Blend together eggs, water, cheese, parsley, salt and pepper. Dip brains into egg mixture, roll in bread crumbs and fry in hot oil until golden brown on all sides. Serve with lemon wedges. Serves 4.

LAMB BRAINS IN WHITE SAUCE

4 lamb's brains	⅛ teaspoon nutmeg
½ cup butter	⅛ teaspoon salt
1 tablespoon flour	⅛ teaspoon pepper
¼ cup milk	2 teaspoons lemon juice

Boil brains in water 1 minute, then remove from water and cut each brain in half, lengthwise. Melt ¼ cup butter in a small pan, blend in flour, mixing well, add milk and nutmeg and boil gently 2 minutes. Remove white sauce from fire and keep warm.

Melt remaining ¼ cup butter in a large frying pan, add brains, sprinkle with salt and pepper and cook 3 or 4 minutes, turning gently so they do not break. Add white sauce and continue cooking slowly 4 minutes. Remove from fire, place in serving dish, sprinkle with lemon juice and serve. Serves 4.

LAMB BRAINS NEAPOLITAN STYLE

4 lamb's brains	1 teaspoon capers
3 tablespoons olive oil	12 ripe black olives, pitted and diced
¼ teaspoon salt	
⅛ teaspoon pepper	2 tablespoons bread crumbs

Put brains in small pan, cover with cold water and let stand 10 minutes. Change water and place pan with brains and fresh water over flame. Allow water to reach boiling point, then remove brains and rinse them in clear, cool water. Dry with towel.

Put 1½ tablespoons olive oil in shallow casserole, add brains, sprinkle with salt and pepper, cover with layer of capers, then a layer of olives. Sprinkle with bread crumbs, pour remaining 1½ tablespoons olive oil over crumbs, and place casserole in hot oven for 10 minutes. Serve in casserole. Serves 4.

LAMB'S CORATELLA WITH ARTICHOKES ROMAN STYLE

4 artichokes	½ onion, chopped
3 tablespoons lard	½ cup dry red wine
¼ teaspoon salt	1 tablespoon chopped parsley
⅛ teaspoon pepper	1 teaspoon lemon juice
1 young lamb's coratella	½ lemon, cut into wedges

Remove outer leaves from artichokes, cut into 8 wedges each and remove chokes. Place in frying pan with 2 tablespoons lard and cook slowly with half the salt and pepper until tender. Add a little water occasionally if artichokes tend to become too dry.

In another large frying pan place 1 tablespoon lard, add the lung portion of the coratella, sliced very thin, and the onion and cook gently about 15 minutes when the lung will make a queer whistling sound. Add remaining salt and pepper and ¼ cup wine and continue cooking until wine has evaporated. Add heart, sliced very thin, and cook 5 minutes. Add liver, also sliced very thin, and continue cooking 8 minutes or until liver has lost its reddish tint. Add rest of wine and artichokes and cook 2 minutes longer. Add parsley and lemon juice, place on serving dish immediately, garnish with lemon wedges and serve. Serves 4.

COTEGHINO OR ZAMPONE WITH LENTILS

1½ pounds coteghino or zampone	1 tablespoon olive oil
2 cans cooked lentils	2 thin slices bacon, chopped
1 small onion, chopped	1 stalk celery, chopped

Boil the coteghino or zampone slowly 1¾ hours. Drain lentils. Place onion in oil in saucepan and brown. Add bacon, brown further and add celery, lentils and 1 cup broth from coteghino or zampone and cook 15 minutes. Place lentils on serving dish, slice coteghino or zampone and serve over lentils. Serves 6.

Variation: Rice may be used instead of lentils.

FRITTO MISTO (Mixed Fry)

A mixed fry is composed of different ingredients, fried separately and served together. The following recipe will be enough for a bountiful mixed fry. You may omit some of the ingredients and substitute others that you prefer.

Sweetbreads, ½ pound. Remove skin, cut into pieces 1-inch thick, roll in flour, dip into beaten egg, roll in bread crumbs and fry in hot butter until golden.

Brains, ½ pound. Let stand 30 minutes in ice water, place on fire and bring water to a boil. Remove skin, cut into large cubes, roll in flour, dip into beaten egg, roll in bread crumbs and fry in hot butter until golden.

Calf's liver, 1½ pounds sliced. Cut into 4 pieces, flour and fry in hot butter 4 minutes on each side.

Zucchini (Italian squash), 1 small squash. Cut into long strips, dip into pastella (see index) and fry in hot oil.

Artichoke, 1. Remove outer leaves, stem and choke. Cut into very thin slices, roll in flour, dip into beaten egg and fry in hot olive oil until crisp and golden.

Cauliflower, 8 small flowerlets. Parboil 5 minutes, drain, roll in flour, dip into beaten egg and fry in hot olive oil.

Apple, 1 large, sliced. Dip slices into pastella (see index), fry in hot butter and sprinkle with a little sugar and cinnamon.

Potato Croquette, 1 recipe potato croquette (see index).

Tomatoes, 2 medium, not too ripe. Cut into thick slices and remove seeds. Dip into pastella (see index) and fry in hot oil. Serve immediately.

GRILLED HEART OF BEEF

1 pound beef heart, sliced very thin	½ teaspoon salt
	¼ teaspoon pepper
2 tablespoons olive oil	½ lemon, cut into wedges

Place slices of heart in dish, add oil and salt and pepper and let stand ½ hour or longer, turning frequently. Place slices of heart in frying pan over brisk flame and cook 8 minutes, turning slices frequently. Remove to serving dish, garnish with lemon wedges and serve immediately. If allowed to stand before serving, the heart will become tough. Serves 4.

BEEF HEART IN ANCHOVY SAUCE

2 tablespoons olive oil	¼ teaspoon salt
1 clove garlic	⅛ teaspoon pepper
1 pound beef heart, sliced thin	2 teaspoons lemon juice
3 anchovy filets, chopped	1 teaspoon chopped parsley

Brown garlic in oil in frying pan, and when brown, remove garlic from pan and add slices of heart. Brown well on both sides over brisk flame for 8 minutes, add anchovies and cook 1 minute longer. Remove from fire, add salt and pepper, lemon juice and parsley and serve immediately. Serves 4.

BEEF HEART WITH MUSHROOMS

2 tablespoons dried
mushrooms
3 tablespoons olive oil
¼ teaspoon salt
⅛ teaspoon pepper

2 tablespoons tomato paste
¾ cup water
1½ pounds beef heart,
sliced thin

Soak dried mushrooms in cold water 30 minutes. Rinse well, drain and place in saucepan with 1 tablespoon olive oil. Add half the salt and pepper and brown lightly. Dilute tomato paste with water, add to mushrooms, cover pan and cook over moderate flame 45 minutes.

Heat remaining 2 tablespoons olive oil in frying pan, add slices of heart, season with remaining salt and pepper and cook over lively fire 5 minutes. Add tomato and mushroom sauce to heart, cook together 1 minute and serve. Serves 6.

BEEF KIDNEY BRAISED

1 beef kidney (about ¾
pound), sliced very thin
2 tablespoons olive oil or
lard
½ onion, chopped

¾ cup white wine or ½ cup
Marsala
½ tablespoon tomato paste
¼ teaspoon salt
⅛ teaspoon pepper
1 tablespoon chopped parsley

Place sliced kidney in frying pan with 1 tablespoon olive oil or lard and fry 2 or 3 minutes over high flame. Remove pan from fire and place kidney on colander. The kidney will start to drip a dark red liquid. Let it drip 10 minutes.

Clean frying pan and put in 1 tablespoon olive oil or lard and the chopped onion. Brown the onion slowly until golden brown in color. Add the kidney, which has dripped 10 minutes, and cook over brisk fire 1 minute. Add white wine or Marsala, tomato paste, salt and pepper and continue cooking 3 minutes. Remove from fire, add chopped parsley and serve on a pre-heated platter. (Pork kidney may be substituted for beef kidney with equally good results.) Serves 4.

GRILLED VEAL KIDNEY

2 veal kidneys, cut into
4 slices lengthwise
2 tablespoons olive oil

½ teaspoon salt
½ teaspoon pepper
2 teaspoons lemon juice

Place sliced kidney on large platter, sprinkle with oil, salt and pepper and let stand 1 hour. Place on hot grill and cook 6 minutes on each side. Place on serving dish and sprinkle with lemon juice. Serves 2.

VEAL KIDNEYS TRIFOLATI

4 veal kidneys	½ teaspoon butter
1 clove garlic	2 filets of anchovies, chopped
2 tablespoons olive oil	1 tablespoon chopped parsley
¼ teaspoon salt	1 teaspoon lemon juice
⅛ teaspoon pepper	

Slice kidneys thin as possible and remove all fat. Brown garlic in oil over gentle fire, and when brown, remove garlic from pan. Add slices of kidney, season with salt and pepper, increase flame and cook briskly 5 minutes. Add butter and chopped anchovies, mix well, remove from fire, add parsley and lemon juice and serve immediately. Serves 4.

LIVER BALLS

¾ pound liver (beef or pork) , chopped	2 egg yolks
¼ pound salt pork, chopped	¼ teaspoon salt
3 slices bread, soaked in water and squeezed dry	⅛ teaspoon pepper
	¾ pound *rete* (to be obtained only in Italian shops)
1 tablespoon chopped parsley	1 egg, beaten 1 minute with fork
2 tablespoons grated Parmesan cheese	3 tablespoons bread crumbs
	4 tablespoons butter

Mix together liver, salt pork, bread, parsley, cheese, egg yolks, salt and pepper. When well mixed, shape into little meat balls. Wrap well with *rete* (optional), dip into beaten egg, then in bread crumbs and fry gently in butter 10 minutes, or until balls are golden brown on all sides. Serves 4.

BEEF LIVER FLORENTINE STYLE

1 pound beef liver, sliced thin	6 fresh sage leaves
2 tablespoons flour	½ teaspoon salt
2 tablespoons olive oil	½ teaspoon pepper
2 cloves garlic, chopped	1 tablespoon olive oil
	2 tablespoons tomato purée

Dredge liver in flour. Place 2 tablespoons olive oil, garlic and sage leaves in frying pan, add liver and fry 4 minutes on each side. Add salt and pepper and remove liver from pan. Add 1 tablespoon oil and tomato purée to pan gravy and cook 1 minute. Return liver to pan, cook 3 or 4 minutes longer and serve. Serves 4.

FRIED BEEF LIVER WITH SAGE

1 pound beef liver, sliced thin	¼ cup butter
1 tablespoon flour	½ teaspoon salt
1 egg, lightly beaten with fork	1 teaspoon fresh sage leaves

Dredge liver with flour and dip into beaten egg. Melt butter in frying pan, add liver and fry 4 minutes on each side. Add salt and place on serving dish. Add sage leaves to butter in pan, mix well and pour over liver. Serves 4.

BEEF LIVER ITALIAN STYLE

1 pound beef liver, sliced very thin	½ teaspoon salt
2 tablespoons flour	¼ teaspoon pepper
¼ cup butter	1 tablespoon butter
	2 teaspoons lemon juice

Remove liver skin and dredge slices in flour. Melt butter in frying pan, add liver and fry over high flame 4 minutes on each side. Add salt and pepper and remove from pan. Add 1 tablespoon butter to pan gravy, melt and add lemon juice. Scrape bottom of pan and mix well. Serve over liver immediately. Serves 4.

BEEF LIVER PISTOIA STYLE

1 pound beef liver, sliced thin	2 cloves garlic
2 tablespoons flour	½ teaspoon salt
2 tablespoons olive oil	½ lemon, cut into wedges

Dredge liver in flour. Place oil in frying pan, add garlic, brown and remove garlic from pan. Add liver and fry 4 minutes on each side. Add salt and remove to serving dish. Garnish with lemon wedges and serve. Serves 4.

FRIED LIVER IN SWEET-SOUR SAUCE

2 tablespoons flour	4 tablespoons bread crumbs
4 large thin slices of liver	4 tablespoons butter
1 egg, beaten 1 minute with fork	1 tablespoon sugar
	4 teaspoons lemon juice

Flour liver, dip in egg and roll in bread crumbs. Melt 3 tablespoons butter in frying pan, add liver and brown on both sides, allowing about 5 minutes a side. Remove liver to serving dish.

Add 1 tablespoon butter and sugar to frying pan and cook very slowly until sugar is melted. Remove from fire, add lemon juice, mix well, return liver to pan and turn in sauce until well covered on both sides. Serve immediately. Serves 4.

LIVER TRIESTE STYLE

2 tablespoons olive oil	¼ teaspoon salt
1 onion, chopped	⅛ teaspoon pepper
1 stalk celery, chopped	6 slices toast
1 carrot, sliced	1 tablespoon bread crumbs
1 pound beef or calf's	2 teaspoons lemon juice
liver, in 1 piece	1 sprig parsley, chopped
1 clove	

Place olive oil and vegetables in saucepan. Remove skin from liver, stick clove in liver, and place over vegetables. Add salt and pepper, enough water to cover, cover pan and bring to boiling point. When boiling, remove cover, lower flame and simmer 2 hours, turning liver occasionally.

Cut toast into triangles and place on serving plate. Slice liver thin, place on toast and pour gravy and vegetables over it. Sprinkle with bread crumbs and lemon juice, garnish with parsley and serve. Serves 4.

LIVER VENETIAN STYLE

2 medium onions, chopped	¼ teaspoon salt
4 tablespoons olive oil	⅛ teaspoon pepper
8 slices liver, sliced thin	

Brown onion thoroughly in oil in frying pan, add liver, salt and pepper and cook 5 minutes, turning once. Serve immediately. Serves 4.

LIVER WITH ARTICHOKES

4 artichokes	¼ teaspoon salt
3 tablespoons olive oil	⅛ teaspoon pepper
½ onion, chopped	1 tablespoon chopped parsley
1 pound beef liver, sliced	2 teaspoons lemon juice
very thin	

Remove outside leaves from artichokes, cut into 8 pieces each, lengthwise, and remove chokes. Place in large frying pan with oil and onion and cook over low fire 15 minutes. Add liver, salt and pepper and cook 5 minutes over high flame, turning liver once. Remove from pan, add parsley, sprinkle with lemon juice and serve immediately. Serves 4.

CALF'S LIVER BIRD STYLE

1 pound calf's liver, sliced thin	½ teaspoon pepper
	2 tablespoons olive oil
2 tablespoons flour	1 teaspoon sage leaves
½ teaspoon salt	2 tablespoons wine vinegar

Dredge liver with flour and sprinkle with salt and pepper. Cook in hot olive oil 3 minutes on each side. Add sage leaves and vinegar, cook 1 minute longer and serve immediately. Serves 4.

CALF'S LIVER MILANESE

8 slices calf's liver, ½ inch thick (about 2 pounds)	3 tablespoons flour
	1 egg, lightly beaten with fork
¼ teaspoon salt	4 tablespoons bread crumbs
⅛ teaspoon pepper	4 tablespoons butter
1 tablespoon chopped parsley	parsley sprigs
	¾ lemon, cut into wedges

Sprinkle liver with salt, pepper and parsley and allow to stand 1 hour. Roll liver in flour, then in egg, then in bread crumbs and fry in butter about 5 minutes on each side until liver is golden brown. Remove liver to serving dish, pour frying butter over it, garnish with parsley and lemon wedges, and serve. Serves 4.

CALF'S LIVER TUSCAN STYLE

4 tablespoons flour	¼ teaspoon salt
8 thin slices calf's liver (about 2 pounds)	⅛ teaspoon pepper
	1 tablespoon chopped fresh sage leaves
4 tablespoons olive oil	1 lemon, cut into quarters

Flour liver, place in frying pan with oil and cook 5 minutes on each side. Add salt, pepper and sage leaves and cook 2 minutes longer on each side. Garnish with lemon quarters and serve immediately. Serves 4.

PORK LIVER

¾ pound pork liver, cut into 10 pieces	10 bay leaves
	10 small squares bread
½ pound pork *rete* (lamb's intestinal membrane—obtainable only in Italian shops)	

Wrap each piece of liver in *rete,* place on skewer and follow with 1 bay leaf and 1 square of bread. Repeat process until skewer is filled. Grill over hot fire or fry in pan with a little bacon fat. Do not cook over 8 minutes. Serve immediately. Serves 4.

PORK LIVER PETRONIUS

¾ pound pork liver, cut into large cubes
½ pound *rete* (lamb's intestinal membrane—obtainable only in Italian shops)

½ loaf long French bread, cut into thin slices
12 bay leaves
2 tablespoons olive oil
½ teaspoon salt
¼ teaspoon pepper
2 tablespoons dry white wine

Wrap each liver cube in a piece of *rete.* Place on skewers 1 piece liver, 1 slice bread and 1 bay leaf and repeat until all liver is used. Place skewers in greased baking dish, sprinkle with oil, salt and pepper and bake in medium oven (375°F.) 10 minutes on one side, then, turning skewers, 10 minutes on the other side. Add wine, mix well and serve with pan gravy. Serves 4.

PORK LIVER TUSCAN STYLE

2 tablespoons bread crumbs
1 clove garlic, chopped
1½ teaspoons fennel seed
1 pound pork liver, cut in 12 1-inch pieces
¼ teaspoon salt

⅛ teaspoon pepper
½ pound *rete* (lamb's intestinal membrane—obtainable only in Italian shops)
2 tablespoons bacon drippings or butter

Mix bread crumbs with garlic and fennel seed and roll each piece of liver in this mixture. Add salt and pepper and wrap each piece in *rete.* Cook on skewer over grill or in frying pan with bacon drippings. Do not cook over 10 minutes. Serve immediately. Serves 4.

SWEETBREADS WITH ARTICHOKES

1 pound sweetbreads
4 artichokes
2 tablespoons olive oil
salt and pepper
1 tablespoon butter

2 thin slices prosciutto, minced
2 tablespoons Marsala or sherry
¼ teaspoon salt
⅛ teaspoon pepper

Place sweetbreads in cold water for 15 minutes. Change water, place in saucepan over fire and bring water to boiling point. Remove sweetbreads and place again in cold water, drain, dry and remove skin.

Remove outer leaves and chokes from artichokes and cut each into 8 pieces. Place in frying pan with oil and cook until tender. Add salt and pepper and a few drops of water if artichokes become too dry.

Place butter in another frying pan, add sweetbreads and cook over high flame 3 minutes on each side or until golden brown in color. Add prosciutto and cook 2 minutes longer. Add Marsala or sherry, season with salt and pepper and cook 1 minute more. Remove from fire and serve. Serves 4.

Variation: 1 pound shelled fresh peas may be substituted for artichokes if desired.

LAMB'S SWEETBREADS WITH PROSCIUTTO

1 pound lamb's sweetbreads	3 thin slices prosciutto or
2 tablespoons butter	lean bacon, cut into slivers
1/4 teaspoon salt	2 tablespoons Marsala or dry
1/8 teaspoon pepper	sherry

Place sweetbreads in cold water for 15 minutes. Change water, place in saucepan and bring water to boiling point. Remove from fire, place again in cold water, drain, dry and remove skin.

Melt butter in frying pan, add sweetbreads, and cook over brisk fire until golden brown in color. Add salt, pepper and prosciutto or bacon and cook 2 minutes. Add Marsala or sherry and cook 2 minutes longer. Remove from fire and serve immediately. Serves 4.

Tripe as sold in most butcher shops is already boiled and therefore should not be difficult to obtain. However, if tripe purchased is not pre-boiled, it must be boiled 4 hours before using in ordinary recipes.

GOLDEN TRIPE ALLA BOLOGNESE

1 tablespoon olive oil	2 pounds parboiled tripe,
1 thin slice salt pork,	cut into 2-inch squares
chopped	3 egg yolks, lightly beaten
1 small onion, chopped	with fork
1/2 clove garlic, chopped	1 teaspoon meat extract,
1 tablespoon chopped	dissolved in
parsley	1/2 cup warm water
1/2 teaspoon salt	2 tablespoons grated Parmesan
1/4 teaspoon pepper	cheese

Place olive oil, salt pork, onion, garlic and parsley in a large frying pan and brown together slowly. Add salt and pepper and tripe and cook slowly 1 hour, mixing frequently.

In a mixing bowl combine egg yolks with meat extract, dissolved in water. Lower flame under tripe as much as possible and add egg and meat extract mixture. Mix well, cover pan and let simmer very slowly 5 minutes. Remove from fire, add Parmesan and mix well. Serve with additional Parmesan sprinkled over tripe, if desired. Serves 6.

TRIPE ALLA MILANESE

2 pounds veal tripe
8 quarts water
2 teaspoons salt
1 stalk celery
1 onion
2 cloves
1 onion, sliced
2 carrots, diced
1 large celery heart, minced
¼ cup butter
¼ pound bacon, minced
1 pound fresh tomatoes,
  skinned and cut into pieces

or 1 medium can tomatoes
¼ teaspoon salt
1 pinch saffron
1 cup warm water
1 can red beans
½ small new white cabbage,
  sliced thin
3 large potatoes, boiled and
  diced
½ teaspoon sage
3 tablespoons grated Parmesan
  cheese
⅛ teaspoon pepper

Clean tripe, place in large pan with water, salt, celery, onion and cloves and boil 2 hours. Remove from water and cut into thin strips. Place in a large pan the sliced onion, carrots, celery heart, butter and bacon and brown well. When browned, add tomatoes and cook 5 minutes. Add tripe, salt, saffron and 1 cup warm water and cook ½ hour. Add beans, cabbage and potatoes and continue cooking 25 minutes longer. Add sage, sprinkle with Parmesan cheese and pepper and cook 5 minutes more. Serves 4.

TRIPE GENOESE STYLE

1 cup olive oil
1 onion, chopped
1 bay leaf
⅛ pound pork fat, chopped
2 pounds parboiled tripe,
  sliced thin
1⅛ cups dry white wine

2 tablespoons tomato paste,
  diluted in ½ cup water
1 clove garlic, chopped
1 teaspoon chopped parsley
½ teaspoon rosemary
½ teaspoon salt
⅛ teaspoon pepper
1 cup stock or water

In large frying pan place oil, onion, bay leaf and pork fat and cook slowly until onion is well browned. Add tripe and wine, cover pan and cook over low fire until wine has evaporated. Add diluted tomato paste, garlic, parsley, rosemary, salt and pepper and cook over low fire 1 hour, adding stock or water a little at a time. Gravy should be very thick.

At end of hour taste tripe to determine if it needs further cooking. If so, continue cooking until it reaches desired tenderness, but take care not to overcook. Serves 6.

TRIPE LUCCA STYLE

1 onion, chopped	¼ teaspoon salt
3 tablespoons butter	⅛ teaspoon pepper
1 pound parboiled tripe, cut into thin strips	3 tablespoons grated Parmesan cheese
	¼ teaspoon cinnamon

Brown onion in 2 tablespoons butter, add tripe, salt and pepper and cook slowly 1 hour, turning often. With fire very low, add Parmesan, cinnamon and remaining butter, mix well and cook 10 minutes longer. Serves 4.

TRIPE ROMAN STYLE

1 onion, chopped	2 pounds parboiled tripe, cut into finger strips
2 sliced bacon or salt pork, chopped fine	½ teaspoon salt
1 tablespoon chopped parsley	¼ teaspoon pepper
½ clove garlic	2 tablespoons grated Parmesan cheese
2 tablespoons tomato paste	1 tablespoon chopped mint leaves
1 cup water	

Place onion, bacon or salt pork, parsley and garlic in frying pan and brown slowly and thoroughly. Add tomato paste and water and cook 10 minutes. Add tripe, lower fire and cook slowly 1 hour or until tripe is as tender as you desire. Add salt and pepper and, if gravy is too thick, add a little water. Remove from pan, sprinkle with Parmesan and mint and serve. Serves 6.

ITALIAN SAUSAGE WITH ENDIVE

¾ pound Italian sausage, sweet or hot	¼ teaspoon salt
1 head endive	¼ teaspoon pepper (omit if hot sausage is used)

Prick sausage with needle, place in large frying pan with 1 tablespoon water and brown slowly. When well browned, remove from frying pan. Add endive, which has been washed and chopped fine, to pan gravy, add a little water if necessary and cook 20 minutes. Add salt and pepper. Cut sausage into 3-inch pieces and serve with endive. Serves 4.

ITALIAN SAUSAGE WITH POTATOES

1 pound Italian sausage,
   sweet or hot
4 medium potatoes, boiled,
   peeled and diced

½ teaspoon salt
½ teaspoon pepper (omit if
   hot sausage is used)

Prick sausage with needle, place in large frying pan with 1 tablespoon water and brown thoroughly. Add potatoes and brown in sausage
fat. Add salt and pepper, cut sausage into 3-inch pieces and serve.
Serves 4.

FRIED ITALIAN SAUSAGE

1 pound Italian sausage
   sweet or hot

water to cover

Prick sausage all over with a needle and place in frying pan. Cover
with cold water and cook over moderate fire 45 minutes. After all water
has evaporated, there will be enough fat in pan to brown sausage
nicely and give it a delicious brown crust. Serves 4.

SAUSAGE WITH BEANS

1 pound Italian sausage,
   sweet or hot
2 tablespoons olive oil
1½ tablespoons tomato paste

¼ teaspoon salt
⅛ teaspoon pepper (omit if
   hot sausage is used)
4 cups boiled kidney beans

Prick sausage with needle and place in frying pan with enough cold
water to cover. Cook over moderate fire until water evaporates, then
cook 30 minutes longer, allowing sausage to brown thoroughly in its
own fat. Remove from pan and keep warm. Add oil to fat in pan, add
tomato paste, salt and pepper and cook 10 minutes. Add sausage and
cook 30 minutes more. Place beans on bottom of serving dish and
place sausage and sauce over them. Serves 4.

7. *Poultry*

CHICKEN

CHICKEN CACCIATORA

4-pound spring chicken, cut into pieces
½ cup flour
1 teaspoon salt
½ cup fat
¼ cup chopped onion
1 clove garlic, chopped fine
¼ cup chopped carrot
3 sprigs parsley
1 basil or bay leaf
4 cups tomatoes
1 teaspoon salt
dash pepper
¼ cup Marsala, sherry or white wine

Dredge chicken in flour, sprinkle with salt and brown in fat until golden on all sides. Place in covered dish in warm place. Brown onion, garlic, carrot, parsley and bay leaf or basil in fat left in frying pan.

Strain tomatoes (when strained you should have 2 cups pulp). Add tomato pulp to browned vegetables in frying pan, add 1 teaspoon salt and dash of pepper and bring to a boil. Add chicken and wine and simmer 30 minutes, or until chicken is tender. Serves 4.

CHICKEN CACCIATORA MADDALENA

4-pound tender chicken, cut into pieces
2 tablespoons olive oil
1 teaspoon chopped parsley
½ stalk celery, chopped
½ clove garlic, chopped
1 teaspoon salt
dash pepper
2 bay leaves
½ cup dry white wine
2 tablespoons water

Place chicken in frying pan with olive oil, chopped parsley, celery, garlic, salt and pepper and brown thoroughly on all sides over moderate flame. When chicken is well browned, add bay leaves and, after 1 minute, the wine. Cook gently until wine is almost evaporated. Add water, cover and simmer about 30 minutes, until chicken is done. Serves 4.

CHICKEN CACCIATORA WITH OLIVES

3 tablespoons olive oil
3 cloves garlic, sliced
4-pound tender chicken, cut into pieces
⅛ teaspoon salt
⅛ teaspoon pepper
½ cup dry white wine
2 tablespoons vinegar
20 ripe black olives, pitted and diced
20 green olives, pitted and diced
2 anchovy filets, chopped

133

Place oil and garlic in frying pan. When oil is hot, add chicken, sprinkle with salt and pepper and brown slowly and thoroughly on all sides. When chicken has a good golden color, add wine and vinegar. Add olives, and after a few minutes, the chopped anchovies. Add several tablespoons water, and leaving fire low, cook until chicken is done and sauce is thick and rich (about 45 minutes). Serves 4.

CHICKEN FRICASSEE ALLA SALVIA

1 tablespoon butter	1/8 teaspoon pepper
1 tablespoon olive oil	1 1/4 cup dry white wine
4-pound tender chicken,	1/8 pound prosciutto with fat,
cut into pieces	sliced thin and shredded
1/4 teaspoon salt	1 tablespoon fresh sage leaves

Melt butter in a large frying pan and add oil and chicken. Sprinkle chicken with salt and pepper and brown slowly and thoroughly on all sides. When well browned, pour wine over chicken and add prosciutto and sage. Lower flame, cover pan and cook slowly until chicken is cooked, about 40 minutes. Serve immediately with gravy. Serves 4.

CHICKEN FRICASSEE ROMAN STYLE

1 tablespoon lard	1/2 clove garlic, chopped
2 slices prosciutto, cut	1/2 teaspoon marjoram
into small pieces	1 cup strong red wine
3 1/2-pound tender chicken,	4 or 5 tomatoes, peeled and
cut into pieces	sliced
salt	stock or water
pepper	

Melt lard in large frying pan. Add prosciutto and chicken. Sprinkle with salt and pepper and brown chicken thoroughly over slow fire, turning frequently. When brown, add chopped garlic, marjoram and wine. Cook until wine has evaporated, then add tomatoes. Add a little stock or water if necessary. Increase heat and cook about 20 minutes. The chicken should be well done by this time. The gravy should be thick, dark and not too abundant. Serves 4.

FRIED CHICKEN FLORENTINE

3 tablespoons olive oil	3 1/2-pound frying chicken,
4 tablespoons lemon juice	cut into pieces
1/4 teaspoon salt	2 cups flour
1/8 teaspoon pepper	1 egg, lightly beaten
2 teaspoons chopped parsley	1 1/2 cups olive oil for frying

Make a marinade of oil, lemon juice, salt, pepper and parsley. Pour over chicken in a casserole and let stand for about 2 hours, turning occasionally. After 2 hours take chicken out of marinade, dry well, flour thoroughly, dip into beaten egg and fry in deep olive oil for about 15 minutes. Serves 4.

CHICKEN GOURMET STYLE

¼ cup butter	2 quarts water
1 tablespoon flour	1 teaspoon salt
1½ cups milk	1 whole boiled chicken,
⅛ teaspoon nutmeg	about 4 pounds
½ teaspoon salt	2 tablespoons grated Parmesan
¼ teaspoon pepper	cheese
½ pound elbow macaroni	

Melt butter in saucepan, blend in flour, add milk, nutmeg, salt and pepper and cook, stirring well, until thickened. Cook elbow macaroni in boiling salted water 10 minutes. Drain and mix with half of cream sauce. Pour creamed macaroni inside boiled chicken. Place chicken in greased baking dish, pour remaining sauce over it and sprinkle with grated cheese. Bake chicken in hot oven (400°F.) 10 minutes, or until cheese has browned. Serves 4.

CHICKEN IN PIQUANT SAUCE

2 tablespoons olive oil	1 cup hot water
1 onion, chopped	½ teaspoon meat extract
3½- to 4-pound chicken,	½ cup vinegar
cut into pieces	2 anchovy filets, chopped
¼ teaspoon salt	fine
⅛ teaspoon pepper	2 small gherkins, chopped fine
½ tablespoon flour	1 tablespoon capers
¾ cup dry white wine	½ teaspoon chopped garlic
1 tablespoon tomato sauce	1 sprig parsley, chopped

Place oil and onion in large frying pan and brown. Add chicken, salt and pepper and brown well. When browned, sprinkle chicken with flour and add wine. Cook until wine evaporates, then add tomato sauce. Let cook for about 5 minutes, add 1 cup hot water and meat extract, lower flame a bit, and let chicken cook thoroughly about 1 hour, so that the sauce will be concentrated.

Place vinegar in small pan and cook until reduced about half in quantity. Put anchovies, gherkins, capers, garlic and parsley, all chopped fine, into a cup and add vinegar. Let sauce stand for 5 minutes, then pour over chicken. Serve immediately. Serves 4.

CHICKEN LIVERS WITH ARTICHOKES

4 artichokes	1 pound chicken livers
2 tablespoons lemon juice	2 slices prosciutto or lean
¼ teaspoon salt	bacon, cut into slivers
3 tablespoons olive oil	1 tablespoon chopped parsley
⅛ teaspoon pepper	juice of ½ lemon
¼ cup butter	

Remove outer tough leaves of artichoke, remove choke and slice each artichoke into 8 pieces lengthwise. Place in cold water to cover, add lemon juice and salt and let stand 15 minutes. Remove from water and dry. Place oil and artichokes in large frying pan, add salt and pepper and cook over moderate heat until well browned, adding a little water from time to time if artichokes tend to become too dry.

In smaller pan, melt butter, add livers and cook 5 minutes. Add prosciutto or bacon to livers, mix and add to artichokes. Mix well and cook 2 minutes. Add parsley and lemon juice, remove from fire and serve. Serves 4.

CHICKEN LIVERS WITH SAGE

¼ cup butter	2 slices prosciutto or lean
1 pound chicken livers,	bacon, cut into slivers
each liver cut into 2	4 slices bread, cut in triangles
or 3 pieces	and fried in butter
¼ teaspoon salt	2 tablespoons Marsala or
⅛ teaspoon pepper	sherry wine
1 teaspoon chopped sage	1 tablespoon butter
leaves	

Melt the ¼ cup butter in shallow pan, add chicken livers, salt, pepper, sage and prosciutto and cook about 5 minutes. Remove livers from pan and place in warm serving dish on fried bread triangles. Add Marsala or sherry to pan gravy, mix well and cook 3 minutes. Add 1 tablespoon butter, mix well and pour over livers and fried bread. Serves 4.

CHICKEN TETRAZZINI

5- to 6-pound stewing	1 large sweet onion, chopped
chicken	4-ounce can roasted peppers,
2 teaspoons salt	chopped
¼ teaspoon pepper	1 large green pepper, chopped
1 pound spaghetti	1 pound grated cheese
3 slices bacon, shredded	1 8-ounce can mushrooms

Cut chicken into pieces, cover with water, add salt and pepper and cook slowly 3 hours, or until meat loosens from bones. Remove meat from bones and cut into small pieces. Cook spaghetti in boiling chicken broth until tender, and drain. Brown bacon in large pot, add onion, brown lightly, add roasted peppers, green pepper, cheese and mushrooms and mix thoroughly. Add chicken and spaghetti and keep over low flame until thoroughly heated. If needed, moisten with a little chicken broth. Serves 12.

CHICKEN WITH EGG SAUCE

¼ cup butter	1 teaspoon butter
1 tablespoon flour	¼ teaspoon salt
1½ cups chicken broth	⅛ teaspoon pepper
1 egg yolk, lightly beaten with fork	4-pound chicken, boiled

Melt butter, blend in flour, add broth and cook slowly, stirring constantly, until slightly thickened. Remove from fire, add beaten yolk, 1 teaspoon butter, salt and pepper. Mix well and serve over chicken. Serves 4.

CHICKEN WITH RICE

4-pound young tender chicken, whole and cleaned	1 stalk celery
	1 bunch parsley
	2 tablespoons butter
water to cover chicken (about 1 quart)	½ onion, chopped
	¾ pound rice
1 teaspoon salt	dash of nutmeg
1 onion	lump of butter
1 clove	2 tablespoons grated Parmesan cheese
1 carrot	

Place chicken in a stewing pan, just large enough to accommodate chicken. Pour in enough water to cover chicken and place over moderate fire. As water gets warm, remove scum that will form on top. When water reaches boiling point, add 1 teaspoon salt, onion, clove, carrot, celery and parsley. Cover pan, lower fire and simmer gently about 1¼ hours.

In another pan, about 20 minutes before chicken is ready, place butter and chopped onion and brown gently and slowly. Wash rice, add to onion and butter, brown slightly and baste with chicken broth. Raise flame and let rice cook well, adding broth a little at a time. Add a little salt, if needed, nutmeg, a good lump of butter and Parmesan.

Place chicken in center of serving dish and arrange rice around it. Pour extra broth over all. Serves 4.

TURKEY

TURKEY BALLS

2 cups cooked turkey, chopped	1 egg yolk
½ teaspoon salt	3 slices bread
¼ teaspoon pepper	1 tablespoon butter
⅛ teaspoon cinnamon	1 teaspoon tomato paste
2 tablespoons grated Parmesan cheese	2 cups stock
	1 tablespoon butter, melted
	1 tablespoon flour

Mix turkey meat with salt, pepper, cinnamon, cheese and egg yolk. Soak bread in water, squeeze dry and add to mixture. Blend all together until mixture is smooth. Make about 12 balls. Place 1 tablespoon butter in large saucepan, melt, add tomato paste and stock and cook 5 minutes. Place turkey balls in stock and simmer 20 minutes. Remove balls from broth and place on serving dish.

Boil broth rapidly until reduced half in quantity. Blend together 1 tablespoon melted butter and 1 tablespoon flour, add to stock, stirring in well, and cook until thickened. Pour this sauce over balls and serve. Serves 4.

BOILED TURKEY

12-pound turkey	2 large tomatoes, or ½ small
8 quarts water	can tomatoes
1½ teaspoons salt	1 carrot
2 stalks celery	1 small onion

Place turkey in cold water in large pan. Bring to boil, remove scum, add salt, celery, tomatoes, carrot and onion and boil gently about 2 hours, or until turkey is tender (cooking time will depend on the turkey). Let turkey cool a little in broth, remove from pan and cool completely before slicing. Save broth for soups or stock. Serves 8.

ROAST TURKEY

1 young turkey, about 15 pounds	1 cup olive oil
2 teaspoons salt	4 slices bacon
2 teaspoons pepper	1 tablespoon flour

Clean and truss turkey. Sprinkle with salt and pepper, place in roasting pan, pour oil over turkey and place bacon slices across the breast. Bake in 400° F. oven 3½ hours, basting frequently. Remove bacon slices from breast, sprinkle with flour and baste with fat from pan. Repeat the basting twice and it will give the breast a golden color. Serves 10.

STUFFED ROAST TURKEY

20 queen olives, pitted and chopped	1 young turkey, about 9 pounds
20 chestnuts, slightly roasted, skinned and chopped	4 slices fat bacon salt and pepper
1 pound sweet Italian sausage, skinned and chopped	2 tablespoons olive oil 1 tablespoon flour
1 black truffle, diced (if available)	

Mix olives, chestnuts, sausage meat and truffle. Stuff turkey cavity with mixture and sew closed. Place turkey in roasting pan, lay bacon slices across breast, season with salt and pepper, and pour oil over all. Cook in slow oven (300°F.) for about 2 hours.

When turkey is nearly done, remove bacon strips, sprinkle turkey with flour and pour pan fat over it. Return to oven for 10 minutes. Repeat the basting 3 times and turkey will have a crisp, crusty skin. Pour fat slowly over flour so as not to remove it. Continue cooking 30 minutes. Serves 8.

STUFFED TURKEY LOMBARDY STYLE

10-pound turkey	heart, liver and gizzard, boiled and chopped
1 pound chopped beef	
½ pound sweet Italian sausage, skinned and chopped	⅛ teaspoon salt
	⅛ teaspooon pepper
2 eggs	½ cup butter
½ cup grated Parmesan cheese	2 slices prosciutto
	1 sage leaf
⅛ teaspoon nutmeg	½ teaspoon rosemary
15 boiled peeled chestnuts, mashed	½ cup wine
	1 teaspoon flour
2 slices fat bacon, diced	1 cup stock or water

Mix the beef, sausage, eggs, Parmesan, nutmeg, chestnuts, bacon, heart, liver and gizzard together and add half the salt and pepper. Stuff turkey and sew up opening. Melt butter in a large iron pot or Dutch oven, place turkey in it, and place prosciutto, sage and rosemary over turkey. Brown turkey well on all sides. When well browned, add wine. Cover pot, lower fire and continue cooking for 3 hours. Occasionally add a little stock or water. Baste frequently.

When turkey is tender, remove from pan and place on serving dish. Blend 1 teaspoon flour with pan gravy and add 1 cup stock or water. Serve this gravy over turkey. Serves 8.

DUCK

DUCK IN SALMI

1 medium-sized duck, cut into pieces	liver, heart and gizzard, chopped very fine
1 large onion, spiked with 3 cloves	½ cup olive oil
	½ cup wine vinegar
2 sage leaves	¼ teaspoon salt
1 bay leaf	⅛ teaspoon pepper

Place duck in large pan with onion, spiked with cloves, sage leaves, bay leaf, liver, heart and gizzard. Add oil, vinegar, salt and pepper. Cover pan with a double sheet of brown paper, tucking in edges of paper. Put pan cover on and cook over a very moderate fire about ½ hour. When meat is done, place in serving dish, strain gravy and serve on toasted bread. Serves 4.

SQUAB

GRILLED SQUAB

4 tablespoons melted butter	½ cup vinegar
4 medium squabs, split	4 or 5 peppercorns
salt and pepper	⅛ teaspoon chopped red pepper
4 teaspoons prepared mustard	1 cup hot water
bread crumbs	1 tablespoon meat extract
4 tomatoes	½ teaspoon tomato paste
salt and pepper	1 teaspoon butter
2 cloves garlic, chopped	1 teaspoon flour
1 tablespoon olive oil	½ tablespoon prepared mustard
1 teaspoon chopped parsley	1 tablespoon capers, chopped

Butter squab, sprinkle with salt and pepper, and grill on open grill or in broiler. When squabs are nearly done, spread with mustard and roll in bread crumbs. Again spread with butter and finish broiling or grilling. Cut tomatoes in half, sprinkle with salt, pepper, garlic, oil and parsley and broil.

In a little saucepan put vinegar, peppercorns and red pepper. Let vinegar cook down to half, then add hot water, meat extract and tomato paste. Mix well and boil 10 minutes.

Melt butter, blend flour, and add to sauce, stirring constantly until thickened. Remove from fire, add mustard and capers and serve over squab, surrounded by tomatoes. Serves 4.

8. Game

WILD DUCK

WILD DUCK WITH LENTILS

1 medium-sized wild duck, cleaned	1 very small onion, sliced
1 teaspoon salt	1 bay leaf
½ teaspoon pepper	1 teaspoon chopped parsley
2 tablespoons olive oil	1 stalk celery, diced
2 slices fat bacon, chopped	1 carrot, sliced
⅓ clove garlic	½ cup dry white wine
	1 large can cooked lentils

Wash and dry duck and sprinkle inside with a little salt and pepper. Place duck in Dutch oven with olive oil, bacon, garlic, onion, bay leaf, parsley, celery, carrot and remaining salt and pepper and brown slowly, turning often until duck is well browned all around. Add wine and cook until it evaporates. Add enough water to cover duck, cover pot and cook over moderate flame 1 hour, or until duck is done to taste. Remove fat from gravy and use this to pour over cooked lentils and duck. Serves 4.

HARE

HARE IN SALMI

1 small hare, skinned, cleaned and cut into pieces	½ teaspoon pepper
1 small onion, chopped	1½ cups dry red wine
1 stalk celery, chopped	2 tablespoons olive oil
1 carrot, sliced	¼ teaspoon salt
1 teaspoon chopped parsley	½ tablespoon flour
1 bay leaf	3 tablespoons water
½ teaspoon thyme	2 anchovy filets, chopped
½ teaspoon rosemary	¼ clove garlic, chopped
¼ teaspoon sage	½ teaspoon chopped parsley
	⅛ cup vinegar
	⅛ cup white wine

Wash and dry hare. Make a marinade of onion, celery, carrot, parsley, bay leaf, thyme, rosemary, sage and pepper with the red wine. Place hare in marinade and let stand for at least 2 hours. Heat oil in large pan or Dutch oven, add hare, sprinkle with salt and flour and brown slowly. When hare is slightly browned, add herbs and vegetables of the marinade and continue browning.

When hare is well browned, add wine from marinade and continue cooking slowly until wine has evaporated. Add water, cover pan and cook for about 1 hour, until hare is well done.

Remove hare from pan. Mix together anchovies, garlic, parsley, vinegar and white wine and add to pan gravy. Mix gravy well and pour over hare in serving dish. Serves 4.

HARE SAINT HUBERT STYLE

3 tablespoons olive oil	10 grains juniper
1 onion, chopped	1 clove garlic, sliced
1 carrot, sliced	2 cups dry red wine
1 stalk celery, diced	¼ cup wine vinegar
1 clove	1 medium hare, cut
2 sage leaves	into pieces
1 bay leaf	2 tablespoons olive oil
1 teaspoon thyme	1 cup stock
½ teaspoon rosemary	1 teaspoon grated orange
½ teaspoon marjoram	rind

Place olive oil in saucepan, add onion, carrot and celery and brown lightly. Add clove, sage, bay leaf, thyme, rosemary, marjoram, juniper and garlic and cook 2 minutes. Add wine and vinegar, bring to boiling point, mix well and place in casserole. Let cool. Add hare and let stand 12 hours.

When hare is ready for cooking, place 2 tablespoons oil in frying pan, remove hare from marinade, and brown well in oil. Add vegetables from marinade and as hare becomes brown, add a little of the marinade liquid. Let liquid evaporate, then add a little more. Repeat until all liquid is used. Add stock, lower flame, cover pan and cook slowly until hare is done to taste (about 1½ hours). Add orange rind, mix well and serve. Serves 4.

PHEASANT

PHEASANT IN CASSEROLE

1 small pheasant, cleaned	¼ teaspoon pepper
and tied like a chicken	½ cup cognac
3 tablespoons butter	1 cup stock
½ teaspoon salt	¼ teaspoon meat extract

Place pheasant in large Dutch oven with butter, salt and pepper. Cook over slow flame for about 3 hours, turning often. When cooked and golden brown, remove to serving plate. Pour off fat from pan and add cognac, stock and meat extract. Scrape bottom of pan well and cook 1 minute. Pour sauce over pheasant. Serves 4.

PHEASANT WITH CREAM

1 small pheasant	salt and pepper
3 tablespoons butter	1¼ cups heavy cream
½ onion, chopped	1 tablespoon lemon juice

Place pheasant in Dutch oven with butter, onion, salt and pepper. Cook slowly, browning gently on all sides 2¼ hours. Add cream and continue cooking 30 minutes, basting frequently with cream. Just before serving, add lemon juice to gravy and mix. Serve immediately. Serves 4.

RABBIT

BRAISED RABBIT

1 small rabbit, cut into pieces	2 slices prosciutto or bacon
2 tablespoons olive oil	1 tablespoon chopped parsley
salt and pepper	1 cup dry wine
1 clove garlic, chopped	5 fresh tomatoes, skinned and cut into pieces

Place rabbit in frying pan with oil. Add salt, pepper, and garlic, and brown slowly. When well browned, add prosciutto or bacon and parsley and continue browning a few minutes. Add wine and cook until wine has evaporated. Add tomatoes and about ½ cup water, lower flame and cook slowly until meat is tender (about 1 hour). Serves 4.

RABBIT IN EGG SAUCE

1 tablespoon butter	2 tablespoons chopped parsley
1 medium-sized rabbit, cut into small pieces	salt and pepper
1 small onion, chopped	½ tablespoon flour
3 slices prosciutto or lean bacon, chopped	½ cup white wine
	2 egg yolks, lightly beaten
	1 tablespoon lemon juice

Place butter in large pan, melt, and add rabbit. Cook over hot fire 2 or 3 minutes. Add onion, prosciutto or bacon, 1 tablespoon parsley, salt and pepper. Brown the meat thoroughly, then sprinkle with flour. Mix well and add wine. Cook until wine evaporates, then add enough water to cover. Lower heat, cover pan, and cook until meat is tender (about 1 hour), and the sauce rich and concentrated. Mix egg yolks with lemon juice and rest of parsley. Remove rabbit from stove, add egg mixture to sauce and mix well. Cover pot and let stand in warm place 5 minutes before serving. Serves 4.

RABBIT SWEET-SOUR

1 medium-sized rabbit, cut into pieces	½ teaspoon chopped parsley
2 cups dry red wine	2 bay leaves
½ onion, chopped	½ teaspoon thyme
2 cloves	5 peppercorns
	2 tablespoons flour

Wash rabbit well and dry. Make a marinade of the other ingredients, excluding flour, and warm over slow fire, but do not boil. Pour over rabbit and let stand for at least 4 hours—the longer the better. Remove meat from marinade, dry well and sprinkle with flour. You will now use the following ingredients:

1 onion, chopped	2 tablespoons sugar
2 tablespoons bacon drippings or lard	½ cup vinegar
1 cup stock or water	½ cup raisins
	½ cup pine nuts

In a large skillet brown onion in bacon drippings or lard. Add meat and fry it slowly to a crusty brown. When well browned, add the strained marinade, a little at a time. When the marinade is all used the rabbit should be golden brown. Add salt and pepper to taste. Add enough stock or water to cover meat and cook slowly about 1 hour, or until meat is tender. Skim off surplus fat from the gravy.

In a little saucepan, melt the sugar slowly and when melted and slightly brown, add vinegar. Mix well with a wooden spoon, scraping all sugar from bottom of pan. Add this to the sauce in the pan and also raisins and nuts. Cook 4 or 5 minutes and serve. Serves 4.

9. *Macaroni, Spaghetti and Rice*

AGNOLOTTI OR RAVIOLI

½ pound chopped pork,
   lightly fried
1 cup cooked spinach,
   drained and chopped
1 tablespoon grated
   Parmesan cheese
1 egg yolk

2 slices prosciutto, chopped
2 slices Italian salami, chopped
1 teaspoon sherry wine
¼ teaspoon salt
⅛ teaspoon pepper
⅛ teaspoon nutmeg

Mix the above ingredients together thoroughly.
Make dough using:

4 cups flour
3 eggs

1 teaspoon water

Mix flour, eggs, and water together well and work dough until firm. Cut into 2 pieces and roll each piece into a very thin sheet. On one sheet place 1 teaspoon of mixture every 2 inches until all the sheet is used. Place second sheet of dough over first and press with fingers around each mound. Cut into squares 2 inches on a side, being careful that edges are well closed.

Cook 20 minutes or less in 5 quarts boiling water to which 3 tablespoons salt have been added. Drain. Serve with meat sauce (see index) or with butter and 2 tablespoons Parmesan cheese. Serves 4.

LASAGNE NEAPOLITAN STYLE

1 pound *Ronzoni* curly edge
   lasagne (#80)
1 pound pork shoulder
1 tablespoon olive oil
½ onion, minced
1 clove garlic, sliced
1 teaspoon minced parsley
½ teaspoon salt
½ teaspoon pepper
1½ cans tomato paste

2 cups warm water
5 quarts water
3 teaspoons salt
1 pound ricotta (Italian pot
   cheese)
1 tablespoon hot water
4 tablespoons grated Parmesan
   cheese

Place pork in saucepan with oil, onion, garlic, and parsley and brown thoroughly on all sides. Add salt, pepper and tomato paste, diluted in 2 cups warm water. Cover pan and cook 2 hours, adding a little water from time to time, if necessary. This should make about 2 cups of tomato sauce. Remove pork from sauce, and keep warm.

In another pan bring water to boil, add salt, and drop in lasagne.

Cook 15 minutes, or until tender, stirring almost constantly to prevent lasagne from sticking together. Drain. Mix ricotta with 1 tablespoon warm water, making a soft paste.

In a casserole, arrange lasagne in layers, alternating with sauce, ricotta and Parmesan, until lasagne is all used, and ending with a layer of sauce, ricotta and Parmesan. Bake in moderate oven 20 minutes and serve. Serve pork as second course. Makes 6 large or 8 medium servings.

NEAPOLITAN CARNIVAL LASAGNE

3 cups ragout gravy (see index)	2 teaspoons salt
1 pound *Ronzoni* lasagne	¾ pound ricotta
4 quarts water	¾ cup grated Parmesan cheese

Have gravy already prepared and warm. Cook lasagne in salted boiling water 15 minutes, or until tender. Stir lasagne well while it is cooking as this type of pasta has a tendency to stick together. Drain well. Place 1 layer lasagne in casserole, cover with some of the gravy and ricotta, sprinkle with Parmesan cheese and repeat layers until all is used. Bake in moderate oven (375°F.) 10 minutes. Serves 6.

LASAGNE OLD STYLE

1 pound *Ronzoni* lasagne	½ teaspoon pepper
½ pound ground beef	5 quarts water
½ pound ground pork	3 teaspoons salt
2 tablespoons olive oil	1 pound lasagne
1 medium onion, minced	1 pound mozzarella cheese, sliced thin
1 clove garlic	
1 teaspoon minced parsley	¾ pound ricotta
1½ cans tomato paste	2 tablespoons grated Roman cheese
2 cups water	
½ teaspoon salt	

Brown beef and pork in saucepan with oil, onion, garlic and parsley. Add tomato paste, 2 cups water and salt and pepper and simmer 1½ hours.

Bring 5 quarts water to boil, add salt and lasagne and cook 15 minutes, or until tender, stirring almost constantly to prevent sticking together. Drain. Arrange lasagne in casserole in layers, alternating with layers of sauce, mozzarella and ricotta, until lasagne is all used, and ending in like sequence, ricotta last. Sprinkle with grated cheese. Bake in moderate oven (350°F.) about 20 minutes, or until mozzarella is melted, and serve. Makes 6 large or 8 medium servings.

LASAGNE PIEDMONT STYLE

5 cups all-purpose flour	2 egg yolks
3 tablespoons grated	2 tablespoons water
Parmesan cheese	½ teaspoon salt
2 eggs	

Place flour in a mound on large pastry board. Make a well in the flour and place in the well the cheese, eggs, egg yolks, water and salt. Work the above ingredients into the flour and knead well until all flour is mixed and dough is firm. Divide dough into 4 parts and roll each part paper thin. Place dough sheets on clean tablecloth and let dry 1 hour. Fold sheets and cut dough in ribbons 1 inch wide. Shake ribbons loose. Have ready:

5 quarts boiling water	1½ cups chopped meat sauce
4 teaspoons salt	(see index)
¼ pound butter	½ teaspoon pepper
3 tablespoons grated	⅛ teaspoon nutmeg
Parmesan cheese	

Drop lasagne into boiling salted water and boil 20 minutes. Drain. Place in large casserole, add butter, Parmesan, sauce, pepper and nutmeg and mix well. Keep warm 5 minutes and serve. Serves 6.

GREEN LASAGNE MODENA STYLE

3 cups flour	2 eggs
½ pound spinach, cooked	¼ teaspoon salt
drained and strained	

Make a mound of the flour on large pastry board and scoop out a well in the mound. Place strained spinach, eggs and salt in well and work into flour, knead for 20 minutes, adding a little more flour if necessary. Divide the kneaded dough into two parts and roll each part paper thin. Stretch dough sheets on clean towels to dry. Let dry 1 hour. Fold each sheet and cut across dough with sharp knife, making ribbons ¾ inch wide. Shake ribbons loose and cook in boiling salted water ½ hour, or less, to taste. Drain. Have ready:

3 cups chopped meat sauce	6 tablespoons grated Parmesan
(see index)	cheese
	½ cup butter

In large casserole place a layer lasagne, cover with sauce and Parmesan and dot with butter. Repeat until lasagne is all used, ending with sauce, cheese and butter. Bake in moderate oven ¾ hour. Sprinkle with additional Parmesan and serve. Serves 4.

MACARONI WITH RICOTTA

1 pound macaroni	2 tablespoons warm water
4 quarts boiling water	3 tablespoons sugar
2 tablespoons salt	1 teaspoon cinnamon
¾ pound ricotta	

Add macaroni to boiling salted water and cook about 12 minutes, until tender. Drain.

Add warm water, sugar, and cinnamon to ricotta and mix well. Add to macaroni. Mix well and serve. Serves 4.

MANICOTTI (Little Muffs)

2 cups flour	1 pound ricotta
1 tablespoon butter	2 cups tomato sauce (see
3 eggs	index)
½ teaspoon salt	1 tablespoon fresh chopped basil
1 cup lukewarm water	½ cup grated Roman cheese

Combine flour, butter, eggs and salt, add water gradually and mix to form a medium soft dough. Knead until smooth and roll on floured board until thin. Cut into rectangles 4 by 6 inches. Place 1½ tablespoons ricotta in center of each rectangle, roll dough and close, moistening and pressing edges carefully to prevent ricotta from falling out.

Boil manicotti gently 10 minutes in extra large pan in about 8 quarts water. Remove carefully with flat strainer and place in 1 large casserole, or 2 each in individual casseroles. Cover with tomato sauce, sprinkle with fresh basil leaves and place in hot oven (400°F.) 10 minutes. Serve with grated Roman cheese. Serves 6.

NOODLES WITH BUTTER AND PARMESAN CHEESE*
(Roman Style)

3 eggs	1½ cups butter
4 cups flour	1½ cups grated Parmesan
4 quarts water	cheese
2 tablespoons salt	

Beat eggs lightly and add to flour on pastry board, mixing well. Work until dough is stiff and elastic, adding more flour if needed. Cut dough into 3 parts and roll out each part on floured board as thin as possible. Sprinkle dough sheets with a little flour, let dry a little, roll and cut into strips ¾ inch wide. Cook in 4 quarts boiling water to which salt has been added. Cook about 8 minutes, or until tender but not soft. Cooking time will vary a little depending on thickness of noodles. Drain well and place in large bowl. Add butter and cheese and mix until butter and cheese have been completely absorbed by noodles. Serve immediately with a little added grated cheese. Serves 4 or 6.

PASTELLA FOR FRYING (Number 1)

4 tablespoons flour
1¼ cups cold water
2 tablespoons olive oil

½ teaspoon salt
2 egg whites, beaten stiff

Blend flour with water and beat with rotary beater until smooth. Add oil and salt. Beat egg whites until stiff but not dry. Just before using pastella, fold egg whites into mixture. Makes 2½ cups pastella.

PASTELLA FOR FRYING (Number 2)

4 tablespoons flour
1¼ cups cold water

½ teaspoon salt

Mix together flour, water and salt and beat until smooth. Makes 2 cups pastella.

PENNONI WITH MUSHROOMS

4 tablespoons olive oil
½ clove garlic, chopped
1½ pounds mushrooms,
    cut into pieces
⅛ teaspoon salt
⅛ teaspoon freshly ground
    pepper

2 teaspoons parsley, chopped
1 pound pennoni (type
    of macaroni)
4 quarts boiling water
2 teaspoons salt
4 tablespoons grated Parmesan
    cheese

Place oil, garlic and mushrooms in saucepan and cook gently 15 minutes. Add salt, pepper and parsley and cook 5 minutes longer.

Cook pennoni in salted water 15 minutes and drain. Pour mushroom mixture over pennoni, sprinkle with grated cheese and serve. Serves 4.

RAVIOLI GENOESE STYLE

3⅛ cups flour	5 tablespoons tomato paste
1 egg	1 large head escarolle
4 tablespoons water	½ pound sweet Italian sausage,
dash salt	skinned
2 pounds round steak	1 lamb's brain
1 tablespoon olive oil	1 egg
2 tablespoons leaf lard	2 tablespoons heavy cream
½ medium onion, chopped	½ teaspoon marjoram
½ clove garlic	¼ teaspoon salt
½ teaspoon rosemary	2 tablespoons grated Parmesan
¼ cup dry red wine	cheese
½ pound fresh tomatoes,	4 cups boiling water
peeled and cut into	2 tablespoons salt
pieces, or 1 large can	1 cup grated Parmesan cheese
tomatoes	

Place flour on pastry board. Mix together egg, water and salt and add to flour, working together until you have a soft dough. Cut into 2 pieces, cover and let stand.

Place steak in saucepan with oil and leaf lard and brown well on both sides. Add onion, garlic and rosemary and brown a little longer. Add wine and continue cooking until wine evaporates. Add tomatoes and tomato paste and enough water to cover meat, cover pan and simmer 2 hours.

Clean and cut escarolle, boil in salted water until tender, drain thoroughly and put through food chopper. Put sausage meat, lamb's brain and half of cooked round steak through food chopper, combine with chopped escarolle, add 1 egg, cream, marjoram, salt and Parmesan cheese and mix all together thoroughly.

Roll dough into 2 thin sheets. On one sheet place 1 teaspoon of mixture at 2-inch intervals until mixture is all used. Cover with second sheet. Press with fingers around the little mounds and cut into 2-inch squares, making sure that dough is pressed firmly and edges are well closed. Cook ravioli in boiling salted water 6 minutes, drain and serve with steak gravy, sprinkled with Parmesan cheese. Serves 4.

RAVIOLI WITH RICOTTA

4 cups flour	1 tablespoon water
3 eggs	

Mix the above ingredients together, making a dough, and work until firm. Cut in two and roll into 2 thin sheets. Now take:

1 pound ricotta
1 egg
2 tablespoons grated
   Parmesan cheese

½ teaspoon salt
5 quarts boiling water
3 teaspoons salt

Mix together thoroughly ricotta, egg, Parmesan and salt, and place 1 teaspoon of mixture on one of the dough sheets at 2-inch intervals. Place second sheet over the first and press with fingers around each ricotta mound. Cut into 2-inch squares, making sure that edges are well closed. Cook about 20 minutes, according to taste, in salted boiling water. Serve with meat sauce (see index) or with butter and grated Parmesan cheese. Serves 4.

RICOTTA BALLS

1 pound ricotta
2 tablespoons grated
   Parmesan cheese
1¼ tablespoons flour
¼ teaspoon salt

1 tablespoon chopped parsley
2 eggs
⅛ teaspoon pepper
2 tablespoons flour
4 tablespoons butter
2 cups tomato sauce (see index)

Mix together well the ricotta, cheese, 1¼ tablespoons flour, salt, parsley, eggs and pepper. Place on floured board and knead until firm but soft. Make 18 balls, press lightly between fingers and fry in butter until all sides are evenly browned. Remove from pan, pour tomato sauce over them and serve. Serves 4.

SPAGHETTI ALLA NOVELLI

3 medium onions, chopped
1 tablespoon olive oil
8 anchovy filets, minced
2 tablespoons chopped
   parsley
1 stalk celery, chopped fine
1 teaspoon rosemary
1 teaspoon sage
1 pound fresh ripe tomatoes,
   peeled and cut into pieces

½ cup dry white wine
½ teaspoon salt
¼ teaspoon pepper
4 quarts water
3 tablespoons salt
1 pound spaghetti
2 tablespoons grated Roman
   cheese
2 tablespoons grated Parmesan
   cheese

Brown onions gently in olive oil. Add anchovies, parsley, celery, rosemary and sage and continue browning 5 minutes. Add tomatoes and cook 30 minutes. Add wine and seasoning, cook 1 minute longer and remove from fire.

While sauce is cooking, put water on to boil, adding salt. When water is boiling, put in spaghetti, and boil 12 minutes, or until spaghetti is cooked to your taste. Drain, serve with sauce and sprinkle with grated cheeses. Makes 4 large or 6 medium portions.

SPAGHETTI ALL' ORTICA

1 tablespoon olive oil	4 quarts water
½ pound mushrooms, sliced thin	3 teaspoons salt
	1 pound Ronzoni spaghetti #8
½ teaspoon salt	½ cup olive oil
¼ teaspoon pepper	1 teaspoon freshly ground pepper
1 tablespoon chopped parsley	
1 teaspoon lemon juice	

Place 1 tablespoon olive oil in frying pan, add mushrooms, salt, pepper and parsley and brown 5 minutes. Remove from fire and add lemon juice.

Bring salted water to boiling point, add spaghetti and cook 15 minutes, or until spaghetti is done to your taste. Drain, add ½ cup olive oil and pepper, mix well. Add mushrooms, mix again and serve. Makes 4 large or 6 medium servings.

SPAGHETTI MARINARA

2 cloves garlic, chopped fine	½ teaspoon basil
⅓ cup olive oil	1½ teaspoons salt
4 cups tomatoes, peeled and cut into wedges	¼ teaspoon pepper
	⅛ teaspoon oregano
1 tablespoon chopped parsley	3 tablespoons tomato paste
	grated cheese
	1 pound Ronzoni spaghetti #8

Brown garlic in oil, add tomatoes, parsley, basil, salt and pepper and cook over low flame 30 minutes. Add oregano and tomato paste and continue to cook about 15 minutes, or until sauce thickens.

While sauce is cooking, cook spaghetti in rapidly boiling salted water until tender, drain and place on serving dish. Pour sauce over spaghetti, mix lightly and serve with grated Parmesan or Roman cheese. Serves 4.

MEATLESS SPAGHETTI

1 pound *Ronzoni* spaghetti (#8)	1 green pepper, chopped fine
½ cup olive oil	½ pound mushrooms, peeled
1 large onion, chopped	and chopped
2 cloves garlic, sliced	½ teaspoon salt
½ cup carrots, chopped	¼ teaspoon pepper
1 cup celery, chopped	4 cups tomato sauce
	¼ cup grated Roman cheese

Cook spaghetti in rapidly boiling salted water until tender, drain and place in oiled casserole. Heat olive oil in large frying pan, add onion, garlic, carrots, celery, green pepper, mushrooms, salt and pepper and cook over moderate flame 10 minutes. Add tomato sauce and simmer 15 minutes. Pour sauce over spaghetti and bake in moderate oven (350°F.) until golden brown on top. Serve with grated Roman cheese. Serves 4.

SPAGHETTI SYRACUSE STYLE

1 pound *Ronzoni* spaghetti (#8)	1 tablespoon capers
½ cup olive oil	1 tablespoon minced fresh basil
2 cloves garlic, sliced	3 anchovy filets, cut into
6 large ripe fresh tomatoes,	small pieces
peeled and cut into pieces	½ teaspoon salt
1 small eggplant, diced	1 teaspoon pepper
2 roasted green peppers,	4 quarts boiling water
sliced	3 teaspoons salt
10 Sicilian olives, pitted	

Place oil in large frying pan, add garlic and brown. Remove garlic from oil. Add tomatoes and eggplant to oil and cook 30 minutes, or until eggplant is done. Add peppers, olives, capers, basil, anchovies, salt and pepper. Cover pan and cook 10 minutes longer, adding a little water if needed.

In large saucepan, bring water to a boil, add salt and spaghetti, cook 12 minutes and drain. Serve spaghetti with sauce. Makes 4 large or 6 medium servings.

SPAGHETTI CARBONARA (WITH BACON)

1 pound *Ronzoni* Spaghetti (#8)	3 eggs lightly beaten
¼ pound lean bacon, diced	¼ cup white wine (if desired)
¾ cup grated Romano or	1 tsp. pepper.
Parmesan cheese	

Cook spaghetti in rapidly boiling water until tender. While spaghetti is cooking, fry bacon over low flame until bacon is crisp. Add cheese (and wine) to beaten eggs. Drain spaghetti and return it to the pot. Pour egg mixture over the hot spaghetti; add pepper and two tablespoons of very hot bacon fat. Stir. The heat of the spaghetti should cook the egg mixture. Transfer to a hot platter; garnish with bacon. Serves 4.

SPAGHETTI WITH CHICKEN LIVERS

1 pound *Ronzoni* spaghetti (#8)	¼ teaspoon pepper
1 pound chicken livers	½ cup grated Parmesan cheese
2 tablespoons olive oil	½ pound mushrooms, washed
1 onion, chopped fine	and peeled, or 1 large can
2 cups tomato purée	mushrooms
½ teaspoon salt	¼ pound butter

Cook spaghetti in rapidly boiling salted water until tender, and drain. Heat olive oil in large frying pan, add onion and brown until golden in color. Add tomato purée, salt and pepper. Add grated cheese, a little at a time, blending thoroughly. Add spaghetti and keep over low flame, stirring constantly until thoroughly heated. Sauté mushrooms and chicken livers in butter. Place spaghetti mixture on serving dish, pour over it the mushrooms and chicken livers and serve with a sprinkling of Parmesan cheese. Serves 4.

SPAGHETTI WITH MEATBALLS (Number 1)

1 pound chopped beef	½ teaspoon salt
1 onion, chopped	¼ teaspoon pepper
1 slice bread, soaked in	1 clove garlic, chopped
tomato purée	2 tablespoons olive oil
2 eggs, lightly beaten	1 can tomato purée
dash cinnamon	1 cup chopped celery
dash clove	1 pound *Ronzoni* thin spaghetti (#9)
dash nutmeg	½ cup grated Parmesan cheese

Combine chopped beef, onion, soaked bread, eggs, cinnamon, clove, nutmeg, salt and pepper. Mix thoroughly and shape into little balls. Brown garlic in olive oil and remove from oil. Add meat balls to oil and brown well on all sides. Add tomato purée and an equal quantity of water and the chopped celery and simmer until celery is tender (about 10 minutes).

While sauce is simmering, cook the spaghetti in rapidly boiling water until tender. Drain spaghetti and place on hot serving dish. Place meatballs over spaghetti, pour sauce over all and sprinkle with grated Parmesan cheese. Serves 4.

SPAGHETTI WITH MEATBALLS (Number 2)

½ pound chopped veal
½ pound chopped pork
1 clove garlic, chopped
  fine
2 tablespoons chopped parsley
½ teaspoon salt
¼ teaspoon pepper
½ cup bread crumbs
¼ cup milk
1 egg, lightly beaten

¼ cup flour
¼ cup olive oil
4 tablespoons chopped onion
1 large can Italian tomatoes,
  peeled
1 teaspoon basil
½ teaspoon salt
dash pepper
3 tablespoons tomato paste
1 pound spaghetti

Combine meat, garlic, parsley, salt, pepper, bread crumbs, milk and egg, mix thoroughly and shape into 8 balls. Heat olive oil in frying pan, dredge meatballs in flour and brown on all sides in oil. When meatballs are brown, remove from pan, reserving oil.

Brown onion in oil in same frying pan until golden, add tomatoes, basil, salt and pepper and simmer 30 minutes. Blend in tomato paste, return meatballs to pan with sauce and simmer 20 minutes longer.

While sauce is cooking, cook spaghetti in boiling water until tender, drain and place on serving dish. Pour sauce over spaghetti, mix lightly, arrange meat balls on top and serve with sprinkling of grated Parmesan cheese. Serves 4.

SPAGHETTI WITH SAUSAGE AND TOMATOES

1 pound Italian sausage,
  cut into small pieces
3 medium onions, chopped
1 pound mushrooms
3 cups canned tomatoes

1 teaspoon salt
⅛ teaspoon pepper
1 pound spaghetti
4 ripe olives, pitted and
  chopped

Fry sausage, add onions and brown well. Add mushrooms, brown lightly and add tomatoes, salt and pepper. Let simmer over low fire until thickened.

While sauce is simmering, cook spaghetti in rapidly boiling water until tender, drain and place in oiled baking dish. Add olives to sauce, pour sauce over spaghetti and mix well. Bake in low oven (325°F.) 30 minutes. Serves 4.

SPAGHETTINI WITH VONGOLE (or Little Neck Clams)

2½ pounds vongole with
    shells, or Little Neck clams
1 tablespoon olive oil
½ cup olive oil
1 clove garlic, sliced
4 tablespoons tomato paste
1 teaspoon salt

½ teaspoon pepper
½ cup water
1 teaspoon chopped parsley
4 quarts boiling water
3 teaspoons salt
1 pound spaghettini, thin
    spaghetti or vermicelli

Wash vongole or clams thoroughly, place in large frying pan, add 1 tablespoon olive oil, cover pan and place on hot fire. Mix around often until shells are all open. Remove from fire, separate clams from shells, reserving juice. Strain juice through fine strainer.

Place ½ cup oil in small saucepan, add garlic and brown gently. Remove garlic. Add tomato paste, clam juice, salt and pepper to oil and cook gently 30 minutes. Add a little water if sauce seems too thick. Add clams, boil 1 minute longer, add parsley and remove from fire. Bring water and salt to boil, add spaghettini and cook 12 minutes, or until done to your taste. Do not overcook; spaghettini should be slightly chewy. Drain. Pour sauce over spaghettini, adding more pepper, if desired. Makes 4 large or 6 medium portions.

SPAGHETTINI WITH VONGOLE IN PLAIN SAUCE

2 pounds vongole (little
    clams with shells)
1 tablespoon olive oil
½ cup olive oil
2 cloves garlic, cut into pieces
½ teaspoon salt

1 teaspoon pepper
1 teaspoon chopped parsley
4 quarts boiling water
3 teaspoons salt
1 pound spaghettini or
    thin spaghetti

Wash vongole thoroughly and place in large frying pan with 1 tablespoon olive oil. Cover pan and place over hot fire. Stir around well so that all shells open. When all shells are open, remove from fire, separate clams from shells, reserving juice. Strain juice through fine strainer.

Place ½ cup olive oil in saucepan, add garlic and brown. Add clam juice, salt, pepper and clams. Boil 1 minute. Add parsley and remove from fire.

Bring salted water to boil, add spaghettini and boil 12 minutes. Drain. Pour clam sauce over spaghettini, mix well and serve. Makes 4 large or 6 medium servings.

Additional spaghetti sauces will be found in Chapter 13. See also Sauces in index.

GNOCCHI (DUMPLINGS)

GREEN GNOCCHI

1 pound spinach, boiled, squeezed dry and strained	5 tablespoons flour
2½ pounds potatoes, boiled and mashed	5 quarts boiling water
	3 tablespoons salt
2 egg yolks	¼ pound butter
2 tablespoons grated Parmesan cheese	3 cups tomato sauce (see index)
¼ teaspoon salt	3 tablespoons grated Parmesan cheese

Mix together spinach, potatoes, egg yolks, Parmesan cheese, salt and flour. Roll on floured board in long finger-thin roll and cut into pieces 2 inches long. Cook 10 pieces at a time in boiling salted water. When pieces rise to surface, remove with strainer. Keep water boiling and repeat procedure until all gnocchi are cooked. Place in serving dish, add sauce, sprinkle with grated Parmesan and serve. Serves 4.

POTATO GNOCCHI

5 pounds potatoes	4 cups any favorite tomato sauce
2 cups flour (approximately)	
6 quarts boiling water	4 tablespoons grated Parmesan cheese
3 tablespoons salt	

Boil potatoes until well done. Cool a little, peel and mash thoroughly. Place on floured board and mix well with flour. Some potatoes will require more flour than others. Knead potato dough well. Roll into finger-thin roll and cut into pieces 2 inches long. Press each piece lightly with fork. Place about 20 gnocchi in boiling salted water. When they come to surface, remove from water with strainer and place in serving dish. Keep water boiling briskly, repeat until all gnocchi are cooked. Add sauce, mix well, sprinkle with Parmesan cheese and serve. Serves 6.

POLENTA (CORNMEAL)

POLENTA WITH CHICKEN LIVERS

½ cup butter	⅛ teaspoon pepper
3 slices bacon, diced	1½ cups stock or bouillon
10 chicken livers, diced	1 pound cornmeal
½ teaspoon minced sage leaves	1½ quarts boiling water
¼ teaspoon salt	2 teaspoons salt

Melt butter in saucepan, add bacon, chicken livers, sage, salt and pepper and brown. Add stock, cook 10 minutes longer and set aside. Pour cornmeal slowly into boiling salted water, stirring constantly with wooden spoon. Continue cooking and stirring 30 minutes, or until cornmeal leaves sides of pan easily. Pour into large platter, pour chicken liver sauce over it and serve. Serves 4 or 6.

POLENTA WITH SAUSAGE GRAVY

1 pound Italian sausage	¼ teaspoon salt
(hot or sweet, according	⅛ teaspoon pepper (omit if
to taste)	using hot sausage)
2 tablespoons water	1 medium can tomatoes
1 small onion, chopped	2 small cans tomato purée
1 clove garlic, sliced	

Place sausage in large saucepan with 2 tablespoons water. Prick sausage with needle and let brown in its own fat. Add onion, garlic and salt, brown a little longer. Add tomatoes and tomato purée and simmer 1½ hours. When gravy is ready, take:

1 pound cornmeal	2 teaspoons salt
1¼ quarts boiling water	3 tablespoons grated Roman
	cheese

Pour cornmeal slowly into boiling salted water, stirring constantly with wooden spoon. Continue cooking and stirring 30 minutes or until cornmeal leaves sides of pan easily. Pour cornmeal onto large platter, pour gravy over it and place sausage around it. Sprinkle with cheese and serve. Serves 4 or 6.

RISOTTO (RICE)

ARANCINI SICILIAN STYLE

1 cup rice	¼ teaspoon salt
4 cups boiling salted water	¼ teaspoon pepper
¼ pound chopped beef	½ cup butter
2 chicken livers	3 tablespoons grated Parmesan
2 tablespoons olive oil	cheese
1 clove garlic	2 egg yolks
½ small onion, minced	1 egg, lightly beaten
¼ pound mushrooms, sliced	1 cup bread crumbs
2 tablespoons tomato paste	1 cup olive oil
1 cup warm water	

Wash rice and cook in boiling salted water until tender.

Meanwhile, place chopped beef, chicken livers, oil, garlic and onion in saucepan and brown gently. Add mushrooms and cook 1 minute. Add tomato paste and water and cook 30 minutes. Add salt and pepper.

Drain rice, add butter and Parmesan and cool a little. To this, add egg yolks and the tomato gravy, holding aside the meat and mushrooms. Mix rice well. Make little balls of rice, placing inside each ball some of the meat, livers and mushrooms. Dip rice balls into egg, roll in bread crumbs and fry in hot olive oil until golden brown all over. Serves 4 or 6.

RICE ALLA FREGOLI

½ cup butter
1 very small onion, sliced
5 chicken livers, sliced thin
5 slices prosciutto, cut into slivers
¼ pound sweetbreads, cut into small pieces
2 tablespoons dried mushrooms, soaked in water ½ hour and squeezed dry
½ cup dry white wine
½ cup Marsala or sherry wine

¾ pound rice
1 cup shelled peas
1 truffle (optional), sliced thin
1 tablespoon meat extract, blended with 1 cup warm water
1 cup stock
¼ teaspoon salt
⅛ teaspoon white pepper
¼ cup butter
4 tablespoons grated Parmesan cheese

Place in large pan ½ cup butter, onion, chicken livers, prosciutto, sweetbreads and dried mushrooms and brown gently but thoroughly. Add white wine, Marsala or sherry, rice, peas and truffle slices and continue cooking over low fire, stirring frequently, until all the wine has evaporated.

Add meat extract and water, stock, salt and pepper and cook slowly 20 minutes, or until rice is tender. Add ¼ cup butter, sprinkle with Parmesan and serve. Serves 4.

BAKED RICE GENOA STYLE

¼ cup butter
½ small onion, chopped
½ pound Italian sweet sausage, skinned and minced
1 cup shelled fresh peas
1 artichoke, with outer leaves and choke removed and sliced into thin slivers

4 medium mushrooms, sliced
2 teaspoons meat extract
4 tablespoons warm water
¾ pound rice
4 cups water
1 teaspoon salt
½ cup stock
4 tablespoons grated Parmesan cheese

Melt butter in saucepan, add onion and sausage and brown gently. Add peas, artichoke slices and mushrooms and brown a little longer.

Add meat extract, diluted in warm water, cover pan and cook 10 minutes. Boil rice in boiling salted water 5 minutes. Drain and add to ingredients in saucepan, mixing well.

Place rice mixture in casserole, add ½ cup stock and Parmesan cheese, and bake in moderate oven (375°F.) until rice is cooked and a crust has formed on top. This usually takes ½ hour. Remove from oven and serve. Serves 4.

RICE FRITTERS*

½ cup rice	rind of ½ lemon, grated
1 pint milk	1 tablespoon rum
⅛ teaspoon salt	½ cup flour
1 teaspoon sugar	3 eggs, separated
1 tablespoon butter	

Cook rice in milk in double boiler about 20 minutes. Add salt, sugar, butter and lemon rind and let cool. When cool, add rum, flour and beaten egg yolks and let stand in cool place several hours. When ready to serve, fold in stiffly beaten egg whites, and drop by spoonfuls into deep hot oil or cooking fat. Serve hot, sprinkled with powdered sugar. Serves 4.

RICE SAILOR STYLE

1 very large onion or	¾ pound rice
2 medium onions, chopped	1 sage leaf
2 tablespoons olive oil	¼ teaspoon salt
2 tablespoons water	⅛ teaspoon pepper
8 anchovy filets, minced	½ cup dry white wine
2 tablespoons tomato paste	1 cup water
½ cup water	2 tablespoons grated Roman
2 teaspoons chopped parsley	cheese

Brown onion in olive oil, adding a little water now and then to prevent burning. When onion is very soft add anchovies and brown 5 minutes. Add tomato paste and water and cook 20 minutes. Add parsley. Add rice, sage, salt and pepper to gravy, then add wine and cook until wine is somewhat evaporated. Add 1 cup water and cook about 10 minutes, or until rice is tender. If rice gets too dry in cooking, a little more water may be added. Serve sprinkled with grated cheese. Serves 4.

RICE WITH EGGPLANT

¾ pound rice
1 large eggplant
3 tablespoons frying oil
1 tablespoon olive oil
1 tablespoon butter
1 thin slice salt pork, chopped
½ medium onion, chopped
1 can tomato paste
4 tablespoons water

¼ teaspoon salt
⅛ teaspoon pepper
1 cup stock or bouillon
¼ cup butter
½ pound mozzarella cheese, sliced thin
4 tablespoons grated Parmesan cheese
1 teaspoon chopped sweet basil

Peel eggplant, slice thin and fry golden in frying oil. Set aside. In saucepan place oil, butter, salt pork and onion and brown thoroughly. Add tomato paste, water, salt and pepper and cook 40 minutes, adding more water if necessary. Remove 1 cup sauce from pan and set aside. Add stock or bouillon to rest of sauce and cook rice in it about 12 minutes, or until tender. More water may be added if needed. Add butter to cooked rice mixture.

In a casserole place half the rice, then half the eggplant, then half the mozzarella and half the tomato sauce which you set aside. Repeat and add Parmesan cheese and basil. Place in hot oven (400°F.) and bake 15 minutes. Serves 6.

RICE WITH EGGS SURPRISE

1 cup rice
8 hard cooked eggs
8 slices prosciutto, chopped fine
2 tablespoons cream sauce, cold
1 tablespoon grated Parmesan cheese
2 tablespoons butter

½ medium onion, chopped
¼ pound fresh mushrooms, sliced
2 cups stock
¼ cup butter
3 tablespoons grated Parmesan cheese

Cut eggs in half and separate the whites from yolks. Add chopped prosciutto to cream sauce. Add 1 tablespoon Parmesan cheese and mix well. Fill egg whites with this mixture, reserving yolks for later.

Melt 2 tablespoons butter in saucepan, add onion and mushrooms and brown lightly. Add rice and brown 5 minutes. Add stock and cook gently 15 minutes, or until rice is tender, adding more water or stock, if rice becomes too dry. Add ¼ cup butter and 3 tablespoons Parmesan cheese. Mash egg yolks and sprinkle over rice. Serve with stuffed egg whites. Serves 4.

RICE WITH SAUSAGE

½ medium onion, sliced	1 can tomato purée
1 tablespoon butter	¼ teaspoon salt
¾ pound sweet Italian sausage, skinned and minced	⅛ teaspoon pepper
	2 cups rice
¼ pound mushrooms, sliced	4 cups stock or water
2 large fresh tomatoes or ½ medium can tomatoes, skinned and cut into pieces	2 tablespoons butter
	3 tablespoons grated Roman cheese

Place onion in saucepan with butter and brown a little. Add sausage and continue browning until crisp. Add mushrooms, tomatoes, tomato purée, salt and pepper and cook 20 minutes, adding a little water if necessary.

Cook rice in boiling water or stock about 12 minutes, or until tender, and drain.

Pour sauce over rice, add butter, sprinkle with cheese and serve. Serves 4.

RICE WITH SHRIMPS

1½ pounds shrimps	2 tablespoons cognac
3 cups salted water	½ medium onion, minced
¼ cup butter	1 tablespoon olive oil
½ medium onion, sliced	½ cup butter
1 carrot, diced fine	1 pound rice
1 teaspoon chopped parsley	1 cup dry red wine
⅛ teaspoon thyme	2 cups stock from shells
1 bay leaf	

Shell shrimps. Boil shrimp shells 20 minutes in salted water.

Place ¼ cup butter, onion, shrimps, carrot, parsley, thyme and bay leaf in saucepan and sauté until golden brown. Add cognac and cook until evaporated.

In another larger pan place minced onion, olive oil and ½ cup butter. Brown onion a little and add rice. Let rice brown a little, stirring frequently, then add wine. Let wine evaporate, add stock and cook until rice is tender, about 15 minutes. Remove from fire. Pour shrimps and sauce over rice and serve. Serves 4.

RICE WITH SQUID

2 large (or 4 small) squid	salt and pepper
2 tablespoons olive oil	2 tablespoons tomato purée
½ medium onion, sliced	2 cups warm water
½ clove garlic, minced	1½ cups rice
¾ cup dry red wine	

Clean squid, removing inside bone and bladder. Remove skin from body, cut off head, keeping tentacles, and cut all into very small pieces. Wash thoroughly in running water. Place squid pieces in large pan with oil, onion and garlic and brown gently but thoroughly. Add wine, salt and pepper and continue cooking until wine evaporates. Add tomato purée and warm water, cover and cook 1 hour over low fire. Add rice and cook 20 minutes longer, adding more warm water if rice seems too dry. Serves 4.

RICE WITH SWEETBREADS

¼ cup butter	⅛ teaspoon pepper
½ medium onion	1 pound sweetbreads
⅛ pound prosciutto, cut	2 tablespoons butter
into slivers	2 tablespoons Marsala or
1 cup rice	sherry wine
½ cup Marsala or sherry wine	2 tablespoons butter
3 cups stock	3 tablespoons grated Parmesan
¼ teaspoon salt	cheese

Melt ¼ cup butter in saucepan, add onion and brown slowly. When light brown, add prosciutto, heat through thoroughly and add rice. Let rice brown 5 minutes, stirring frequently, add Marsala or sherry and cook slowly until wine evaporates. When wine has evaporated, add stock, salt and pepper and cook about 20 minutes, or until rice is tender.

Soak sweetbreads in cold water in saucepan for ½ hour, place on fire and bring to a boil. Remove sweetbreads and place in cold water for a few minutes, then drain and remove skin. Cut into 4 or 5 pieces, place in saucepan with 2 tablespoons butter, salt and pepper, and braise 5 or 6 minutes. Add Marsala or sherry, scrape bottom of pan and remove from fire. Pour over cooked rice, add 2 tablespoons butter, sprinkle with Parmesan and serve. Serves 4.

RICE ALLA MILANESE*

4 tablespoons butter	1 small box saffron dissolved in
1 small onion, minced	2 tablespoons broth
1½ cups rice	4 tablespoons grated Parmesan
2 quarts chicken broth	cheese
¼ cup butter	

Melt the 4 tablespoons butter in saucepan, add onion and brown. When brown, add rice and stir well until all the butter is absorbed. Add broth a little at a time. Do not let rice become too dry. Cook 40 to 45 minutes over low flame. Stir constantly. When done, add ¼ cup butter and saffron and mix well. Sprinkle with Parmesan cheese and serve. Serves 2.

RICE WITH BUTTER AND CHEESE*

2 cups rice	1 clove garlic
4 cups water or stock	1 sage leaf
½ teaspoon salt	4 tablespoons grated Parmesan
½ cup butter	cheese

Cook rice in boiling salted water or stock until tender, and drain. Melt butter, add garlic and sage leaf and sauté 3 minutes. Remove garlic and sage leaf and pour butter over cooked rice. Sprinkle with cheese and mix well. Serves 4.

Other recipes for rice dishes will be found in Chapters 5 and 6.

10. Pizza

BREAD DOUGH FOR PIZZA*

4⅔ cups sifted flour	¼ teaspoon pepper
2 tablespoons leaf lard	1¼ envelopes yeast
¼ teaspoon salt	1⅛ cups warm water

Place flour on pastry board, add lard, salt, pepper, yeast and warm water and work well until smooth. Place in large pan, cover and let rise in warm place 2 hours, or until double in bulk. Place on floured board and pound lightly to deflate it. Divide into 2 pieces and stretch each piece on bottom of greased 12-inch pie plate. Dough may be prepared in this manner, may be purchased from a baker, or a prepared dough mix may be used.

CASATIELLA

4 tablespoons leaf lard	4 hard cooked eggs
1 teaspoon freshly ground pepper	2 tablespoons butter or oil
1 recipe bread dough for pizza (see index)	¼ teaspoon salt

Add leaf lard and pepper to bread dough and mix thoroughly. Form dough into large doughnut shape and make 8 holes, at regular intervals, all around the surface. In each hole place half of a hard cooked egg, close hole, brush with butter or oil, sprinkle with salt and bake on greased pie plate in moderate oven (350°F.) 45 minutes. Serves 4.

NEAPOLITAN STUFFED CALZONE

1 recipe bread dough for pizza (see index)	⅛ pound Italian salami, cut into slivers
¼ cup leaf lard	⅛ teaspoon salt
½ pound mozzarella cheese, diced	¼ teaspoon pepper
¼ pound sliced prosciutto, cut into slivers	2 cups tomato sauce (see index)
	2 tablespoons grated Roman cheese

Cut dough into 4 parts and press and roll each part until you get 4 large disks about ¼ inch thick. Coat each disk with leaf lard and place on each a quarter of the mozzarella, prosciutto, salami, salt and pepper. Fold each disk in half, pressing around the edges and making sure that the stuffing is well closed in. Coat each calzone with more leaf lard and place on pie plate in hot oven for about 20 minutes.

Remove, pour sauce over all, sprinkle with grated cheese and serve. Serves 4.

PIZZA

1 recipe bread dough for pizza (see index)
2 tablespoons olive oil
1/4 pound anchovy filets
1 medium can tomatoes
3/4 pound mozzarella cheese, sliced thin
1/4 teaspoon salt
1/8 teaspoon freshly ground pepper
1/2 teaspoon oregano

Pull dough with your hands until it is about 1/2 inch thick and large enough to cover a round pie plate about 18 inches across (or 2 12-inch plates). Sprinkle with oil until dough is well covered. Place anchovies, tomatoes and mozzarella cheese all over dough, add salt, pepper, oregano and a little more oil and place in hot oven (400°F.) for about 20 minutes. Serves 4.

PIZZA DI SCAMMERO

4 3/8 cups flour, sifted
2 tablespoons leaf lard
1/4 teaspoon salt
1/4 teaspoon pepper
1 1/4 envelopes yeast
1 1/8 cups warm water
2 heads endive, cleaned, shredded and parboiled
3 tablespoons olive oil
1 clove garlic
1/4 teaspoon salt
1/8 teaspoon pepper
1 tablespoon olive oil
2 tablespoons capers
6 anchovy filets, cut into pieces
6 black olives, pitted and cut into pieces
1 tablespoon raisins

Place flour on pastry board, add lard, salt, pepper, yeast and warm water and work well until smooth. Place in large pan, cover and let rise in warm place 2 hours, or until doubled in bulk.

Place endive in pan with oil, garlic, salt and pepper and cook 15 minutes. Remove garlic and let endive cool.

When dough is ready, return it to floured board and pound it lightly to deflate it. Divide it into 2 pieces and spread out 1 piece over bottom of an oiled, 12-inch earthen pie plate. Place endive over dough in pie plate, leaving clear a 1-inch border all around. On the endive place capers, anchovies, olives and raisins and cover with the other piece of dough, pressing carefully around edges to make sure filling is closed in well. Cut off excess dough around edges with knife. Place casserole in moderate oven (375°F.) for 45 minutes. Let cool and serve. Serves 6.

RUSTIC PIZZA

3⅛ cups flour	2 small eggs
1½ tablespoons leaf lard	2 tablespoons grated Parmesan
⅛ teaspoon salt	cheese
⅛ teaspoon pepper	⅛ teaspoon salt
1 envelope yeast, diluted in	⅛ teaspoon pepper
1 cup warm water	¼ pound prosciutto, cut into
1½ pounds ricotta	slivers

Place flour on pastry board, add leaf lard, salt, pepper and yeast in warm water, and work together well until dough is elastic and smooth. Place in deep dish, cover and let stand in warm place 2 hours, or until doubled in volume.

In a bowl place ricotta, eggs, Parmesan, salt and pepper and mix together well with wooden spoon.

When dough is ready, cut into 2 pieces and stretch 1 piece over bottom of greased, 12-inch shallow casserole dish. Spread ricotta mixture over this, leaving 1-inch border clear. Place prosciutto over ricotta mixture and place second sheet of dough over all, pressing edges closed carefully and cutting off excess dough around edges. Bake pizza in moderate oven (375°F.) 45 minutes. Serve cool. Serves 4.

PIZZA WITH ANCHOVIES*

1 recipe bread dough for pizza	¼ teaspoon salt
(see index)	½ teaspoon pepper
1 large can tomatoes, drained	3 tablespoons olive oil
18 anchovy filets	1 teaspoon oregano

Stretch dough over 2 12-inch pie plates. Spread tomatoes over dough. Place anchovies over tomatoes, sprinkle with salt, pepper, olive oil and oregano and bake in hot oven (400°F.) 20 minutes, or until edges of dough are crisp. Serves 2 or 4.

PIZZA WITH MOZZARELLA*

1 recipe bread dough for pizza	¾ pound mozzarella cheese,
(see index)	sliced thin
1 large can tomatoes, drained	3 tablespoons olive oil
½ teaspoon salt	1 teaspoon oregano (optional)
½ teaspoon freshly ground	
pepper	

Spread out dough over bottoms of 2 12-inch pie plates. Arrange half the tomatoes over dough in each plate, sprinkle with salt and pepper and arrange mozzarella slices over tomatoes. Sprinkle with olive oil and oregano and bake in hot oven (400°F.) 20 minutes, or until cheese is melted and edges of dough are crisp. Serves 2 or 4.

PIZZA WITH ONIONS

4⅔ cups flour, sifted	4 tablespoons olive oil
2 tablespoons leaf lard	4 large onions, sliced thin
¼ teaspoon salt	⅛ teaspoon salt
¼ teaspoon pepper	⅛ teaspoon pepper
1¼ envelopes yeast	20 black olives, pitted and
1⅛ cups warm water	cut into pieces

Place flour on pastry board, add lard, salt, pepper, yeast dissolved in warm water and work together until smooth. Place dough in large pan, cover and let rise in warm place 2 hours, or until dough has doubled in bulk.

Put oil in saucepan, add onions and brown lightly, taking care not to burn. Add salt and pepper. When dough is ready, cut it in two and stretch one part over bottom of a greased, 12-inch earthen pie plate. Spread with onions, then olives and cover with second sheet of dough. Press edges together until tightly closed, cut off surplus dough around edges and bake in moderate oven (375°F.) 45 minutes. Cool and serve. Serves 6.

PIZZA WITH SAUSAGE*

This pizza may be made with sweet or hot sausage, according to your taste. If hot sausage is used, omit pepper.

1 envelope dry yeast	1 large can tomatoes, drained
1 cup lukewarm water	½ teaspoon basil
3⅛ cups flour	½ cup grated Roman cheese
2 tablespoons olive oil	2 tablespoons olive oil
½ pound Italian sausage,	½ teaspoon salt
cut into thin slices	½ teaspoon pepper

Blend yeast with 2 tablespoons lukewarm water and let stand 5 minutes. Place flour on pastry board, add yeast and remaining lukewarm water and knead well 15 minutes, or until dough is soft and malleable. Add olive oil and work into dough. Let rise in warm place 2 hours, or until dough is doubled in bulk.

Place sausage in saucepan with a few drops water and brown lightly. Add tomatoes, basil and cheese and simmer 15 minutes. Stretch dough as thin as possible over large baking sheet or pie plate. Sprinkle with olive oil, spread tomato and sausage over dough and sprinkle with salt and pepper. Bake in hot oven (400°F.) 15 minutes. Lower heat to 375°F. and continue baking 30 minutes. Serves 4.

11. Vegetables

ARTICHOKES

BOILED ARTICHOKES

3 artichokes
½ cup melted butter

juice of ½ lemon

Cut off tips and stalks of artichokes and remove tough outer leaves. Cut each into about 8 pieces, removing center chokes. Boil in water with salt for 15 minutes, or until tender. Serve with melted butter and lemon juice. Serves 4.

FRICASSEE OF ARTICHOKES

4 artichokes
2 tablespoons flour
1 egg, lightly beaten
4 tablespoons oil, cooking
   or olive
2 tablespoons butter

½ cup stock
½ teaspoon salt
½ teaspoon pepper
4 eggs, lightly beaten
juice of ½ lemon
½ tablespoon chopped parsley

Cut off tips and stalks of artichokes, discard tough outer leaves, and cut into thin slices, removing chokes from centers. Roll slices in flour, dip into egg and fry in oil and butter until golden in color. Drain.

Place in skillet with stock, salt and pepper and cook over moderate flame 5 minutes. Add lemon juice and parsley to beaten eggs and pour over artichokes. Lower flame as far as possible, stir constantly and continue cooking 4 minutes. Serve immediately. Serves 4.

FRIED ARTICHOKES

2 artichokes
2 cups water
juice of ½ lemon
1 cup flour

2 eggs, lightly beaten
1 teaspoon salt
½ teaspoon pepper
1½ cups olive oil

Cut off tips and stalks of artichokes, discard tough outer leaves, and cut in halves, removing chokes from centers. Cut into very thin slices. Dip into 2 cups of water to which lemon juice has been added, drain, dry and roll in flour. Add salt and pepper to beaten eggs. Dip floured artichoke slices into egg mixture and fry in hot olive oil until golden brown. Serve hot. Serves 4.

169

FRIED STUFFED ARTICHOKES

4 artichokes
½ teaspoon salt
¼ teaspoon pepper
1 tablespoon chopped parsley
2 tablespoons olive oil
2 tablespoons water
½ medium onion, sliced
1 teaspoon chopped parsley
2 tablespoons butter
¼ pound veal, chopped

1 cup fresh peas, shelled, or
  ½ large can peas, drained
½ pound mushrooms, chopped
  fine
¼ teaspoon salt
¼ teaspoon pepper
4 tablespoons flour
1 cup water
2 tablespoons oil, olive
  or vegetable
2 cups oil, olive or vegetable

Cut off tips and stems of artichokes, discard tough outer leaves, and press open centers of artichokes. Sprinkle centers with salt, pepper and a little parsley. Place artichokes, standing up, in saucepan with olive oil and water, cover pan and cook over medium flame 15 minutes.

Brown onion lightly in pan with parsley and butter, add veal, peas, mushrooms, salt and pepper and cook over very low flame 20 minutes. Remove from fire and cool.

When mixture is cool, use as a filling to stuff centers and inside leaves of parboiled artichokes. Mix flour with water and oil, blending together well. Dip stuffed artichokes into this batter and fry, standing up, in deep oil until crisp. Frying time should be about 10 minutes on each end. Serve immediately. Serves 4.

ARTICHOKES IN ANCHOVY SAUCE

4 artichokes
2 tablespoons olive oil
2 tablespoons dry white wine
½ teaspoon salt
½ teaspoon pepper
½ cup stock

4 anchovy filets, chopped
½ clove garlic, chopped
1 tablespoon chopped parsley
2 tablespoons dry white wine
2 tablespoons butter

Cut off tips and stems of artichokes, remove tough outer leaves and cut each artichoke into 8 or 10 slices. Place slices in large skillet with olive oil and cook slowly until artichokes begin to brown. Add wine, salt and pepper, and continue cooking until wine evaporates. Add stock, cover pan and continue cooking over low flame until artichokes are tender to the fork.

Remove from skillet. To pan gravy add anchovies, garlic and parsley and cook 2 minutes. Add more wine and a little more stock if gravy is too thick. Add butter, pour over artichokes and serve. Serves 4.

ARTICHOKES PARMESAN STYLE

4 artichokes	1 cup warm water
3 tablespoons flour	½ teaspoon salt
1 egg, lightly beaten	½ teaspoon pepper
1 cup olive oil	4 tablespoons grated Parmesan
2 slices bacon, chopped	cheese
1 very small onion, sliced	2 tablespoons butter
3 tablespoons tomato paste	

Cut off stalks and tips of artichokes and remove tough outer leaves. Cut into very thin slices, roll in flour and in egg and fry a few slices at a time in olive oil until golden brown.

Brown bacon and onion in small saucepan, add tomato paste, water, salt and pepper and cook 10 minutes. Place a layer of fried artichoke slices in greased casserole, cover with some of the sauce, sprinkle with some of the Parmesan cheese, dot with butter and repeat layers until all artichokes are used, ending with a layer of Parmesan. Bake in moderate oven (375°F.) 20 minutes. Serves 4.

ARTICHOKES ROMAN JEWISH STYLE

4 artichokes	1 teaspoon pepper
juice of 1 lemon	3 cups olive oil
1 teaspoon salt	

Clean artichokes of outer tangle of leaves, pare the stalk and cut off tips of the leaves. Press the artichokes down, holding them by the stems to spread leaves. Wash artichokes in water containing lemon juice and drain well. Sprinkle inside leaves with salt and pepper. Place oil in deep frying pan and cook artichokes until crisp and tender (25 minutes or longer, according to tenderness of artichokes), turning during cooking so that they are well browned all over. Serve very hot. Serves 4.

ARTICHOKES SICILIAN STYLE

4 artichokes	1 cup bread crumbs
½ small onion, chopped	½ teaspoon salt
1 clove garlic, chopped	½ teaspoon pepper
1 tablespoon chopped parsley	¼ cup olive oil
2 tablespoons grated Roman	2 tablespoons water
cheese	2 tablespoons olive oil

Cut off stalks and tips of artichokes and remove some of the tough outer leaves. Spread remaining leaves open. Mix onion, garlic, parsley, cheese, bread crumbs, salt and pepper, moisten with ¼ cup olive oil and

2 tablespoons water and fill each leaf with a tiny bit of this mixture. Fill the center of each artichoke with this mixture also.

Place artichokes in baking dish, sprinkle with olive oil and pour a little water in bottom of the dish. Bake in slow oven (325°F.) 45 minutes, or until the bottoms of the artichokes are soft to the fork. Serves 4.

ARTICHOKES TUSCAN STYLE

4 small tender artichokes	4 eggs
juice of 1 lemon	½ teaspoon salt
2 tablespoons flour	½ teaspoon pepper
1 cup olive oil	2 tablespoons milk

Cut off tips and stems of artichokes and remove tough outer leaves. Cut into thin slices, removing chokes from centers. Place artichoke slices in water and lemon juice and let stand 5 minutes. Drain, dry well and roll in flour. Fry in olive oil until nicely browned.

Place fried slices in buttered shallow baking dish. Mix eggs, salt, pepper and milk and beat lightly with fork. Pour egg mixture over artichoke slices and bake in moderate oven (375°F.) 15 minutes. Serve immediately. Serves 4.

ARTICHOKES WITH MINT

4 artichokes	½ teaspoon pepper
3 tablespoons olive oil	1 teaspoon chopped mint leaves
½ teaspoon salt	3 tablespoons water

Cut off stems and tips of artichokes and remove outer leaves. Cut each into about 10 slices, removing center chokes. Place in skillet with oil, salt, pepper and mint and cook slowly 30 minutes, or until artichokes are tender. Add a little water during cooking, if necessary. Serves 4.

ARTICHOKES WITH PROSCIUTTO

4 artichokes	6 tablespoons grated Parmesan
4 quarts water	cheese
1 teaspoon salt	4 slices prosciutto, shredded
1 egg yolk	⅛ teaspoon nutmeg
2 cups cold cream sauce	2 tablespoons melted butter
(see index)	

Cut off tips and stems of artichokes and remove outer leaves. Cut into halves, removing chokes from centers. Boil in salted water 8 minutes and drain well.

Mix together egg yolk, cream sauce, Parmesan cheese, prosciutto and nutmeg. Place artichoke halves in greased baking dish, top with the cream sauce mixture and sprinkle with Parmesan cheese and melted butter. Bake in moderate oven (375°F.) 15 minutes, or until cheese has melted. Serves 4.

ASPARAGUS

ASPARAGUS WITH EGGS MILANESE

1 small bunch asparagus	4 tablespoons grated Parmesan
4 poached eggs	cheese
½ cup butter, melted	1 teaspoon salt
	½ teaspoon pepper

Clean asparagus and cut off tough part of stalk. Boil briskly about 15 minutes, or until tender. Exact time for boiling depends on thickness and tenderness of the asparagus. Drain very well. Place poached eggs in center of baking dish, arrange asparagus around eggs, sprinkle with melted butter, Parmesan, salt and pepper and bake in very hot oven (450°F.) 3 or 4 minutes. Serves 4.

ASPARAGUS TIPS WITH PROSCIUTTO

24 asparagus tips	½ cup butter
8 long thin slices	3 tablespoons grated Parmesan
prosciutto or ham	cheese

Use canned tips or cook fresh ones in briskly boiling water 10 minutes, or until tender. Drain well. Wrap 3 tips in each slice prosciutto and fasten with toothpick. Place in greased baking dish, sprinkle with half the butter and the Parmesan and bake in hot oven (400°F.) 5 minutes. Remove from oven, pour on remaining butter and serve. Serves 4.

BEANS

BEANS TUSCAN STYLE

¾ pound white beans	1 large fresh tomato, peeled
2 tablespoons olive oil	and cut into pieces
½ teaspoon sage	1 teaspoon salt
2 cloves garlic, sliced	½ teaspoon pepper
4 cups water	2 tablespoons olive oil

Place well-washed beans in large saucepan with oil, sage, garlic, water and tomato. Cover pan, and cook over low flame 3 hours, or until tender. Add salt, pepper and olive oil before serving. Serves 4.

BEANS WITH HAM RIND

1 pound white beans	1 tablespoon leaf lard
½ pound ham rind	1 small can tomato sauce
½ salt pork, chopped	1 cup water in which beans
½ clove garlic	are boiled
1 tablespoon minced parsley	1 teaspoon salt
1 small onion, sliced	½ teaspoon pepper

Soak beans 8 hours. Cut ham rind into pieces 2 inches square and boil with beans 1 hour, or until beans are almost tender. Drain and save water.

Place salt pork, garlic, parsley, onion and leaf lard in large saucepan and brown. Add tomato sauce, water in which beans were boiled, salt and pepper and bring slowly to boiling point. Add beans and ham rind and cook 4 minutes over low flame, or until beans are completely cooked. Add more water from the beans during final cooking, if necessary. Serves 8.

BEANS WITH LETTUCE

½ pound kidney beans	1 teaspoon chopped parsley
½ cup olive oil	2 tablespoons tomato sauce
1 clove garlic	1 cup stock
2 heads romaine lettuce,	½ teaspoon salt
shredded	½ teaspoon pepper

Soak beans overnight. Boil in water 1 hour and drain.

Place olive oil and garlic in large pan, brown garlic and remove, Add lettuce and parsley and cook 15 minutes. Add tomato sauce, stock, salt, pepper and boiled beans and cook 30 minutes, or until beans are tender. Serves 4.

FRESH BEANS IN TOMATO SAUCE

2 pounds fresh beans	1 tablespoon chopped parsley
⅛ pound salt pork, chopped	1 large can tomatoes
1 tablespoon leaf lard	¾ teaspoon salt
1 small onion, chopped	½ teaspoon pepper
1 stalk celery, chopped	

Shell beans and boil in water 20 minutes. Drain and save water. Place salt pork and leaf lard in large saucepan, add onion, celery and parsley and brown slowly. Add tomatoes, beans, salt and pepper and cook 20 minutes longer, or until beans are really tender. If any more liquid should be needed during cooking add a little of the water in which beans were boiled. Serves 4.

Broccoli and Brussels Sprouts

BROCCOLI ROMAN STYLE

1 small bunch broccoli	½ teaspoon salt
3 tablespoons olive oil	½ teaspoon pepper
2 cloves garlic, sliced	1½ cups dry red wine

Trim broccoli of tough leaves and stems, cut into small flowerlets, wash well and drain. Place olive oil and garlic in large skillet and brown garlic. Add broccoli, salt and pepper and cook 5 minutes. Add wine, cover skillet and cook over very low flame 20 minutes, or until broccoli is tender, stirring gently so as not to break flowerlets. Serves 4.

BROCCOLI SICILIAN STYLE

1 small bunch broccoli	¼ pound provolone cheese,
4 tablespoons olive oil	diced fine
1 large onion, sliced	½ teaspoon salt
10 black olives, pitted and	½ teaspoon pepper
cut into pieces	1 cup dry red wine
4 anchovy filets, cut into pieces	

Clean broccoli and cut into very thin slices. Pour 1 tablespoon olive oil in bottom of pan, place thin layer of sliced onions, some olives, some anchovies and 1 layer sliced broccoli in pan. Add a sprinkling of cheese, some salt and pepper and sprinkle with olive oil. Repeat procedure until ingredients are all used. Pour remaining olive oil over top and add wine. Cover pan and cook over very low flame about 30 minutes, or until broccoli is tender. Do not stir. Serves 4.

BROCCOLI SOUR

1 bunch broccoli	½ teaspoon pepper
¼ cup olive oil	juice 1 lemon
½ teaspoon salt	

Wash and clean broccoli thoroughly. Cook in 2 quarts boiling water 15 minutes, taking care not to overcook, and drain. Place broccoli on serving dish, sprinkle with oil, salt, pepper and lemon juice and serve. Serves 4.

BROCCOLI WITH PROSCIUTTO

1 medium bunch broccoli	½ teaspoon pepper
1½ tablespoons leaf lard	3 thin slices prosciutto or
½ clove garlic	ham, shredded
½ teaspoon salt	

Remove all tough leaves and stems from broccoli. Cut into pieces and boil in salted water 15 minutes, or until tender. Drain. Melt leaf lard in skillet, add garlic and brown a little. Add cooked broccoli and mash with fork. Add salt and pepper and cook 5 minutes. Add prosciutto or ham and cook 2 minutes longer. Serves 4.

BRUSSELS SPROUTS

1 small box Brussels sprouts	1 teaspoon meat extract
2 tablespoons butter	½ cup warm water
½ teaspoon salt	

Clean Brussels sprouts, removing outside yellow or brown leaves. Wash well and boil in salted water 12 minutes. Drain. Melt butter in skillet, add sprouts and salt and cook gently 5 minutes. Blend meat extract with warm water, add to sprouts and cook 2 minutes longer. Serve immediately. Serves 4.

CABBAGE

NEW CABBAGE IN VINEGAR

1 small new cabbage	½ teaspoon salt
(about 1½ pounds)	½ teaspoon pepper
1 tablespoon leaf lard	½ cup water
1 tablespoon chopped	½ cup vinegar
salt pork	½ teaspoon sugar
½ clove garlic	

Boil cabbage 10 minutes in lightly salted water. Drain and shred. Melt leaf lard in skillet, add salt pork and garlic and brown. Add shredded cabbage, salt and pepper and cook 15 minutes. Pour water, vinegar and sugar over cabbage, cover skillet and cook 10 minutes longer. Serves 4.

CARROTS

BUTTERED CARROTS

4 large carrots	½ teaspoon sugar
¼ cup butter	1½ teaspoons flour
½ teaspoon salt	1 cup stock or water

Scrape carrots and cut into ½-inch strips. Melt butter in skillet, add carrots and cook 5 minutes. Add salt and sugar and sprinkle with flour, mixing well. Add stock or water, cover skillet and cook gently 20 minutes. Serves 4.

MARINATED CARROTS

1 bunch large carrots	¼ cup olive oil
2 cloves garlic, sliced	2 tablespoons wine vinegar
½ teaspoon salt	1 teaspoon oregano
½ teaspoon pepper	

Scrape carrots and cut into thick slices. Boil in water 10 minutes, or until tender, taking care not to overcook. Drain well and place in bowl with garlic, salt, pepper, oil, vinegar and oregano, stirring and mixing well. Let stand in marinade 12 hours before serving. Serves 8.

STUFFED CARROTS

4 large carrots	1 teaspoon parsley
1 small can tuna fish, grated	¼ clove garlic, chopped
1 slice bread, soaked in	2 tablespoons olive oil
water and squeezed dry	1 cup tomato sauce (see index)

Scrape carrots and cut into halves lengthwise. Scoop out centers of carrot halves. Mix together tuna fish, bread, parsley and garlic and fill scooped-out carrots with this mixture. Place carrots in baking dish, sprinkle with olive oil and pour tomato sauce over carrots. Cover baking dish and bake in moderate oven (375°F.) 35 minutes, or until carrots are tender. Serves 4.

CAULIFLOWER

CAULIFLOWER AU GRATIN

1 small cauliflower	1½ tablespoons grated Parmesan
1½ cups thin cream sauce	cheese
(see index)	1½ tablespoons bread crumbs
	¼ cup butter

Break off flowerlets and cook in 2 quarts boiling salted water 10 minutes. Drain well and place in buttered baking dish. Cover with cream sauce, sprinkle with cheese and bread crumbs and dot with butter. Bake in hot oven (400°F.) 20 minutes. Serves 4.

CAULIFLOWER HARLEQUIN

1 small cauliflower	¼ pound boiled ham, diced
4 tablespoons butter, melted	2 hard cooked eggs, diced
2 tablespoons grated	2 tablespoons fine bread crumbs
Parmesan cheese	

Cook cauliflower flowerlets in boiling salted water 15 minutes. Drain and place in well-buttered casserole. Add 2 tablespoons butter, sprinkle with Parmesan cheese, diced ham, diced egg and bread crumbs and pour rest of melted butter over crumbs. Bake in moderate oven (375°F.) 20 minutes. Serves 4.

CAULIFLOWER PUDDING

1 small cauliflower	2 tablespoons grated Parmesan
1½ cups cream sauce	cheese
(see index)	2 eggs, lightly beaten
¼ teaspoon salt	1 cup cream sauce (see index)
⅛ teaspoon nutmeg	

Remove leaves from cauliflower and cut flowerlets into small pieces. Cook in slightly salted water 20 minutes, drain and strain. Mix with cream sauce, salt, nutmeg, cheese and eggs. Mix well and place in buttered 1-quart mold. Place mold in boiling water and cook 1 hour. Unmold and serve with additional cream sauce. Serves 4.

CELERY

CELERY IN TOMATO SAUCE

1 large bunch celery	1 teaspoon chopped parsley
2 quarts water	2 tablespoons tomato paste
½ teaspoon salt	1 cup stock or water
3 slices bacon, chopped	¼ teaspoon salt
1 small onion	½ teaspoon pepper

Clean celery, cut off leaves and cut stalks into 4-inch pieces. Boil in salted water 5 minutes, drain and reserve liquid. Place bacon, onion and parsley in saucepan and brown. Add tomato paste and stock or water (the water in which the celery was boiled will do well here). Add salt, pepper and celery and simmer gently 10 minutes longer, or until celery is completely cooked. Serves 4.

CELERY IN CASSEROLE

1 large bunch celery	½ teaspoon salt
1 small onion	½ cup grated Parmesan cheese
⅛ pound salt pork	½ cup butter, melted

Remove leaves from celery, cut stalks into 5-inch pieces and wash well. Place in 2 quarts boiling water with onion, salt pork and salt; boil 15 minutes, or until celery is tender. Drain. Place 1 layer cooked celery in greased casserole, sprinkle abundantly with cheese and with butter, and repeat layers until all celery is used, ending with cheese. Bake in hot oven (400°F.) 7 minutes. Serves 4.

CELERY PARMIGIANA STYLE

1 very large bunch celery	2 slices bacon
2 quarts stock or water	1 cup tomato sauce (see index)
1 small onion	½ cup grated Parmesan cheese
1 clove	

Clean celery, remove leaves and cut stalks into 5-inch pieces. Cook in boiling stock or water with onion, clove and bacon 15 minutes, or until celery is tender. Place 1 layer celery in greased shallow casserole, top with tomato sauce, sprinkle with Parmesan and repeat layers until celery is all used, ending with tomato sauce and cheese. Bake in hot oven (400°F.) 10 minutes. Serves 4.

CHESTNUTS

CHESTNUT PUREE

1 pound chestnuts	½ teaspoon sugar
½ cup milk	½ cup butter
¼ teaspoon salt	

Peel chestnuts, boil in water 30 minutes, or until tender, remove from fire and peel off second skin. Place chestnuts in saucepan with milk, mash with fork until smooth, add salt, sugar and butter and mix well over low fire. Serves 4.

SOUFFLE OF CHESTNUTS

1½ pounds chestnuts	1½ cups stock
¼ teaspoon salt	2 egg whites, beaten stiff
1 tablespoon butter	

Peel chestnuts, boil 30 minutes, or until tender, remove from fire and remove second skin. Force through strainer. Place in saucepan, add salt, butter and stock and cook, stirring well, until stock has evaporated. Cool. Fold in stiff egg whites and pour mixture into greased casserole. Bake in moderate oven (375°F.) 20 minutes. Serves 4.

STEWED CHESTNUTS

1 pound chestnuts, peeled	1 celery stalk
1 teaspoon sugar	4½ teaspoons butter
¼ teaspoon salt	1 teaspoon meat extract

Place peeled chestnuts in moderate oven (375°F.) 5 minutes to loosen second skin. Remove skin. Place chestnuts in large skillet in 1 layer, add enough water to cover and add sugar, salt and celery stalk. Bring to boil and add butter and meat extract. Mix gently, cover skillet and cook 30 minutes, or until chestnuts are tender. Serves 4.

CHICK PEAS (CECI)

CHICK PEAS MARINARA STYLE

½ cup olive oil
4 anchovy filets, chopped
½ teaspoon pepper

1 tablespoon chopped parsley
¼ teaspoon salt
1 can cooked chick peas

Heat oil, add anchovies, pepper, parsley and salt and mix together well over low flame 2 minutes. Heat ceci in own broth, add to the anchovy mixture, mix well and serve. Serves 4.

CHICORY

BRAISED CHICORY

2 small heads chicory
3 tablespoons olive oil
1 clove garlic, sliced
½ teaspoon chopped basil

¼ teaspoon chopped mint leaves
½ teaspoon salt
½ teaspoon pepper

Cut off stems of chicory, wash well and shred not too finely. Place in stew pan with oil, garlic, basil, mint, salt and pepper, cover pan and cook over low flame 1 hour, stirring occasionally. Serves 4.

CHICORY ROMAN STYLE

2 small heads chicory
¼ cup olive oil
3 cloves garlic
6 anchovy filets, cut into
    pieces

3 fresh tomatoes, peeled and cut
    into pieces, or 1 small can
    tomatoes
½ teaspoon salt
½ teaspoon pepper
½ cup stock

Clean chicory and shred not too fine. Place oil in pan with garlic; brown garlic and remove. Add anchovies to oil and mix well. Add tomatoes, salt, pepper and chicory, cover pan and cook gently 30 minutes, adding stock a little at a time as needed. Serves 4.

EGGPLANT

BAKED EGGPLANT SICILIAN STYLE

1 large eggplant, or 2 small ones	1½ cups tomato sauce (see index)
1 cup olive oil	½ cup grated Parmesan cheese
½ teaspoon salt	1 egg beaten lightly with
1 cup cooked leftover meat, chopped	2 tablespoons grated Parmesan cheese

Cut off stalk of eggplant, peel and cut into thin slices. Fry in olive oil until well browned on both sides, sprinkle with salt and drain on paper.

Place 1 layer fried eggplant in casserole, cover with some of the chopped meat, some of the tomato sauce and sprinkle with Parmesan cheese. Repeat procedure until all eggplant is used. Mix egg and cheese together well and pour over eggplant. Place casserole in hot oven (400°F.) 20 minutes. Serve hot. Serves 4.

BROILED EGGPLANT

2 small eggplants, cut in halves	½ teaspoon salt
4 tablespoons olive oil	½ teaspoon pepper
	1 clove garlic, sliced

Make little criss-cross cuts on inside part of eggplant halves. Brush well with oil, salt, pepper and garlic. Place eggplant, cut side up, in broiler and broil gently 30 minutes, brushing frequently with oil. Serves 4.

EGGPLANT CROQUETTES

2 large eggplants	dash nutmeg
3 tablespoons grated Parmesan cheese	2 slices bread, soaked in water and squeezed dry
1 tablespoon chopped parsley	2 eggs
1 tablespoon chopped basil	½ cup flour
¾ teaspoon salt	1 cup olive oil
½ teaspoon pepper	

Cut eggplants into 4 parts each and boil 20 minutes, or until tender. Drain well and chop fine. Mix together well with the Parmesan cheese, parsley, basil, salt, pepper, nutmeg, bread and eggs and shape as croquettes. Flour and fry in olive oil until golden brown on all sides. Serve with tomato sauce (see index) or plain. Serves 4.

EGGPLANT FOGGIA STYLE

2 medium eggplants	1 teaspoon chopped parsley
1 clove garlic, sliced	¼ teaspoon sugar
2 tablespoons olive oil	2 tablespoons bread crumbs
1 small can tomatoes	½ cup water
½ teaspoon salt	2½ tablespoons olive oil
½ teaspoon pepper	1 small can tomato purée
½ teaspoon chopped basil	

Cut tops off eggplants and save. Scoop out eggplant and chop the pulp. Brown garlic in 2 tablespoons olive oil in saucepan, add tomatoes and cook 10 minutes. Add eggplant pulp, salt, pepper, basil, parsley and sugar and cook 5 minutes longer. Add bread crumbs, mixing well, and fill eggplants with this mixture.

Place eggplants, standing up, in casserole, replace tops of eggplants, pour water, oil and tomato purée in casserole and bake in moderate oven (375°F.) 1 hour. Cut eggplants in halves, pour sauce from casserole over them and serve. Serves 4.

FRIED EGGPLANT

1 medium eggplant, peeled	½ teaspoon salt
and cut into ½-inch slices	½ teaspoon pepper
½ cup flour	½ cup olive oil
1 egg, lightly beaten	

Flour eggplant slices and dip into egg to which salt and pepper have been added. Fry in olive oil 6 minutes on each side, or until slices are golden brown. Serves 4.

EGGPLANT GOURMET STYLE

1 medium eggplant, cut	2 tablespoons butter
into 8 parts	3 tablespoons grated Parmesan
1 cup olive oil	cheese
2 cups tomato sauce	

Cut eggplant into 8 parts lengthwise and fry in olive oil until brown and tender. (Cooking time will be about 10 minutes for each part.) Place tomato sauce in casserole, add eggplant, sprinkle well with cheese. Dot with butter and bake in moderate oven (375°F.) 15 minutes. Serves 4.

EGGPLANT IN SKILLET

3 tablespoons olive oil
½ clove garlic
1 medium eggplant, cut into
   large dices (do not peel)
½ teaspoon salt

½ teaspoon pepper
2 tomatoes, peeled and cut into
   pieces
1 teaspoon oregano

Place olive oil and garlic in skillet and brown garlic slightly. Add diced eggplant, salt and pepper and cook gently 20 minutes. Add tomatoes and oregano and cook 15 minutes longer. Serves 4.

EGGPLANT MARINARA

1 large eggplant with skin
   on, cut into large cubes
½ cup wine vinegar
1 teaspoon salt
½ teaspoon pepper

2 cloves garlic, sliced
1 teaspoon chopped oregano
½ teaspoon chopped basil
1 cup olive oil

Boil large eggplant cubes in water 10 minutes and drain well. Place in large bowl with vinegar, salt, pepper, garlic, oregano and basil. Mix well and let stand in this marinade at least 12 hours. Before serving add olive oil and mix well. This will keep for at least 1 week in refrigerator and is a good dish to have ready at all times. Serves 8.

EGGPLANT ONORATO

1 medium eggplant, with
   skin on, diced
¼ cup olive oil
1 cup tomato sauce
   (see index)

¼ teaspoon salt
¼ teaspoon pepper
12 black olives, pitted and cut
   in pieces
1 tablespoon capers

Fry the diced eggplant in olive oil 10 minutes. Add tomato sauce, salt, pepper, olives and capers, cook 10 minutes and serve. Serves 8.

EGGPLANT PARMIGIANA

1 large eggplant, or 2
   small ones
1 cup olive oil
1¼ cups tomato sauce
   (see index)

3 tablespoons grated Parmesan
   cheese
½ pound mozzarella cheese,
   sliced thin

Peel eggplant and cut into thin slices. Fry in oil until brown and drain well on paper. Place 1 layer fried eggplant in casserole, cover with sauce, sprinkle with Parmesan and cover with layer of mozzarella. Re-

peat procedure until all eggplant is used, ending with mozzarella.
Bake in hot oven (400°F.) 15 minutes and serve hot. Serves 4.

EGGPLANT PROVENZALE

4 small eggplants	1 slice prosciutto, minced
1 tablespoon chopped salt pork	2 anchovy filets, cut into pieces
¼ clove garlic, chopped	1 egg
1 small onion, chopped	½ teaspoon salt
2 slices bread, soaked in water and squeezed dry	½ teaspoon pepper
	3 tablespoons bread crumbs
¼ pound mushrooms, sliced thin	¼ pound butter, melted
	1½ teaspoons lemon juice

Cut eggplants into halves and scoop out some of the insides. Mix
together well the salt pork, garlic, onion, bread, mushrooms, prosciutto,
anchovies, egg, salt and pepper and stuff eggplant halves with this mixture. Sprinkle with bread crumbs and melted butter. Place eggplants
in well-greased baking dish and bake in moderate oven (375°F.) 40 minutes. Remove from oven, sprinkle with lemon juice and serve. Serves 4.

EGGPLANT SANDWICHES

2 medium eggplants	2 tablespoons grated Parmesan cheese
½ cup flour	
1½ cups olive oil	¼ teaspoon salt
2 egg yolks	1 egg, lightly beaten
½ pound mozzarella cheese, diced fine	½ cup bread crumbs

Peel eggplants and cut into ½-inch slices. Roll in flour and fry in
olive oil. Drain well on paper. Save oil. Mix together well egg yolks,
mozzarella, Parmesan cheese and salt. Spread 1 tablespoon of this mixture on 1 side of each eggplant slice and cover with another slice. Dip
sandwich into beaten egg, roll in crumbs and fry in oil until golden
brown on both sides. Serves 4.

SKEWERS NEAPOLITAN STYLE

1 medium eggplant	½ teaspoon salt
8 small tomatoes	¼ teaspoon pepper
¾ pound mozzarella cheese, sliced	½ cup milk
	1 cup flour
16 slices French or Italian bread (long loaf)	2 eggs, lightly beaten
	2 cups olive oil

Peel eggplant and cut into ½-inch slices. Cut each slice in half.
Peel tomatoes, cut off tops, drain off juice and cut in two. Cut moz-

zarella in slices about as large as eggplant slices. Have 8 skewers ready. Start skewer with slice of bread, then eggplant, mozzarella, half tomato, then eggplant, etc., until skewer is filled, ending with bread slice. Sprinkle with a little salt and pepper, dip skewers into milk, roll in flour and dip into egg. Fry in hot oil until golden brown on both sides. Serves 4.

WHOLE EGGPLANT SICILIAN STYLE

1 medium eggplant	¼ teaspoon salt
2 cups olive oil	¼ teaspoon pepper

Cut off stem and peel eggplant. Make vertical cuts in eggplant so as to make it resemble a tassel. Do not cut all the way to the top but leave top part whole. Heat oil and fry eggplant until dark brown. Sprinkle with salt and pepper and serve. Serves 4.

EGGPLANT WITH ANCHOVIES

2 medium eggplants	6 anchovy filets, cut into pieces
1 cup oil, olive or cooking	1 tablespoon chopped parsley
½ clove garlic	1 tablespoon vinegar
3 tablespoons olive oil	

Remove stem and peel eggplant. Cut into ½-inch slices and fry in oil until golden brown. Drain well on paper. Place 3 tablespoons oil and garlic in frying pan and brown garlic. Remove garlic when brown and add anchovies. Cook gently 3 minutes. Add parsley and vinegar and cook 1 minute. Pour sauce over fried eggplant and serve either hot or cold. Serves 4.

Fennel (Finocchi)

FENNEL AND CHARD AU GRATIN

6 very small stalks fennel	4 tablespoons fine bread crumbs
1 bunch chard, cut into 2-inch pieces	3 tablespoons grated Parmesan cheese
2 cups cream sauce (see index)	2 tablespoons butter

Cut each fennel into 4 parts and boil with chard 10 minutes. Drain. Grease casserole and sprinkle some bread crumbs on bottom and sides. Place fennels and chard in casserole, pour cream sauce over them, sprinkle with bread crumbs and cheese, and dot with butter. Bake in moderate oven (375°F.) 20 minutes, or until cheese is melted and crumbs are light brown. Serves 4.

FENNEL IN SKILLET

6 very small stalks fennel | ½ teaspoon salt
1 clove garlic, sliced | ½ teaspoon pepper
2 tablespoons olive oil | ½ cup stock or water

Cut off tough outer leaves and ends of fennels. Cut each into 4 parts and wash well. Drain, place in skillet with garlic, oil, salt and pepper and cook 10 minutes, stirring frequently. Add stock or water, cover skillet and cook slowly 20 minutes, or until tender. Serves 4.

KOHLRABI

KOHLRABI AL CRUDO

1 pound kohlrabi | ½ teaspoon salt
1 tablespoon olive oil | ½ teaspoon pepper
1 tablespoon leaf lard | 1 cup stock or water
1 clove garlic

Clean kohlrabi and wash well. Place oil and leaf lard in skillet with garlic. Brown garlic and remove. Add salt, pepper and kohlrabi to oil, cover skillet and cook gently 30 minutes, or until tender, adding a little stock or water from time to time as needed. Serves 4.

MUSHROOMS

MUSHROOMS AU GRATIN

12 large mushrooms | 2 tablespoons water
2 tablespoons butter | 2 tablespoons cold cream
1 small onion, chopped | sauce (see index)
½ teaspoon salt | 2 tablespoons fine bread crumbs
½ teaspoon pepper | 2 tablespoons butter
1 tablespoon parsley |

Remove stems from mushrooms and wash well. Chop stems and fry in 2 tablespoons butter with onion. Brown lightly, add salt, pepper, parsley and water and cook 5 minutes longer. Remove from fire and add cream sauce, mixing well. Fill mushrooms caps with this stuffing, top with bread crumbs, dot with butter and place in well-greased baking dish in moderate oven (375°F.) 15 minutes. Serves 4.

BROILED MUSHROOM CAPS

12 large mushroom caps | ¼ clove garlic, minced
2 tablespoons fine bread | 2 tablespoons olive oil
  crumbs | ½ teaspoon salt
1 tablespoon chopped parsley | ½ teaspoon pepper

Wash mushroom caps well and dry. Mix together bread crumbs, parsley and garlic. Brush mushroom caps with oil and roll in bread crumbs. Sprinkle with salt and pepper and place under broiler 5 minutes on each side. Sprinkle with more oil if necessary. Serves 4.

DRIED MUSHROOMS ON TOAST

¼ pound dried mushrooms	½ cup Marsala or sherry wine
½ teaspoon salt	4 slices bread, cut into triangles
½ teaspoon pepper	3 tablespoons butter
2 tablespoons butter	2 slices prosciutto, cut into slivers

Soak mushrooms in warm water for 1 hour. Squeeze dry, chop, add salt and pepper and cook in butter 8 minutes. Add Marsala and continue cooking 20 minutes, adding 1 tablespoon water whenever needed.

Fry bread triangles in butter and pour mushroom mixture over them. Place prosciutto slivers over mushrooms and serve. Serves 4.

FRIED MUSHROOMS

24 small solid mushrooms	1 tablespoon milk
½ cup flour	½ teaspoon salt
1 egg, lightly beaten	1 cup olive oil

Wash mushrooms well and dry. Roll in flour. Add milk and salt to egg and beat a little. Dip mushrooms into egg mixture and fry in medium hot olive oil until light brown in color. Drain on paper and serve hot. Serves 4.

MUSHROOMS GENOA STYLE

¾ pound mushrooms, sliced thin	½ teaspoon pepper
2 tablespoons olive oil	1 large clove garlic, chopped
½ teaspoon salt	1 teaspoon oregano

Place mushrooms in frying pan with oil, salt and pepper and cook until all water from mushrooms has evaporated. Add garlic and oregano, mix well and cook 1 minute longer. Serves 4.

MUSHROOMS IN BRODETTO

¼ cup butter	1 cup hot water
¾ pound mushrooms, sliced	1 teaspoon meat extract
½ teaspoon salt	2 egg yolks
½ teaspoon pepper	juice of 1 lemon
1 tablespoon flour	1 tablespoon chopped parsley
½ cup dry white wine	

Melt butter in frying pan, add mushrooms, salt and pepper and cook over brisk flame until all the water from the mushrooms has evaporated. Add flour and wine, mix well and continue cooking until wine has evaporated. Add warm water and meat extract, mix well and cook 30 minutes.

Turn off fire, add egg yolks, lemon juice and parsley and mix well. Cover pan and keep on stove with fire turned out for 5 minutes. Serves 4.

MUSHROOMS IN CREAM

1 tablespoon olive oil	¾ pound mushrooms, sliced
1 tablespoon butter	½ teaspoon salt
1 scallion, chopped	½ teaspoon pepper
1 very small onion, chopped	½ cup heavy cream

Place oil and butter in skillet with scallion and onion and brown gently until scallion and onion are golden brown in color. Add sliced mushrooms, salt and pepper and cook over low flame 10 minutes. Add cream and cook 4 minutes longer, stirring constantly. Serves 4.

MUSHROOMS IN PATTY SHELLS

¾ pound mushrooms, sliced thick	½ teaspoon salt
	½ teaspoon pepper
2 tablespoons butter	2 egg yolks
1 tablespoon chopped parsley	½ cup heavy cream
1 tablespoon flour	4 patty shells
½ cup stock	

Place mushrooms in pan with butter and parsley and cook until lightly browned. Sprinkle with flour, add stock, salt and pepper, lower flame and continue cooking 15 minutes. Keep pan on stove but turn off flame. Mix egg yolks with cream and pour over mushroom mixture, blending in very well. Keep pan on stove 5 minutes.

Warm patty shells in oven, then fill with mushroom mixture and serve. Serves 4.

MUSHROOMS IN SHELLS

¾ pound mushrooms, sliced	½ teaspoon meat extract
¼ cup butter	½ cup stock
1 tablespoon chopped parsley	2 tablespoons butter
½ black truffle, sliced	2 tablespoons fine bread
1 tablespoon flour	crumbs

Place mushrooms and butter in frying pan and cook 5 minutes. Add parsley and truffle, sprinkle with flour and mix until well blended. Add meat extract and stock and cook 10 minutes. Remove from fire.

Butter 4 large shells or individual casseroles and fill with mushroom mixture. Dot with butter, sprinkle with bread crumbs and bake in moderate oven (375°F.) 10 minutes. Serves 4.

MUSHROOMS IN SKILLET

2 tablespoons olive oil
¼ clove garlic, minced
3 anchovy filets, chopped
¾ pound mushrooms, cut into large pieces

2 fresh tomatoes, peeled and cut into pieces, or 1 tablespoon tomato sauce
¼ teaspoon chopped mint leaves
½ teaspoon salt
½ teaspoon pepper

Heat oil in skillet with garlic. Add anchovies, mushrooms, tomatoes or sauce, mint, salt and pepper. Cover skillet and cook over brisk flame 15 minutes, stirring very often. Serve on toast. Serves 4.

STUFFED MUSHROOMS

12 large mushrooms
2 tablespoons olive oil
1 small onion, chopped
½ clove garlic
4 anchovy filets, chopped
1 tablespoon chopped parsley
¼ teaspoon salt

½ teaspoon pepper
1 slice bread, soaked in water and squeezed dry
1 egg
2 tablespoons bread crumbs
1 tablespoon olive oil

Cut off stems from mushrooms and wash very well. Chop the stems and cook in olive oil with onion and garlic 5 minutes. Add anchovies, parsley, salt and pepper and cook 5 minutes longer over brisk flame. Remove from stove, add bread and egg and mix together until smooth.

Fill each mushroom cap with stuffing, rounding stuffing up on top. Sprinkle with bread crumbs, then with oil and place in greased baking dish in hot oven (400°F.) 20 minutes. Serves 4.

STUFFED MUSHROOM BALLS

16 medium mushrooms
1 tablespoon butter
1 cup leftover cooked meat, chopped (beef, veal or chicken)
¼ teaspoon salt
¼ teaspoon pepper
2 tablespoons cold cream sauce (see index)

1 tablespoon chopped parsley
1 tablespoon grated Parmesan cheese
½ cup flour
1 egg, lightly beaten
1 cup fine bread crumbs
2 cups olive oil
½ lemon, cut into wedges

Cut off stems from mushrooms and wash thoroughly. Chop stems and cook in butter 5 minutes. Mix mushroom stems with chopped meat, salt, pepper, cream sauce, parsley and Parmesan cheese. Mix well and stuff mushroom caps, placing two together to form balls.

Roll in flour, dip into egg, roll in bread crumbs and fry in olive oil over medium flame until little balls are golden brown. Serve hot with lemon wedges. Serves 4.

STUFFED MUSHROOMS GENOA STYLE

12 large mushrooms	½ teaspoon salt
1 tablespoon olive oil	½ teaspoon pepper
½ clove garlic, chopped	½ teaspoon marjoram
1 veal brain, parboiled	2 egg yolks
and chopped	1 tablespoon grated Parmesan
1 pork brain, parboiled	cheese
and chopped	2 tablespoons olive oil

Cut off stems of mushrooms and wash well. Chop stems and brown in olive oil with garlic 5 minutes. Add chopped parboiled brains, salt, pepper and marjoram and cook 5 minutes longer. Remove from stove, add egg yolks and Parmesan and mix very well.

Fill the mushroom caps with this mixture. Place in shallow baking dish, sprinkle with olive oil and bake in moderate oven (375°F.) 40 minutes. Serves 4.

MUSHROOMS TRIFOLATI

2 tablespoons olive oil	½ teaspoon pepper
1 clove garlic	1 tablespoon butter
¾ pound mushrooms,	4 anchovy filets, chopped
sliced thin	1 tablespoon chopped parsley
½ teaspoon salt	juice of ½ lemon

Place oil and garlic in skillet and brown garlic. Remove garlic, add mushrooms, salt and pepper and cook briskly until all the water from the mushrooms has evaporated. Add butter, anchovies and parsley and cook 5 minutes. Remove from fire, add lemon juice and serve. Serves 4.

ONIONS

BOILED ONIONS

4 large onions	½ teaspoon salt
1 teaspoon chopped parsley	½ teaspoon pepper
½ teaspoon chopped oregano	¼ cup olive oil

Peel onions, cut in halves crosswise and boil in water ½ hour. Drain well and place in serving dish. Sprinkle with parsley, oregano, salt, pepper and olive oil. Serves 4.

ONIONS BORDOLESE

4 very large onions	½ cup butter
8 chicken livers, chopped	1 tablespoon flour
¼ teaspoon pepper	1½ cups water
½ teaspoon salt	½ teaspoon meat extract
½ black truffle, diced	1 jigger cognac
fine (optional)	

Peel onions, cut in halves and scoop out centers to make room for stuffing. Mix together chicken livers, pepper, salt, truffle and ¼ cup butter and stuff onion halves with this mixture. Place onions in well-buttered, covered baking dish and bake in moderate oven (375°F.) 20 minutes.

Melt rest of butter in small saucepan, blend in flour, add water and meat extract and cook 1 minute. Pour sauce over onions and continue baking in moderate oven 15 minutes longer, or until onions are tender. Remove from oven, sprinkle onions with cognac and serve. Serves 4.

FRIED ONION RINGS

2 medium onions	1 cup olive oil
1 cup flour	salt to taste

Peel and slice onions and drop in boiling water for 5 minutes. Remove and transfer onions to iced water. Keep in iced water 3 minutes. Drain well, roll in flour and fry in hot olive oil until golden brown and crisp. Sprinkle with a little salt to taste. Serves 4.

GRILLED ONIONS

4 large onions	½ teaspoon salt
1½ teaspoons chopped parsley	½ teaspoon pepper
2 tablespoons olive oil	

Peel onions and boil in water 10 minutes. Drain well and cut into halves crosswise. Place on grill and sprinkle with parsley, olive oil, salt and pepper and cook under low flame 30 minutes, adding more oil before serving. Serves 4.

STUFFED ONIONS

4 very large onions	¼ pound chopped veal or beef
1½ tablespoons butter	1 tablespoon butter
½ teaspoon salt	1 egg yolk
½ teaspoon pepper	½ teaspoon chopped parsley
2 slices white bread, soaked	2 tablespoons olive oil
in water and squeezed dry	2 tablespoons bread crumbs

Peel onions and cut in halves, crosswise. Boil in water 8 minutes. Cool by placing in cold water for few minutes. Drain well. Cut out 3 or 4 layers from center of each onion to make place for stuffing. Place these layers in small pan with butter, fry 5 minutes and chop.

Mix together salt, pepper, bread, meat, butter, egg yolk, parsley and chopped fried onion. Mix well and stuff onion halves with this mixture. Place stuffed onions in greased baking dish, sprinkle with bread crumbs and oil and bake in moderate oven (375°F.) 1 hour. Serves 4.

PEARL ONIONS†

BAKED PEARL ONIONS

1 pound pearl onions	½ teaspoon pepper
¼ cup olive oil	1 tablespoon wine vinegar
½ teaspoon salt	¼ clove garlic, chopped

Place onions on baking sheet with skins on and bake in moderate oven (375°F.) 15 minutes, or until tender. Remove from oven, peel and place in salad bowl with oil, salt, pepper, vinegar and garlic. Mix well and serve either hot or cold. Serves 4.

PEARL ONIONS IN DARK SAUCE

1 pound pearl onions	1½ teaspoons sugar
½ cup butter	3 tablespoons stock
½ teaspoon salt	

Peel onions and place in ice water 5 minutes. Drain, place in skillet with butter and cook 3 minutes. Add salt and sugar, cover skillet and continue cooking over low flame until onions are light brown in color. Stir gently. Add stock and cook 10 minutes longer. Serves 4.

† Tiny white onions

PEARL ONIONS IN TOMATO SAUCE

1 pound pearl onions
1 tablespoon butter
1 tablespoon olive oil
½ teaspoon salt

½ teaspoon pepper
1½ teaspoons sugar
1 cup tomato sauce (see index)
½ cup stock

Peel onions. Melt butter in large skillet, add olive oil and lay in the onions in a single layer. Add salt, pepper, sugar, tomato sauce and stock, cover skillet and cook over moderate flame 25 minutes, or until onions are tender, adding more stock, if necessary. Serves 4.

PEARL ONIONS IN WHITE SAUCE

1 pound pearl onions
½ cup butter

1½ cups stock

Peel onions and soak in very cold water 5 minutes. Drain, place in skillet with butter and cook gently 5 minutes. Add stock, cover skillet and cook until onions are tender and sauce is slightly thick, turning over once. Serves 4.

PEARL ONIONS SWEET-SOUR (Number 1)

1 pound pearl onions
⅛ pound salt pork, chopped
2 tablespoons butter
1 tablespoon sugar

¼ cup vinegar
½ teaspoon salt
½ teaspoon pepper

Peel onions and soak in ice water 5 minutes. Drain. Place salt pork and butter in frying pan and brown well. Add sugar and blend in well. Add vinegar, stirring in well. Add onions, salt and pepper, cover pan and cook slowly about 30 minutes, or until tender, adding a little water, if necessary. Serves 4.

PEARL ONIONS SWEET-SOUR (Number 2)

1 pound pearl onions
2 tablespoons butter
½ teaspoon salt
½ teaspoon pepper

1½ tablespoons sugar
½ cup vinegar
½ teaspoon flour
½ cup stock

Peel onions and soak in ice water 5 minutes. Drain. Melt butter in large skillet, add onions in single layer, sprinkle with salt, pepper and sugar and add vinegar. Cover skillet and cook 5 minutes over brisk flame. Lower flame and continue cooking 20 minutes, or until onions are tender. Do not stir. Onions will be dark in lower section and white on top. Remove to serving dish.

Add flour to pan gravy, blend well and add stock. Cook 2 minutes and pour gravy over cooked onions. Serves 4.

Peas

PEAS IN CREAM (Bordure)

¼ cup butter	⅛ teaspoon nutmeg
2 tablespoons flour	2 cups peas with prosciutto
1½ cups milk	Roman style (see
2 eggs	following recipe)
½ teaspoon salt	

Melt butter in saucepan, blend in flour, cook 1 minute, add milk and cook until thickened, stirring constantly. Allow to cool.

Add eggs, salt and nutmeg and mix together very well. Pour into well-greased and floured circular mold, place mold in pan of water and bake in moderate oven (375°F.) 30 minutes. Turn out on serving dish, place cooked peas in center and serve. Serves 4.

PEAS WITH PROSCIUTTO ROMAN STYLE

¼ cup butter	½ teaspoon pepper
1 small onion, sliced	2 tablespoons stock or water
2 cups shelled fresh peas,	6 slices prosciutto, shredded
or 1 package frozen peas	¼ teaspoon sugar
¾ teaspoon salt	

Place butter and onion in saucepan and brown onion gently. Add peas, salt, pepper and stock and cook briskly 10 minutes, stirring frequently. Add prosciutto, lower flame and cook until peas are tender. (Cooking time about 10 minutes, depending on the quality of peas.) Add sugar and a little more stock, if required, and serve. Serves 4.

Peppers

PEPPERS AU GRATIN

4 large green peppers	4 tablespoons olive oil
1 tablespoon capers	2 tablespoons fine bread crumbs
4 anchovy filets, cut into	½ teaspoon salt
pieces	½ teaspoon pepper
8 black olives, pitted and	
cut into pieces	

Roast peppers in very hot oven (450°F.) 10 minutes, or until skin is easily removed. Peel, remove seeds and cut into wide slices. Place in oiled baking dish, dot with capers, anchovies, olives and sprinkle with oil, bread crumbs, salt and pepper. Bake in moderate oven (375°F.) 20 minutes and add more olive oil. This dish can be served either hot or cold. Serves 4.

FRIED PEPPERS

3 large peppers	½ cup flour
2 tablespoons oil	1 egg, lightly beaten
½ teaspoon salt	1 cup olive oil
½ teaspoon pepper	

Roast peppers in very hot oven (450°F.) 10 minutes, or until peppers peel easily. Peel, remove seeds and cut into thin slices. Place in dish, add oil, salt and pepper and let stand ½ hour.

Drain off oil, roll in flour, dip into egg and fry in very hot olive oil until golden brown. Serves 4.

PEPPERS ROMAN STYLE

4 large peppers	3 tomatoes, peeled and cut
1 small onion, sliced fine	into pieces
1 tablespoon leaf lard	½ teaspoon salt
1 tablespoon olive oil	¼ teaspoon pepper

Cut peppers in halves, remove stalks and seeds and cut into thin slices. Place onion, oil, and leaf lard in skillet and brown lightly. Add tomatoes and cook 5 minutes.

Add peppers, salt and pepper, cover skillet and cook slowly 30 minutes, adding water if necessary, and stirring frequently. Serves 4.

STUFFED PEPPERS NEAPOLITAN STYLE

4 large peppers	1 tablespoon chopped parsley
½ cup olive oil	1 tablespoon chopped basil
1 cup toasted bread crumbs	2 tablespoons capers
3 tablespoons seedless raisins	½ teaspoon salt
12 black olives, pitted and	½ teaspoon pepper
cut into pieces	4 tablespoons olive oil
6 anchovy filets, cut into	½ cup tomato sauce (see index)
small pieces	

Wash peppers thoroughly. With sharp knife cut all around the stem, removing it together with all the seeds inside, thus leaving an opening through which stuffing may be pushed.

Mix together olive oil, bread crumbs, raisins, olives, anchovies, parsley, basil, capers, salt and pepper. Mix very well, and if stuffing seems too dry, add more oil.

Stuff peppers and place them, standing up, in deep baking dish. Pour oil over peppers and top each with 1 tablespoon tomato sauce. Bake in moderate oven (375°F.) 1 hour. Can be served either hot or cold. Serves 4.

PEPPERS WITH BACON

5 medium peppers	½ teaspoon salt
1 tablespoon olive oil	½ teaspoon pepper
1 medium onion, sliced	¼ pound bacon, sliced thin and
2 tablespoons water	cut into small squares
6 fresh tomatoes, peeled and	
cut into pieces	

Wash peppers, remove stalks and seeds and cut into thin slices. Place oil and onion in large frying pan and brown onion slightly. Add water, tomatoes, salt, pepper and peppers and cook slowly 20 minutes, stirring frequently. Add bacon and continue cooking 10 minutes. Serves 4.

POTATOES

POTATO BRIOCHES

½ recipe for potatoes	1 egg, lightly beaten
duchessa (see index)	2 tablespoons fine bread
¼ pound mozzarella cheese,	crumbs
cut into large cubes	

Grease about 8 muffin tins or small jelly molds. Fill ¾ full with potatoes duchessa and place 1 cube mozzarella cheese in center of each. Brush top with egg, sprinkle with bread crumbs and bake in hot oven (400°F.) 8 to 10 minutes. Unmold immediately and serve. Serves 4.

CREAMED POTATOES

1½ pounds potatoes	1 tablespoon butter
½ teaspoon salt	¼ cup milk
¼ teaspoon pepper	¾ cup heavy cream
⅛ teaspoon nutmeg	

Peel potatoes, quarter and cook in water 15 minutes, or until tender to fork. Drain, place back in pan over low flame and mash potatoes with masher. Add salt, pepper, nutmeg, butter and milk and stir well 5 minutes.

Heat cream. Pour potatoes in covered vegetable dish, pour warm cream over potatoes, cover dish and let stand 3 or 4 minutes. Serves 4.

POTATO CROQUETTES

½ recipe for potatoes
   duchessa (see index)
2 tablespoons flour

1 egg, lightly beaten
1 cup fine bread crumbs
1 cup olive oil

Make prepared potato mixture into croquettes the size of very small eggs. Dip into flour, then into egg; roll in crumbs and fry in hot oil until very brown on all sides. Serve immediately. Serves 4.

POTATO CUTLETS

2 tablespoons butter
8 chicken livers, chopped
¼ cup Marsala or sherry wine
½ cup mushrooms, sliced
1 slice prosciutto, slivered
¼ teaspoon salt

¼ teaspoon pepper
1 recipe potatoes duchessa
   (see recipe below)
1 egg, lightly beaten
1 cup bread crumbs

Place butter and chicken livers in saucepan and braise gently. Add Marsala or sherry, mushrooms, prosciutto, salt and pepper and cook until dry.

Shape potatoes as chops and place 1 tablespoon liver mixture in center of each. Dip into egg, roll in bread crumbs, place in greased baking dish and bake in moderate oven (375°F.) 20 minutes. Serve immediately. Serves 6.

POTATOES DUCHESSA

2 pounds potatoes
¼ cup butter
½ teaspoon salt

¼ teaspoon pepper
⅛ teaspoon nutmeg
1 egg yolk

Peel potatoes, quarter and boil in water 15 minutes, or until tender to fork. Drain, place over low fire and heat so as to dry potatoes of any excess moisture. Put potatoes through ricer and return to pan with butter, salt, pepper and nutmeg. Mix well with wooden spoon, remove from fire, add egg yolk and mix very well 3 minutes. This is the base for many potato dishes. Serves 4.

FRIED POTATOES

4 small potatoes
½ teaspoon salt

1 cup olive oil

Peel potatoes and slice very thin. Place in plate and sprinkle with salt. Tilt plate to one side so the salty water will run off. Let potatoes stand in this way 1 hour.

Heat olive oil in frying pan, squeeze potato slices dry and fry a few slices at a time. When golden brown, drain on paper and serve. Serves 4.

MASHED POTATOES

1½ pounds potatoes	½ teaspoon salt
¼ cup butter	¼ teaspoon pepper
1¼ cups milk	⅛ teaspoon nutmeg

Peel potatoes, quarter and cook in slightly salted water 15 minutes or until tender to fork. Drain, place back on fire with butter and mash thoroughly with masher. Add milk, salt, pepper and nutmeg and beat 5 minutes with wooden fork. Serves 4.

PAN-COOKED POTATOES

1 medium onion, sliced	3 medium tomatoes, peeled and
2 cloves garlic, chopped	cut into pieces, or 1 small
2 tablespoons olive oil	can tomatoes
⅛ pound salt pork,	½ teaspoon salt
diced fine	¼ teaspoon pepper
2 pounds new potatoes,	1 teaspoon chopped basil
peeled and sliced	1 teaspoon chopped parsley

Brown onion and garlic in oil in a large frying pan. Add salt pork and sliced potatoes and continue cooking until potatoes are lightly browned. Add tomatoes, salt, pepper, basil and parsley and cover pan. Cook 20 minutes, or until potatoes are cooked to taste. Serves 6.

POTATOES PARMIGIANA

4 medium potatoes, peeled	½ teaspoon salt
and diced fine	¼ teaspoon pepper
2 tablespoons butter	2 tablespoons butter, melted
1 teaspoon meat extract,	3 tablespoons grated Parmesan
blended in 1 tablespoon	cheese
water	

Cook potatoes in butter 7 minutes, or until tender. Add meat extract and water. Place potatoes and gravy in greased baking dish, sprinkle with salt, pepper, melted butter and cheese and bake in hot oven (400°F.) 10 minutes. Serves 4.

POTATOES PIZZAIOLA

2 pounds potatoes	½ teaspoon salt
2 tablespoons olive oil	½ teaspoon pepper
1 clove garlic	½ teaspoon oregano
3 fresh tomatoes, peeled and	
cut into pieces, or ½	
large can tomatoes	

Parboil potatoes 15 minutes, drain, peel and cut into thin slices. Brown garlic in olive oil. Remove garlic from oil, add tomatoes, salt, pepper and oregano and cook 5 minutes. Add sliced potatoes and cook 10 minutes. Serve immediately. Serves 8.

POTATO ROSETTES

½ recipe for potatoes   1 egg, lightly beaten
duchessa (see index)

Place potatoes in confectionery tube and squeeze out onto greased baking sheet in rounds resembling rosettes. Brush rosettes lightly with egg and bake in hot oven (400°F.) 5 minutes. Serve around meat. Serves 4.

SAUSAGE STUFFED POTATOES

8 medium potatoes   1 tablespoon stock
¾ pound Italian sausage,   1 egg yolk
  sweet or hot   2 tablespoons butter
2 slices bread, soaked in   ¼ teaspoon salt
  water and squeezed dry   ¼ teaspoon pepper (omit if hot
1 tablespoon butter   sausage is used)
1 tablespoon chopped parsley

Boil potatoes with skins on 10 minutes. Drain, peel and with teaspoon scoop out a deep hole for stuffing.

Skin sausage, add bread, butter, parsley, stock and egg yolk, mixing together very well, and stuff potatoes carefully. Place potatoes in greased baking dish, dot with butter, sprinkle with salt and pepper and bake in hot oven (400°F.) 15 minutes. Serve hot. Serves 4.

POTATO SOUFFLE

2 pounds potatoes, peeled   ½ cup light cream
  and quartered   ½ teaspoon salt
½ cup butter   ⅙ teaspoon pepper
⅛ teaspoon nutmeg   2 egg whites, beaten stiff
2 egg yolks

Boil potatoes in slightly salted water 15 minutes, or until tender. Drain and mash well. Add butter, nutmeg, egg yolks, light cream, salt and pepper and mix well. Fold in egg whites and place in greased casserole, the latter large enough to be only two-thirds filled by the potato mixture. Bake in moderate oven (375°F.) 20 minutes. Serve immediately. Serves 6.

POTATO STICKS

4 medium potatoes   salt
2 cups olive oil

Peel potatoes and cut into long, very thin sticks. Place in cold water, drain, dry with towel and fry in hot olive oil until golden and crisp. Sprinkle with salt and serve immediately. Serves 4.

STUFFED POTATOES

4 medium potatoes, peeled
1 medium onion, chopped
1 clove garlic
1 tablespoon olive oil
4 medium tomatoes,
  skinned and chopped
½ teaspoon chopped basil

½ teaspoon chopped parsley
1 tablespoon capers
4 anchovy filets, in pieces
½ teaspoon pepper
¼ pound mozzarella, diced
2 tablespoons olive oil

Scoop out insides of potatoes from the tops. Brown onion and garlic in oil in small saucepan. Add tomatoes, basil, parsley, capers, anchovies and pepper, mix well and cook 20 minutes. Fill potatoes with mixture and add 1 or 2 dices of mozzarella.

Place potatoes, standing up, in greased baking dish. Sprinkle potatoes with olive oil and bake in slow oven (275°F.) 35 minutes. Do not open oven during baking as cold air may cause potatoes to split. Serve immediately. Serves 4.

POTATO SURPRISE

4 medium potatoes
¼ cup butter
2 tablespoons flour
2 cups milk
½ teaspoon salt
¼ teaspoon white pepper

⅛ teaspoon nutmeg
1 egg
1 egg yolk
1 cup Swiss type cheese,
  diced very fine
2 tablespoons melted butter

Parboil potatoes 10 minutes, drain, peel and cut into halves. Scoop out the potato halves and reserve pulp. Melt butter in frying pan, blend in flour, cook 2 minutes and add milk. Mix well, add salt, pepper and nutmeg and cook 5 minutes. Remove from fire and let cool.

When cool, add whole egg and egg yolk and diced cheese and mix very well. Fill the potato half shells with this mixture and cover with potato pulp which was scooped out and reserved. Place stuffed potatoes in greased baking dish, sprinkle with melted butter and bake in moderate oven (375°F.) 25 minutes. Serve immediately. Serves 4.

POTATO TART ALLA TARANTO

3 medium potatoes, boiled
and mashed
1¼ cups flour
¼ teaspoon salt
4 tablespoons olive oil
½ medium can tomatoes,
drained

¼ pound mozzarella cheese, diced
2 tablespoons Parmesan cheese,
grated
¼ teaspoon freshly ground
pepper
1 tablespoon oregano

To mashed potatoes add flour and salt and work together thoroughly. Grease a large shallow casserole and place potato mixture on bottom in a layer about ½ inch thick. Sprinkle well with 2 tablespoons olive oil, add layer of tomatoes, mozzarella cheese, Parmesan cheese and sprinkle with pepper and oregano. Sprinkle with remaining 2 tablespoons olive oil and place in hot oven (400°F.) 30 minutes, or until cheese is light brown. Serves 4 to 6.

POTATO TIMBALE FINANZIERA

2½ pounds potatoes, boiled
and mashed
2 tablespoons grated
Parmesan cheese
1 egg yolk
¼ cup butter
¼ teaspoon salt
1 tablespoon butter
1 cup bread crumbs
1 egg, lightly beaten

½ pound mushrooms, sliced
1 tablespoon butter
½ pound sweet Italian sausage,
skinned and minced
4 chicken livers, sliced thin
1 teaspoon flour
2 tablespoons tomato purée
2 slices prosciutto, slivered
1 hard cooked egg, diced

Mix mashed potatoes with Parmesan, egg yolk, ¼ cup butter and salt.

Butter 1-quart casserole and sprinkle with bread crumbs. Pour lightly beaten egg into casserole and roll it around until bread crumbs in casserole are all wet. Add 1 more layer bread crumbs. Place potato mixture in casserole, leaving a large hole in center, and reserving some of the potato mixture.

Place mushrooms, 1 tablespoon butter, sausage and chicken livers in saucepan and brown thoroughly. Add flour and tomato purée and cook 15 minutes, adding a teaspoon of water, if necessary. Add prosciutto and hard cooked egg.

Remove from fire and place entire mixture in center of potatoes in casserole. Cover with remaining potatoes, dot with butter and place in moderate oven 45 minutes. Remove from oven, let stand 5 minutes and unmold. Serves 4.

POTATOES WITH JACKETS ON

4 large potatoes   1 teaspoon salt

Boil potatoes in enough water to cover, with salt added, 8 minutes. Remove from water and place in moderate oven (375°F.) 30 minutes. Serve with butter. Serves 4.

POTATOES WITH SALT PORK

1 tablespoon olive oil	¼ teaspoon pepper
1 medium onion, sliced	½ teaspoon flour
¼ pound salt pork, diced fine	1 cup stock
1½ pounds potatoes	1 tablespoon chopped parsley
¼ teaspoon salt	

Place olive oil in large frying pan, add onion and brown lightly. Add salt pork and brown until pork is transparent. Peel potatoes and cut into large dices. Sprinkle with salt, pepper and flour, mix well and add stock. Cover frying pan and cook slowly 15 minutes, or until potatoes are done. If sauce should get too thick, add a little more stock. Add parsley and serve. Serves 4.

PUMPKIN

PUMPKIN HUNTER STYLE

½ cup olive oil	½ teaspoon salt
2 cloves garlic	½ teaspoon pepper
1 pound pumpkin, sliced thin and cut into squares	1 teaspoon rosemary

Place olive oil in pan with garlic. Brown garlic and remove. Add pumpkin, salt, pepper and rosemary and cook gently 20 minutes, stirring frequently. Serves 4.

PUMPKIN PUDDING

1 medium can cooked pumpkin	1½ tablespoons flour
1 tablespoon butter	1 cup milk
1 teaspoon salt	3 egg yolks
½ teaspoon pepper	1 tablespoon grated Parmesan cheese
¼ cup butter	

Place pumpkin and butter in saucepan and cook gently until pumpkin is dry. Cool and add salt and pepper. Melt ¼ cup butter, blend in flour, cook 1 minute, add milk, stirring thoroughly and cook until thick. Add sauce to pumpkin and mix well. Add egg yolks, one at a time, mixing well after each addition. Add cheese. Place mixture in greased mold. Place mold over pan of boiling water and cook 45 minutes or until pudding is firm. Turn over onto serving dish. Serves 4 or 5.

SPINACH

SPINACH AND RICOTTA BALLS

1 pound spinach, washed and chopped	2 egg yolks
¾ pound ricotta	2 tablespoons flour
½ teaspoon salt	2 quarts simmering water
2 tablespoons grated Parmesan cheese	¼ cup melted butter
	2 tablespoons grated Parmesan cheese

Cook spinach in 1 cup water 5 minutes. Squeeze spinach dry and mix with ricotta, salt, cheese and egg yolks. When well mixed, shape as very small eggs, dust with flour and drop into simmering water, a few at a time. The little balls will come to the surface of the water. Counting from the time that they rise to the surface, simmer 4 minutes and remove from water. Repeat until all the little balls are cooked. Sprinkle with melted butter and Parmesan and serve immediately. Serves 4.

SPINACH PARMESAN (Number 1)

1 pound spinach, washed and chopped, or 1 package frozen chopped spinach	⅛ teaspoon nutmeg
2 tablespoons butter	2 eggs, lightly beaten
¼ teaspoon salt	3 tablespoons grated Parmesan cheese

Cook spinach in 1 cup water 5 minutes, drain, and chop fine. Place in saucepan with butter, salt and nutmeg and cook 4 minutes, stirring well. Shut off flame and keep pan on hot stove plate. Add eggs, mix well, add Parmesan cheese and continue stirring 2 or 3 minutes. Serve immediately. Serves 4.

SPINACH PARMESAN (Number 2)

1 pound spinach, washed and chopped	½ teaspoon pepper
¼ cup butter	⅛ teaspoon nutmeg
½ teaspoon salt	3 tablespoons grated Parmesan cheese

Place spinach in pan with butter and cook 8 minutes, or until tender. Add salt, pepper, nutmeg and Parmesan cheese and mix well. Serve. Serves 4.

SPINACH PIEDMONTESE STYLE

1 pound washed spinach	½ teaspoon pepper
¼ cup butter	4 anchovy filets, chopped
½ teaspoon salt	½ clove garlic, chopped

Cook spinach in 1 cup water 5 minutes and drain well. Place butter in skillet and brown lightly. Add well-drained spinach, salt, pepper, anchovies and garlic and cook 4 or 5 minutes longer. Serves 4.

SPINACH ROMAN STYLE

1 pound washed spinach	½ teaspoon salt
2 tablespoons leaf lard or	½ teaspoon pepper
bacon drippings	1 tablespoon shelled pine nuts
	1 tablespoon raisins

Cook spinach in 1 cup water 5 minutes and drain well. Melt leaf lard or drippings in saucepan, add spinach, salt and pepper and cook 5 minutes longer. Add nuts and raisins and serve. Serves 4.

SQUASH

FRIED ITALIAN YELLOW SQUASH

4 very thin slices squash, cut	½ teaspoon salt
into 4-inch pieces	1 egg, lightly beaten
½ cup flour	1 cup olive oil

Roll squash in flour, dip into salted egg and fry in hot oil until light brown in color on both sides. Serves 4.

ITALIAN YELLOW SQUASH SICILIAN STYLE

1 pound squash, sliced thin	½ teaspoon salt
2 tablespoons olive oil	½ teaspoon sugar
½ clove garlic, chopped	1 teaspoon chopped mint leaves
1½ tablespoons wine vinegar	

Place squash in skillet with oil and garlic and cook gently until squash is tender. Add vinegar, salt, sugar and mint leaves and cook 2 minutes longer. Serves 4.

STRING BEANS

STRING BEANS AL CRUDO

1 pound string beans	½ teaspoon salt
1 tablespoon leaf lard	¼ teaspoon pepper
1 medium onion, sliced	1½ cups stock or water
1 small can tomatoes	1 teaspoon chopped parsley

Wash and clean beans. Brown onion in leaf lard in skillet. Add to-matoes, salt, pepper and beans, cover skillet and cook beans slowly 40 minutes, or until tender, adding stock or water as needed. Add parsley before serving. Serves 4.

FRIED STRING BEANS

1 pound tender string beans	1 cup olive oil
1 cup flour	salt

Parboil string beans 10 minutes and drain well. Roll in flour and fry in hot olive oil until crisp and golden brown. Sprinkle with salt and serve immediately. Serves 4.

STRING BEAN PUDDING

1 pound string beans	2 eggs, lightly beaten with
2 tablespoons butter	2 tablespoons grated
¼ teaspoon salt	Parmesan cheese
1 cup cream sauce (see	2 tablespoons fine bread crumbs
index)	2 tablespoons butter

Wash string beans and cut into very small pieces. Boil in water 18 minutes and drain. Place beans in saucepan with butter and salt and cook gently 5 minutes. Remove from fire and add cream sauce, eggs and Parmesan.

Grease a 1-quart mold and sprinkle with bread crumbs. Pour in bean mixture, top with more bread crumbs and dot with butter. Bake in hot oven (400°F.) 45 minutes, or until mixture is firm. Remove from oven and let stand 4 minutes before unmolding. Serves 4.

STRING BEAN SOUFFLE

1 pound string beans	2 tablespoons grated Parmesan
2 quarts boiling water	cheese
½ teaspoon salt	4 egg whites
1 cup thick cream sauce	
(see index)	

Wash beans and cook in boiling salted water 20 minutes, or until tender. Drain and pass beans through strainer. Mix with cream sauce and cheese. Beat egg whites until stiff and fold gently into bean mixture. Pour into greased casserole and bake in moderate oven (375°F.) 25 minutes. Serve immediately. Serves 4.

STRING BEAN TIMBALE

1 pound string beans	2 tablespoons stock
3 tablespoons butter	1 cup cream sauce (see index)
½ pound beef or pork, chopped	1 tablespoon grated Parmesan cheese
5 chicken livers, chopped	2 tablespoons bread crumbs
¼ teaspoon salt	2 tablespoons butter

Boil beans in salted water 20 minutes, or until tender, and drain. Place butter, chopped meat and chicken livers in skillet and brown gently. Add salt, stock, cream sauce and cheese and remove from fire. Pour half the beans into greased casserole, cover with meat mixture and place remaining beans on top of meat. Sprinkle with bread crumbs, dot with butter and bake in hot oven (400°F.) 10 minutes. Serves 4.

STRING BEANS WITH PROSCIUTTO

1 pound tender string beans	3 slices prosciutto, shredded
3 tablespoons butter	¼ teaspoon pepper

Wash beans and boil in salted water 20 minutes. Drain well and place in skillet with butter and cook 5 minutes. Add prosciutto and pepper, mix well. Cook 4 or 5 minutes longer and serve. Serves 4.

Swiss Chard

SWISS CHARD GENOA STYLE

1 large bunch Swiss chard	2 eggs, lightly beaten
¼ teaspoon salt	½ teaspoon pepper
¾ cup olive oil	2 tablespoons grated Parmesan cheese
2 medium onions, sliced	
1 tablespoon chopped parsley	½ teaspoon salt
2 cloves garlic	½ cup fine bread crumbs
¼ pound mushrooms, sliced	

Remove stalks from chard, wash and shred. Place in saucepan with ¼ teaspoon salt and no water, cover pan and cook over moderate flame 10 minutes, stirring often. Remove from fire and squeeze dry. Place onions and oil in saucepan and brown onions slightly. Add parsley, garlic, mushrooms and chard, cook 5 minutes, remove from fire and cool. Add eggs, pepper, Parmesan and salt. Grease casserole and sprinkle with some bread crumbs. Pour chard mixture into casserole and top with remaining bread crumbs. Bake in moderate oven (375°F.) 20 minutes. Serve either hot or cold. Serves 4.

TOMATOES

TOMATOES IN SKILLET

4 large tomatoes, halved	½ teaspoon sugar
2 tablespoons olive oil	½ teaspoon chopped basil
½ teaspoon salt	½ teaspoon chopped parsley
½ teaspoon pepper	½ teaspoon chopped mint leaves

Place tomatoes in large greased skillet, cut side up. Sprinkle with oil, salt, pepper, sugar, basil, parsley and mint leaves and cook slowly 10 minutes. Cover skillet and cook 5 minutes longer. Serves 4.

TOMATO SOUFFLE

2 pounds ripe tomatoes, or	4 tablespoons flour
2 large cans tomatoes	2 cups milk
¼ cup butter	2 tablespoons grated Parmesan
1 small onion, sliced	cheese
1 teaspoon crushed basil leaf	¼ pound Swiss type cheese,
½ teaspoon salt	diced
¼ teaspoon pepper	4 egg yolks
½ cup butter	4 egg whites, beaten stiff

Peel fresh tomatoes and cut into pieces. Melt butter, add onion and brown lightly. Add basil, tomatoes, salt and pepper and cook until tomatoes are thick.

Make a cream sauce as follows: Melt butter, blend in flour, add milk and cook slowly until thick and creamy, stirring constantly. Remove from fire, add grated and diced cheese, the tomato sauce and egg yolks and mix well. Fold in gently the egg whites which have been beaten stiff but not dry. Pour into a 1-quart buttered form and bake in moderate oven (375°F.) 1 hour. Remove and serve immediately. Serves 4.

TOMATOES STUFFED WITH BREAD CUBES

4 large tomatoes	½ teaspoon salt
3 slices stale or toasted	½ teaspoon pepper
bread, cubed	¼ teaspoon sugar
1 teaspoon chopped basil	¼ clove garlic, chopped
1 tablespoon chopped parsley	¼ cup olive oil

Cut off tops of tomatoes and scoop out pulp. Strain pulp and save liquid. Fill tomatoes with bread cubes. Sprinkle over the top of each tomato the basil, parsley, salt, pepper, sugar, garlic and some of the olive oil. Pour tomato liquid over each tomato and cover with tomato top. Sprinkle tomatoes with remaining oil and place in well-oiled baking dish. Bake in moderate oven (375°F.) 30 minutes, adding a little water during baking, if necessary. Serves 4.

TOMATOES STUFFED WITH RICE

4 large tomatoes	2 tablespoons olive oil
1 cup rice	¼ clove garlic, chopped
½ teaspoon sugar	½ teaspoon salt
⅛ teaspoon cinnamon	½ teaspoon pepper
1 teaspoon chopped parsley	2 tablespoons olive oil

Split tomatoes, leaving lower part much larger than top part. Scoop out pulp, strain and save liquid.

Mix together rice, sugar, cinamon, parsley, olive oil, garlic, salt and pepper. Stuff lower parts of tomatoes with this mixture, filling to very top. Pour tomato liquid over each stuffed tomato, sprinkle with olive oil and cover each tomato with its own top. Place in well-oiled baking dish, cover and bake in moderate oven (375°F.) 1 hour, or until rice is well cooked. Serves 4.

STUFFED TOMATOES SICILIAN STYLE

4 large tomatoes	2 tablespoons bread crumbs
2 tablespoons olive oil	½ teaspoon salt
1 very small onion, chopped	¼ teaspoon pepper
4 anchovy filets, cut into pieces	⅛ teaspoon nutmeg
½ tablespoon chopped parsley	2 tablespoons bread crumbs
1 tablespoon capers	2 tablespoons olive oil

Cut tops off tomatoes and scoop out centers. Place onion and olive oil in small frying pan and brown onion lightly. Remove from fire and add anchovies, parsley, capers, bread crumbs, salt, pepper and nutmeg, mixing and blending well. Stuff tomatoes. Mix remaining bread crumbs with olive oil and spread over tops of tomatoes.

Place tomatoes in well-oiled baking dish, sprinkle with more oil and bake in moderate oven (375°F.) 30 minutes. Serves 4.

TOMATOES WITH ELBOW MACARONI

4 large tomatoes	1 tablespoon chopped parsley
8 tablespoons elbow macaroni	1 teaspoon chopped basil
½ teaspoon salt	¼ clove garlic, chopped
½ teaspoon pepper	3 tablespoons water
2 tablespoons olive oil	2 tablespoons olive oil

Cut off tops of tomatoes, scoop out pulp and strain, saving liquid and tomato caps. Mix together macaroni, salt, pepper, oil, parsley, basil and garlic. Mix well and stuff tomatoes with mixture. Sprinkle with more oil, cover with tomato caps and place in well-oiled baking dish. Cover bottom of baking dish with water and bake in moderate oven (375°F.) 40 minutes, adding more oil, if needed. Serves 4.

TOMATOES WITH TUNA

4 large tomatoes	½ teaspoon chopped basil
½ teaspoon salt	2 slices bread, soaked in water
½ teaspoon pepper	and squeezed dry
1 medium can tuna fish,	¼ clove garlic, chopped
grated	¼ teaspoon oregano
4 anchovy filets, chopped	2 tablespoons butter
1 tablespoon chopped parsley	

Cut tops off tomatoes and scoop out pulp. Strain pulp and mix with salt, pepper, tuna, anchovies, parsley, basil, bread, garlic, oregano and butter. Mix well and stuff tomatoes with mixture. Place tomatoes in well-oiled baking dish and bake in moderate oven (375°F.) 20 min-utes, adding more oil, if needed. Serves 4.

TURNIPS

WHITE TURNIPS IN SUGAR

3 tablespoons butter	½ teaspoon pepper
4 small white turnips,	1 teaspoon sugar
skinned and sliced thin	1 teaspoon flour
½ teaspoon salt	½ cup stock

Melt butter in pan, add turnips, salt, pepper and sugar and sprinkle with flour. Mix well, add stock and cook over low flame 18 minutes, or until tender. Serves 4.

ZUCCHINI

ZUCCHINI AU GRATIN

4 small zucchini	2 tablespoons butter
½ teaspoon salt	4 tablespoons grated Parmesan
1 cup flour	cheese
1 cup olive oil or	2 tablespoons fine bread crumbs
vegetable oil	½ cup meat sauce (see index)

Cut zucchini into halves crosswise and cut into thin slices. Place slices on shallow dish, sprinkle with salt, tilt dish to one side and let stand in this manner 1 hour. Dry, flour and fry in oil until light brown.

Place in shallow baking dish, dot with butter, sprinkle with cheese and crumbs and add meat sauce. Bake in hot oven (400°F.) 15 minutes. Serves 4.

ZUCCHINI GENOA STYLE

4 medium zucchini, cut into thin strips	½ teaspoon pepper
	½ clove garlic, chopped
3 tablespoons olive oil	1 tablespoon chopped parsley
½ teaspoon salt	1 teaspoon oregano

Place zucchini in skillet with oil and cook over high flame 10 minutes. Add salt, pepper, garlic, parsley and oregano, lower flame and cook 5 minutes longer. Serves 4.

ZUCCHINI IN CASSEROLE

4 medium zucchini	2 tablespoons grated Parmesan
1 tablespoon butter	cheese
1½ cups cold cream sauce (see index)	¼ teaspoon salt
	¼ teaspoon pepper
2 eggs, lightly beaten	

Slice zucchini and fry in butter until light brown, taking care not to overcook. Mix together cream sauce, eggs, Parmesan, salt and pepper and fold in fried zucchini.

Butter and flour a casserole, pour into it the zucchini mixture and place casserole in pan of water in moderate oven (375°F.) 40 minutes. Let stand 5 minutes after removing from oven before turning out on serving dish. Serves 4.

ZUCCHINI IN SKILLET

4 medium zucchini	1 teaspoon salt
1 small onion, sliced	½ teaspoon pepper
2 tablespoons olive oil	1 bay leaf
2 fresh tomatoes, peeled and cut into pieces	½ teaspoon basil leaves

Clean zucchini and slice into 1-inch pieces. Brown onion a little in olive oil in skillet, add tomatoes and cook 5 minutes. Add zucchini, salt and pepper and cook gently 20 minutes, or until tender, adding a little water if necessary. Add bay leaf and basil leaves and cook 2 minutes longer. Serves 4.

MARINATED ZUCCHINI

4 large zucchini
1 cup olive oil
1 clove garlic, chopped
1 tablespoon chopped basil
  leaves

1 tablespoon chopped parsley
½ teaspoon salt
½ teaspoon pepper
1 cup wine vinegar

Cut zucchini into 1-inch slices, fry in hot oil until light brown and drain on paper. In a casserole place 1 layer fried zucchini, dot with chopped garlic, basil and parsley, sprinkle with salt and pepper and repeat procedure until all zucchini are used. Boil vinegar 5 minutes and pour over zucchini. Let marinate at least 12 hours, drain and serve. (The zucchini will keep fresh in this marinade 15 days at least.) Serves 8.

ZUCCHINI PARMESAN (Number 1)

8 small zucchini
½ pound chopped beef
1 egg yolk
1 slice bread, soaked in
  water and squeezed dry
½ teaspoon salt
½ teaspoon pepper
1 tablespoon grated Parmesan
  cheese

⅛ teaspoon nutmeg
½ black truffle, sliced (optional)
1 cup flour
1 egg, lightly beaten
1 tablespoon melted butter
1 cup tomato sauce (see index)
2 tablespoons grated Parmesan
  cheese

Scoop out insides of zucchini with apple corer. Mix together beef, egg yolk, bread, salt, pepper, cheese, nutmeg and truffle and fill the zucchini with this mixture. Cut zucchini into 2 pieces crosswise, flour, dip into beaten egg and fry in drippings or oil until light brown.

Place zucchini in greased baking dish, sprinkle with butter, tomato sauce and Parmesan cheese and bake in moderate oven (375°F.) 10 minutes. Serves 4.

ZUCCHINI PARMESAN (Number 2)

3 large zucchini
1 tablespoon butter

½ teaspoon salt
3 tablespoons grated Parmesan
  cheese

Parboil zucchini 10 minutes. Slice and place in buttered baking dish. Sprinkle with butter, salt and Parmesan and bake in moderate oven (375°F.) 5 minutes, or until cheese has melted. Serve immediately. Serves 4.

ZUCCHINI PIE

4 large zucchini	3 tablespoons grated Parmesan
2 tablespoons flour	cheese
1 cup olive oil	1 cup tomato sauce (see index)
	½ pound mozzarella, sliced thin

Cut zucchini into 1-inch slices, sprinkle with flour and fry in olive oil until light brown. In greased casserole place 1 layer of fried zucchini, sprinkle with Parmesan cheese, add a little of the sauce, cover with thin layers of mozzarella and repeat procedure until zucchini and other ingredients are all used, ending with mozzarella. Bake in moderate oven (375°F.) 30 minutes. Serves 4.

STUFFED ZUCCHINI

8 small zucchini	½ teaspoon pepper
½ pound chopped beef	1 tablespoon leaf lard
1 egg	2 tablespoons butter
2 tablespoons grated Parmesan	1 very small onion, chopped
cheese	1 tablespoon chopped parsley
1 slice bread, soaked in	1 slice lean bacon, chopped
water and squeezed dry	2 tablespoons tomato paste
2 slices prosciutto, shredded	1 cup water
½ teaspoon salt	

With an apple corer remove inside of zucchini, taking care not to break the skin. Mix together well the beef, egg, Parmesan, bread, prosciutto, salt and pepper and stuff zucchini with this mixture.

Melt leaf lard and butter in a large skillet, add onion, parsley and bacon and brown well. Add tomato paste and water and cook 5 minutes. Place zucchini in this sauce. If the sauce is not enough to cover zucchini, add water. Bake in moderate oven (375°F.) 30 minutes. Serves 4.

STUFFED ZUCCHINI LIGURIA STYLE

8 small zucchini	1 egg yolk
1 slice bread, soaked in	1 tablespoon grated Parmesan
water and squeezed dry	cheese
½ teaspoon salt	1 slice lean prosciutto, diced
½ teaspoon pepper	⅛ pound mushrooms, diced
½ teaspoon oregano	2 tablespoons olive oil
2 tablespoons cold cream	1 egg, lightly beaten
sauce (see index)	¼ teaspoon salt

Boil zucchini 4 minutes in water, cut into halves lengthwise, scoop out pulp and save. Mix together pulp from zucchini, bread, salt, pepper, oregano, cream sauce, egg yolk, cheese, prosciutto and mushrooms.

Place zucchini halves in greased baking dish and fill each zucchini half with some of the prepared mixture. Sprinkle with olive oil, brush with beaten egg and a little salt. Bake in moderate oven (375°F.) 30 minutes. Serves 4.

ZUCCHINI WITH MINT

4 medium zucchini	½ teaspoon pepper
2 tablespoons olive oil	1 teaspoon chopped mint
½ teaspoon salt	leaves

Parboil zucchini 10 minutes and cut into strips. Place in skillet with oil, salt, pepper and mint and cook 5 minutes, stirring frequently. Serves 4.

ZUCCHINI WITH TUNA FISH

4 medium zucchini	1 tablespoon olive oil
2 slices bread, soaked in water and squeezed dry	1 clove garlic
	1 small can tomato purée
1 tablespoon olive oil	½ teaspoon salt
1 tablespoon chopped parsley	¼ teaspoon pepper
½ teaspoon pepper	½ cup water or stock
1 medium can tuna fish, grated	

Scoop out zucchini with apple corer. Mix together bread, olive oil, parsley, pepper and tuna fish and fill zucchini with this stuffing.

Brown garlic in oil, add tomato purée, salt, pepper and stock and cook 15 minutes. Place stuffed zucchini in this sauce and bake in moderate oven (375°F.) 45 minutes, or until zucchini are tender to touch. Serves 4.

12. Salads

VEGETABLE SALADS

GYPSY SALAD

¼ cup olive oil
1 tablespoon wine vinegar
½ teaspoon prepared mustard
2 anchovy filets, chopped
½ heart escarole, shredded fine

½ heart endive, shredded fine
1 heart fennel, cut into small pieces
2 radishes, sliced

Mix well oil, vinegar, mustard and chopped anchovies. Pour over mixed greens in salad bowl. Mix well. Serves 2.

SALAD MUSETTA

½ cup olive oil
¼ teaspoon salt
¼ teaspoon pepper
1 tablespoon wine vinegar
1 tablespoon mayonnaise
1 celery heart, in pieces
1 fennel heart, in pieces
2 small boiled potatoes, diced

⅛ pound Swiss cheese, diced
4 artichoke hearts in oil
4 mushrooms in oil
head of 1 head chicory, shredded fine
2 anchovy filets, in pieces
1 teaspoon capers
1 hard cooked egg, sliced

Mix olive oil with salt, pepper, vinegar and mayonnaise. Place other ingredients in salad bowl, pour oil mixture over them and mix gently but thoroughly. Serves 4.

SALAD NEAPOLITAN STYLE

1 medium cauliflower
2 tablespoons olive oil
1 tablespoon wine vinegar
½ teaspoon salt
½ teaspoon pepper

6 anchovy filets
1 tablespoon capers
12 black olives, pitted and cut into pieces

Cut cauliflower flowerlets from head and cook lightly in slightly salted water about 10 minutes. Drain, rinse in cold water and place in salad bowl. Add all other ingredients and mix together well without breaking flowerlets. Serves 6.

RED BEAN SALAD

1 large can red beans,
  drained
½ cup vinegar
½ teaspoon marjoram
½ teaspoon basil
1 teaspoon parsley
2 celery stalks, diced
1 very small onion, minced

1 clove garlic, minced
1 medium can tuna fish,
  in pieces
2 anchovy filets, in pieces
½ cup olive oil
½ teaspoon salt
½ teaspoon pepper

Combine ingredients and let stand in salad bowl at least 4 hours, stirring often. Serves 4.

SICILIAN SALAD

4 hard ripe tomatoes
½ clove garlic, chopped
¼ cup olive oil
½ teaspoon salt

½ teaspoon pepper
½ teaspoon wine vinegar
1 tablespoon basil leaves

Wash tomatoes and cut into large pieces. Sprinkle with garlic, oil, salt, pepper and vinegar and add basil leaves. Chill 5 minutes and serve. Serves 4.

SICILIAN OLIVE SALAD*
(Olive Schiacciate)

2 pounds green Sicilian
  olives (imported)
1 head celery, diced
1 cup capers
2 cloves garlic, sliced
1 small onion, sliced
1 cup olive oil
1 teaspoon freshly ground
  black pepper

2 large red vinegar peppers, in
  pieces
1 carrot, sliced thin
salt, if needed
½ teaspoon fennel seed
1 tablespoon wine vinegar,
  if desired

Pound each olive until broken so that the pits show, but do not remove the pits. Place in large bowl and add all ingredients. The salt must be added only if needed, because the olives vary in saltiness. Mix well and long, cover and let stand in cool place at least 24 hours before serving.

These olives are a fine addition to an antipasto, or will be welcomed with meats, poultry and vegetables. A cup of these olives added to any Italian salad will do wonders. They keep in jars in the refrigerator for an indefinite time.

TYPICAL ITALIAN SALAD*

1 clove garlic
¼ cup olive oil
½ teaspoon salt
½ teaspoon pepper
1 tablespoon wine vinegar
1 small head crisp lettuce,
   shredded

2 firm tomatoes, cut into pieces
½ cucumber, peeled and sliced
4 radishes, sliced
¼ green pepper, cut into small
   pieces

Rub garlic over sides of salad bowl. Mix together oil, salt, pepper and vinegar. Place greens in salad bowl and pour dressing over them. Mix very well 5 minutes. Serves 4.

GARLIC BREAD*

1 long loaf Italian or
   French bread
2 cloves garlic

½ cup good olive oil
   salt and pepper to taste

Cut bread into 1-inch slices and toast in oven. While hot, rub with garlic on one side of each slice, brush with olive oil, sprinkle with salt and pepper and serve hot with salads.

FRUIT SALAD

FRUIT SALAD

1 cup fresh or canned
   pineapple, diced
2 bananas, sliced
1 orange, peeled and cut
   into pieces
2 sweet apples, peeled,
   cored and diced

4 walnuts, quartered
6 lettuce leaves
½ cup heavy cream
½ teaspoon sugar
⅛ teaspoon salt
1 tablespoon lemon juice

Mix fruit together. Line fruit bowl with lettuce leaves and place fruit in center.

Mix cream, sugar, salt and lemon juice and pour over fruit. Chill 5 minutes before serving. Serves 4.

FISH SALADS

SALAD HARLEQUIN

1 small smoked herring, skinned, boned and cut into pieces	2 cooked potatoes, diced
	2 cooked beets, sliced
	⅛ teaspoon salt
3 small gherkins, sliced	½ teaspoon pepper
8 black olives, pitted and cut into pieces	1 teaspoon prepared mustard
	3 tablespoons heavy cream
2 hard cooked eggs, quartered	juice of ½ lemon

Place all ingredients in salad bowl and mix lightly but thoroughly. Serves 4.

SHRIMP SALAD

¼ head lettuce, shredded	2 tablespoons olive oil
2 boiled potatoes, sliced	1 teaspoon wine vinegar
1 tablespoon capers	2 tablespoons mayonnaise
2 anchovy filets, chopped	¼ teaspoon salt
10 large shrimp, sliced	¼ teaspoon pepper

Line salad bowl with lettuce, add potatoes, capers, anchovies and shrimp and mix together well.

Combine oil, vinegar, mayonnaise, salt and pepper and pour over salad. Serves 2.

Other salad recipes will be found in Chapter 1.

13. Sauces

AROMATIC SAUCE WITH ANCHOVY PASTE

2 tablespoons butter
1 tablespoon flour
1½ cups fish stock or water
1 teaspoon meat extract
3 teaspoons anchovy paste

¼ cup butter
2 sweet gherkins, chopped
½ tablespoon capers
1 tablespoon chopped parsley
⅛ teaspoon pepper

Melt 2 tablespoons butter in saucepan, blend in flour and cook 1 minute. Add fish stock or water and meat extract and cook until slightly thickened. Remove from fire and keep warm. Blend together well the anchovy paste and butter and add to sauce a little at a time, beating with rotary beater 1 minute after each addition. Add gherkins, capers, parsley and pepper. Serve on fish. Makes 2½ cups.

BAGNA CAUDA (Hot Bath Sauce)

1 cup butter
4 tablespoons olive oil
4 cloves garlic, minced

6 anchovy filets, chopped
⅛ teaspoon salt
1 small truffle, sliced thin

Heat butter, oil and garlic in top of double boiler until butter is melted and oil is hot. Shut off fire but keep on stove over hot water. Add filets of anchovies, salt and truffle. Keep warm 20 minutes and serve on vegetables or boiled meats. Makes 1½ cups.

CAPER SAUCE FOR FISH*

2 tablespoons butter
1 tablespoon flour
¼ teaspoon salt
¼ teaspoon pepper

2 tablespoons stock
2 tablespoons capers in vinegar
1 teaspoon vinegar

Melt 1 tablespoon butter, blend in flour, cook until slightly brown and add remaining butter. Add salt, pepper and stock and cook until slightly thickened. Add capers and vinegar and mix well. Makes enough sauce for 1 pound of fish.

CRABMEAT SAUCE

3 tablespoons olive oil
½ clove garlic
3 cups canned tomatoes
1 green pepper, chopped fine

½ teaspoon salt
¼ teaspoon pepper
13-ounce can crabmeat
1 egg, well beaten

Place oil in skillet, add garlic and brown slightly. Add tomatoes gradually, stirring well, and cook until creamy and smooth, stirring constantly. Add green pepper, salt, pepper, crabmeat and, last of all, the egg. Cook 2 minutes. Use on spaghetti. Enough for 1 pound spaghetti.

CREAM SAUCE

½ cup butter   1 quart milk
6 tablespoons flour   1 teaspoon salt

Melt butter over very low flame, blend in flour, cook 2 minutes, stirring well, add milk gradually and salt and bring to boiling point. Cook at a simmer until thickened, stirring constantly. Makes 5 cups.

THICK CREAM SAUCE

¼ cup butter   ¼ teaspoon salt
¼ cup flour   dash nutmeg
1¼ cups milk

Melt butter and blend in flour until smooth. Add milk gradually, salt and nutmeg and simmer, stirring constantly, until thickened. Makes 1¾ cups thick cream sauce.

SAUCE GOURMET

½ cup butter   ½ teaspoon meat extract,
2 egg yolks   dissolved in
⅛ teaspoon salt   2 tablespoons warm water

Melt butter over very low fire and add to egg yolks, beating constantly with wire beater until well mixed. Add salt and diluted meat extract and continue beating 5 minutes. Serve on any roasted meat. Makes about 1 cup.

GREEN SAUCE

2 anchovy filets, chopped   1 very small boiled potato,
1 tablespoon chopped parsley   mashed
1 tablespoon capers, chopped   ¼ clove garlic, chopped
3 very small vinegar pickles,   ¼ small onion, grated
  chopped   2 tablespoons olive oil
                                1 tablespoon vinegar

Mix all ingredients except vinegar with oil, beating with beater 5 minutes. Add vinegar. Makes excellent sauce for fish or cold meat. Makes 1¼ cups.

HOT PIQUANT SAUCE

¼ pound prosciutto, sliced
   very thin and chopped fine
1 very small onion, chopped
2 sprigs parsley, minced
1 stalk celery, chopped
1 clove
1 bay leaf
½ clove garlic, chopped
⅛ teaspoon salt

⅛ teaspoon pepper
1 cup vinegar
1 cup stock
1 teaspoon potato flour, in thin
   paste in 1 teaspoon water
1 teaspoon prepared mustard
2 tablespoons capers
2 teaspoons butter

Place prosciutto, onion, parsley, celery, clove, bay leaf, garlic, salt, pepper and vinegar in saucepan; cover and simmer until vinegar is reduced to ⅓ original amount.

Heat stock in another pan, add potato flour and cook slowly, stirring constantly, until thickened. Strain vinegar mixture and add to stock. Add mustard and capers. Keep sauce warm but not boiling, add butter, mix well and serve on cold meats. Makes 1½ cups.

MEAT SAUCE*

4 thin slices salt pork
1 large onion, chopped
1 carrot
2 stalks celery
¼ cup butter
1 pound lean beef, cut
   into slices

¼ teaspoon salt
⅛ teaspoon pepper
3 cloves
4 cups cold water
4 bouillon cubes, dissolved in
   1¼ quarts boiling stock or
   water

Place salt pork in large saucepan, add onion, carrot, celery, butter, slices of beef, salt, pepper and cloves and cook over medium fire until meat is well browned. Add 1 cup cold water and continue cooking until water is absorbed. Add water in this manner 3 times. When water has been evaporated for fourth time, add the boiling stock or water containing the bouillon cubes. Cover. Simmer 5 hours, strain and cool, removing fat which floats on top. This meat sauce may be used for many purposes. Makes approximately 3 cups sauce.

PIZZAIOLA SAUCE

2 tablespoons olive oil
1 clove garlic, sliced
1 medium can tomatoes
¼ teaspoon salt

¼ teaspoon pepper
½ teaspoon oregano
1 teaspoon chopped parsley

Brown garlic in oil, add tomatoes, salt and pepper and cook over high flame 15 minutes. Add oregano and parsley. Serve on steaks, chops or fish. Makes 1 cup.

TOMATO SAUCE

3 tablespoons olive oil	1 medium can tomato purée
½ stalk celery, finely chopped	½ teaspoon salt
1 small onion, chopped	½ teaspoon pepper
1 teaspoon parsley, minced	½ teaspoon basil leaf, minced
1 clove garlic	½ teaspoon oregano
1 large can Italian tomatoes	1 bay leaf

Place oil, celery, onion, parsley and garlic in saucepan and brown lightly. Add tomatoes and tomato purée, salt and pepper and simmer gently for about 45 minutes. Add the basil, oregano and bay leaf. Cook for 10 minutes longer. Makes sufficient sauce for 1 pound of spaghetti or macaroni.

Variation: ⅛ pound butter may be substituted for the olive oil, if preferred.

VENETIAN SAUCE FOR FISH

½ cup butter	½ cup fish stock
1 tablespoon flour	⅛ teaspoon white pepper
½ cup meat stock	2 teaspoons chopped parsley

Melt half the butter in small saucepan, blend in flour well, add meat stock and fish stock, mixing well, and simmer 5 minutes. Add pepper and remaining butter gradually, beating constantly with wire beater. When all the butter is melted and well mixed, add parsley and serve on boiled fish. Makes 1½ cups.

WHITE SAUCE FOR VEGETABLES

½ cup butter	½ cup vinegar
1 tablespoon flour	3 peppercorns
1 cup milk	2 tablespoons heavy cream

Melt half the butter in small saucepan, blend in flour, add milk gradually and cook over low fire, stirring constantly until slightly thickened. Remove from fire and keep warm.

Place vinegar and peppercorns in another small pan and boil gently until reduced half in quantity. Strain vinegar and add to white sauce. Add remaining butter a little at a time, stirring constantly, then add cream. Mix well and serve. Makes 1½ cups.

WHITE WINE SAUCE FOR FISH

¼ cup butter	½ cup light cream
1 tablespoon flour	⅛ teaspoon salt
1 cup fish broth	⅛ teaspoon pepper
¼ cup white wine	

Melt butter, blend in flour well, add fish broth and wine and simmer 5 minutes. Add light cream slowly, mixing constantly. Add salt and pepper and serve on boiled fish. Makes 2 cups.

CHOPPED MEAT SAUCE FOR SPAGHETTI*

½ pound each of beef and pork, chopped together
1 tablespoon olive oil
1 clove garlic
½ medium onion, chopped
1 teaspoon chopped parsley
1 medium can tomatoes

2 small cans tomato purée
⅛ teaspoon salt
⅛ teaspoon pepper
½ teaspoon chopped basil
2 bay leaves
1 tablespoon butter

Place chopped meat, oil, garlic, onion and parsley in saucepan and brown slowly, stirring frequently to prevent meat from cooking in lumps. Remove garlic as soon as browned. Add tomatoes, tomato purée, salt and pepper, cover pan and simmer 1 hour. Add basil, bay leaves and cook 1 minute longer. Remove from fire and add butter. Makes enough sauce for 1 pound spaghetti or other forms of macaroni.

SPAGHETTI SAUCE HOME STYLE

1 tablespoon lard or butter
½ medium onion, minced
1 stalk celery, chopped fine
1 carrot, chopped
⅛ pound bacon or salt pork, chopped fine
½ clove garlic

2 teaspoons chopped parsley
3 tablespoons tomato paste
1 cup water
¼ teaspoon salt
⅛ teaspoon pepper
½ teaspoon sugar (if desired)

Place butter, onion, celery, carrot, salt pork, garlic and parsley in saucepan and brown slowly 10 minutes, adding 1 tablespoon water if necessary. When mixture is well browned and the pork fat is melted, add tomato paste which has been diluted in 1 cup water. Add salt and pepper and simmer gently 30 minutes. Add sugar, if desired. Makes enough sauce for 1 pound of spaghetti.

JIFFY SPAGHETTI SAUCE*

1 small can tomato purée
1 tablespoon water

¼ cup butter

Heat purée in small saucepan, add water and butter and simmer 1 minute. Serve on spaghetti. Makes enough for ½ pound spaghetti.

SAUSAGE SPAGHETTI SAUCE*

1 pound Italian sausage, sweet or hot as preferred	1 medium can tomatoes
2 tablespoons water	2 small cans tomato purée
1 medium onion, chopped	¼ teaspoon salt
1 stalk celery, chopped	⅛ teaspoon pepper (omit if hot sausage is used)
1 teaspoon chopped parsley	2 bay leaves

Prick sausage with needle and place in saucepan with water. Cook until water evaporates and sausage begins to fry. Add onion, celery and parsley and brown sausage well, turning often. Add tomatoes, tomato purée, salt and pepper, cover pan and simmer 1 hour and 15 minutes or until sausage is tender to fork. Add bay leaves, cook 1 minute and serve. Makes enough for 1 pound spaghetti or other macaroni, or ¼ pound rice.

TUNA FISH SPAGHETTI SAUCE*

1 medium can grated tuna fish	⅛ teaspoon pepper
1 clove garlic, chopped	1 large can tomatoes
1 tablespoon chopped parsley	1 small can tomato purée
1 tablespoon olive oil	⅓ teaspoon oregano
¼ teaspoon salt	½ teaspoon chopped basil

Brown tuna fish, garlic and parsley in oil over gentle fire 10 minutes. Add salt, pepper, tomatoes and tomato purée and simmer 1 hour. Add oregano and basil and cook 5 minutes. Serve over spaghetti or fine noodles. Makes enough for 1 pound spaghetti.

SPAGHETTI SAUCE WITH MEATBALLS*

½ pound each of beef and pork, chopped together	¼ teaspoon salt
1 tablespoon grated Roman cheese	⅛ teaspoon pepper
	3 tablespoons lard or olive or vegetable oil
4 slices bread, soaked in water and squeezed dry	1 medium can tomatoes
1 tablespoon chopped parsley	2 small cans tomato purée
1 egg	¼ teaspoon salt
½ teaspoon grated onion	⅛ teaspoon pepper
¼ clove garlic, chopped	2 bay leaves
	½ teaspoon chopped sweet basil
	¼ cup butter

Place chopped meat, cheese, bread, parsley, egg, grated onion, garlic, salt and pepper in mixing bowl. Mix together thoroughly and shape into small balls. Place lard or oil in frying pan and fry meat balls over brisk fire 5 minutes on each side or until well browned.

Place tomatoes and tomato purée in saucepan, bring to a boil and add meat balls. Add salt and pepper and simmer 1 hour. Add bay leaves, basil, and butter. Pour sauce over spaghetti or other macaroni, place meat balls around spaghetti and serve. Makes enough for 1 pound spaghetti or macaroni.

WHITE SPAGHETTI SAUCE*

¼ pound bacon, cut into small pieces

1 clove garlic, chopped or ground

½ teaspoon coarsely ground pepper

¼ cup grated Roman cheese

Fry bacon, garlic and pepper together until bacon is crisp. Spread over spaghetti and sprinkle with cheese. Makes enough for ½ pound spaghetti.

Dessert sauces will be found in Chapter 14. See also Chapter 9 and index for additional spaghetti sauces.

14. *Desserts*

CAKES AND COOKIES

AMARETTI ORESTANO
(Italian Macaroons)

½ pound almonds	2 egg whites
1 cup sugar	½ teaspoon almond extract

Blanch almonds and place in warm oven 5 minutes to dry completely. Chop almonds very fine until reduced to a powder. Add sugar and mix well. Beat egg whites until stiff but not dry and add to almonds and sugar. Add almond extract and blend all together gently but thoroughly.

Butter and flour a baking sheet and drop batter on baking sheet by spoonfuls. Leave a space of 1 inch between cookies, shaping spoonfuls of batter into ovals. Sprinkle with confectioners' sugar. let stand 2 hours and bake in moderate oven (375°F.) 5 minutes, or until delicately brown in color. Makes 14.

BISCOTTI AI PIGNOLI
(Biscuits with Pine Nuts)

1½ cups sugar	2⅛ cups pastry flour
4 eggs	2 tablespoons confectioners'
¼ teaspoon grated lemon	sugar
rind	3 tablespoons pine nuts

Place sugar and eggs in top of double boiler, over hot but not boiling water, and beat until egg mixture is lukewarm. Remove from over hot water and continue beating until foaming and cool. Add lemon rind and flour slowly and blend in gently.

Drop by teaspoonfuls on buttered and floured baking sheet, leaving a space of 1 inch between them. Sprinkle with confectioners' sugar and pine nuts. Let stand 10 minutes and bake in moderate oven (375°F.) 15 minutes. This recipe makes about 40 cookies.

BISCOTTI ALL' ANACI (Anise Biscuits)

2 eggs	1¼ cups pastry flour, sifted
⅝ cup sugar	1 teaspoon anise seeds

Place eggs and sugar in bowl and beat well 10 minutes. Add flour slowly, blending gently and thoroughly. Add anise seeds. Butter and

If the recipe calls for pastry flour, cake flour can be substituted.

flour a loaf pan 4 inches wide, pour in batter and bake in moderate oven (375°F.) 20 minutes.

Remove from pan, leaving oven on, cut loaf into 1-inch slices and place slices on buttered baking dish. Place again in oven. Brown slices first on one side and then on the other. Browning will take about 5 minutes for each side. Makes about 20 biscuits.

ERITREA TART

1½ pounds shelled almonds	1½ cups butter, creamed
1 cup sugar	½ teaspoon vanilla extract
1 egg	1 teaspoon potato flour
4 egg yolks	6 egg whites, beaten stiff
5 squares cooking chocolate	

Toast almonds, chop very fine and grind to powder. Add sugar and mix well. Add 1 egg and 4 egg yolks and blend into smooth paste. Melt chocolate over very low flame and add to creamed butter, mixing very well until thoroughly blended. Add to almond mixture. Add vanilla, potato flour and stiff egg whites and blend gently but thoroughly. Pour into a greased and floured fairly deep 12-inch cake pan. Bake in moderate oven (375°F.) 1 hour. Serves 12.

FRIED RICOTTA

½ pound macaroons	1 egg, lightly beaten
1 pound ricotta	1 cup bread crumbs
¼ teaspoon cinnamon	1 cup butter
2 eggs	

Mash macaroons very fine, add ricotta, cinnamon and eggs and mix well. Shape into small balls, dip into beaten egg, roll in bread crumbs and fry in hot butter until golden. Serves 6.

GENOA TART

1½ cups sugar	1 teaspoon grated lemon rind
5 eggs	1¼ cups pastry flour, sifted

Place sugar, eggs and lemon rind in saucepan, place over very low flame and beat with rotary beater until lukewarm. Remove from fire and continue beating until cold and foaming. Sprinkle flour into egg mixture slowly, stirring constantly with wooden spoon.

Pour into a buttered and floured 18-inch cake pan and bake in moderate oven (375°F.) 40 minutes. Turn over on serving dish and sprinkle with powdered sugar.

If the recipe calls for pastry flour, cake flour can be substituted.

GNOCCHI DI LATTE ROMAN STYLE
(Milk Gnocchi)

6 egg yolks	2 cups milk
3 tablespoons flour	dash nutmeg
1 tablespoon cornstarch	4 tablespoons grated Parmesan
1 tablespoon sugar	cheese
1 tablespoon potato flour	1½ teaspoons cinnamon
¼ teaspoon salt	¼ cup butter, melted

Mix together egg yolks, flour, cornstarch, sugar, potato flour and salt, add milk and nutmeg, and mix well. Place over low flame and continue stirring about 10 minutes, or until mixture is thick and smooth.

Wet a smooth surface or a large cake pan, spread the mixture over it about ½ inch thick and let cool completely. When cool, cut into small squares about 1 inch across and place in layers on buttered baking dish. Sprinkle each layer with Parmesan cheese, cinnamon and melted butter. Bake in moderate oven (375°F.) 20 minutes, or until golden in color. Serve hot. Serves 6.

BOCCA DI DAMA (Lady's Mouth)

¼ cup shelled almonds	1¾ cups sugar
¼ cup sugar	1¾ cups pastry flour, sifted
1 egg, lightly beaten	½ teaspoon grated lemon rind
7 eggs, at room temperature	¼ teaspoon cinnamon
3 egg yolks, at room	¼ cup chopped candied orange
temperature	peel

Place almonds in saucepan with a little water and bring to a boil. Remove from fire and cool. Remove almond skins, dry well and chop and pound to a fine paste. Add sugar and 1 egg and mix well until a smooth paste is obtained.

Place eggs, egg yolks and 1¾ cups sugar in top of double boiler and place over hot, but not boiling, water. Beat eggs and sugar until mixture is lukewarm. Remove from over hot water and continue beating until yellow and very thick. Add almond mixture and sprinkle in flour, a little at a time, blending flour in thoroughly. Add lemon rind, cinnamon, and candied orange peel and mix thoroughly.

Butter and flour a deep 12-inch cake pan and pour in cake batter. The batter should not fill the pan more than ⅔ full. Bake in moderate oven (375°F.) 40 minutes.

If the recipe calls for pastry flour, cake flour can be substituted.

MADDALENA CAKE

4 eggs
2 egg yolks
1½ cups sugar
1 cup pastry flour

½ cup potato flour
¼ cup butter, melted
½ teaspoon grated lemon rind

Place eggs, egg yolks and sugar in top of double boiler, place over hot but not boiling water and beat with rotary beater until lukewarm. Remove from over water and continue beating until cool and thick.

Sift the two flours together 3 times and add gradually to egg mixture, mixing well. Add melted butter and lemon rind. Pour into a buttered and floured 12-inch cake pan and bake in moderate oven (375°F.) 45 minutes.

MARGHERITA TART

6 egg yolks
1¾ cups confectioners' sugar
6 egg whites

1⅓ cups potato flour
½ cup butter, melted
1 teaspoon grated lemon rind

Combine egg yolks and sugar and beat until yellow and foaming. Beat egg whites until they stand in peaks. Fold together yolks and whites gently and add potato flour gradually, mixing well but gently. Add melted butter and lemon rind.

Butter and flour a 10-inch cake pan, pour in batter and bake in moderate oven (375°F.) 30 minutes. Turn over on cake rack and cool.

MARITOZZI

1 envelope dry yeast, in 2 tablespoons lukewarm water
2 cups pastry flour, sifted
2 tablespoons lukewarm water
¼ teaspoon salt
2 tablespoons olive oil

2½ tablespoons sugar
1 tablespoon chopped pine nuts or chopped walnuts
3 tablespoons seedless raisins
1 tablespoon candied orange peel, cut fine
1 tablespoon sugar
1 teaspoon water

Soak yeast in 2 tablespoons lukewarm water 5 minutes, add 2 tablespoons flour and 1 tablespoon water, mix well and let stand in warm place 15 minutes, or until double in bulk.

Place remaining flour on pastry board, form a well in center and add yeast dough, 1 tablespoon water, salt and olive oil, kneading well to make a soft, pliable dough. Continue to knead and when dough does not stick to board or fingers, add sugar and work in well. Sprinkle dough with a little flour, shape into a ball and let stand, covered, in warm place 1 hour.

If the recipe calls for pastry flour, cake flour can be substituted.

Return dough to floured board, add nuts, raisins and orange peel and mix well so that fruit and nuts will be well distributed. Roll dough into a thick tube and cut into 12 slices and shape each slice into an egg-shaped ball. Place on buttered baking sheet about 3 inches apart and let stand, covered, in warm place 3 hours, or until puffy.

Bake in very hot oven (450°F.) 7 minutes. While they are baking, mix together sugar and water. Remove cakes from oven, brush with sugar and water mixture and return to a cooling oven for a few minutes. Makes 12 maritozzi.

ORANGE CAKE

¾ cup butter, at room temperature	1 cup chopped candied orange and lemon peel
⅞ cup sugar	2 jiggers rum
3 eggs	1 cup pastry flour
½ teaspoon grated orange peel	¾ cup potato flour

Cream butter, add sugar and mix until smooth and creamy. Add eggs, one at a time, mixing well. Add orange peel. Steep candied fruits in rum 1 hour and add to batter. Sift together the two flours and add to other ingredients, mixing until smooth. Line a deep cake form with greased paper and pour batter into it. Bake in hot oven (400°F.) 45 minutes.

PAN DI SPAGNA (Italian Sponge Cake)

5 egg yolks	1 teaspoon vanilla
1½ cups sugar	½ teaspoon grated lemon rind
1¼ cups pastry flour, sifted	5 egg whites

Place egg yolks and sugar in mixing bowl and beat until lemon colored. Add flour, a little at a time, blending in well. Add vanilla and lemon rind. Beat egg whites until stiff but not dry and fold into cake mixture. Butter and flour a cake pan about 8 inches square. Pour in cake batter and bake in moderate oven (375°) 40 minutes. Turn over on cake rack and cool.

PANETTONE DI MILANO

5 cups pastry flour	4 egg yolks, room temperature
1 envelope yeast	2 eggs, room temperature
2 teaspoons lukewarm water	1 cup sugar
¼ teaspoon salt	½ cup lukewarm water
¾ cup butter, melted	⅔ cup seedless raisins
	½ cup candied citron peel, cut in small pieces

If the recipe calls for pastry flour, cake flour can be substituted.

This cake should be started the day before the actual baking.

Sift and measure flour. Blend yeast with water and let stand 5 minutes. Add yeast to ½ cup flour and mix well. Make a little ball of the dough and place it in a bowl in warm place 2 hours. When ball of dough has doubled in size, put 2 cups flour on pastry board, place yeast dough in middle, add enough lukewarm water to make a soft pliable ball and knead carefully. Cover well and let stand in warm place 3 hours. Place 1 cup flour on pastry board, add yeast dough and enough lukewarm water to make a soft pliable ball of dough and knead well. Let stand in warm place 2 hours.

When dough has risen again, place 1½ cups flour on pastry board, add dough, salt and melted butter and knead together well. Beat together egg yolks, whole eggs, sugar and ½ cup lukewarm water. Beat until frothy. Add to dough a little at a time, kneading constantly until everything is well absorbed. Add raisins and citron and knead well to distribute fruit evenly.

You may make one large panettone, or loaf, or two small ones. If you wish to make two, divide dough into 2 parts. Let rise in warm place 4 to 6 hours, depending upon heat. The loaf or loaves should be double the original size with dough soft to the touch. Make a cross mark with a knife on each loaf and place on buttered paper on baking sheet and place in hot oven (400°F.) 5 minutes. Remove quickly and place ½ tablespoon butter in center of cross mark. Return to oven and bake at 400°F. 15 minutes. Lower heat to 375°F. and continue baking 45 minutes, or longer, according to size of loaf. This cake stays fresh a long time and is ideal served with coffee or wine.

PANFORTE SIENA STYLE

¼ pound shelled, blanched almonds	¾ cup candied citron peel, cut fine
¼ pound hazelnuts, lightly toasted	¾ cup candied lemon peel, cut fine
⅓ cup powdered cocoa	¾ cup honey
1½ teaspoons cinnamon	¾ cup sugar
¼ teaspoon allspice	2 tablespoons confectioners'
½ cup pastry flour	sugar
¾ cup candied orange peel, cut fine	1 tablespoon cinnamon

Mix together well the almonds, hazelnuts, cocoa, cinnamon, allspice, flour, orange peel, citron peel and lemon peel. Place honey and sugar in large saucepan and cook over very low flame, stirring constantly,

If the recipe calls for pastry flour, cake flour can be substituted.

until a little of mixture dropped into cold water forms a ball. Add first mixture to honey and sugar and combine well.

Line a 9-inch cheese cake spring pan with well buttered paper and pour in mixture, evening it up with knife blade. Bake in very slow oven (300°F.) 30 minutes. Remove bottom part of pan, cool and remove sides. Sprinkle with confectioners' sugar and cinnamon.

PAN NERO (Sweet Black Bread)

4 egg yolks	½ cup flour
½ cup sugar	1 tablespoon potato flour
4 egg whites, beaten stiff	1 tablespoon sugar
4 squares cooking chocolate	

Beat together egg yolks and sugar until yellow in color and creamy. Fold in beaten egg whites. Melt chocolate over low flame and add to egg mixture. Sift the two flours together and add gently to the batter.

Butter an 8-inch square, 3 inches high, cake pan; sprinkle buttered surface of pan with 1 tablespoon sugar, spread around as evenly as possible and shake out surplus sugar. Pour in batter and bake in moderate oven (375°F.) 35 minutes.

PARADISE TART

2½ cups butter	2½ cups pastry flour
5 cups sugar	2½ cups potato flour
5 eggs	2 teaspoons grated lemon rind
6 egg yolks	

Cream butter, add sugar and mix until fluffy. Beat together lightly the eggs and egg yolks and add to sugar and butter mixture a little at a time, stirring constantly. Sift the two flours together until blended and add to other ingredients, mixing until very smooth. Add lemon rind and fold in lightly.

Grease and flour a large cake pan about 14 inches across, or two 9-inch cake pans. Pour batter into pan and bake in moderate oven (375°F.) 45 minutes, or until toothpick inserted in center of cake comes out clean. Turn over on cake rack and sprinkle with confectioners' sugar. This cake will stay fresh a very long time.

PASTA MARGHERITA

3 eggs	1 cup pastry flour
5 egg yolks	1 cup potato flour
1¾ cups sugar	⅜ cup butter, melted
1 teaspoon vanilla	

If the recipe calls for pastry flour, cake flour can be substituted.

Place eggs, egg yolks, sugar and vanilla in top of double boiler over hot but not boiling water and beat with rotary egg beater until eggs are warm. Remove from over hot water and beat until eggs are thick and velvety.

Sift pastry flour and potato flour together 3 times and add to eggs 1 tablespoon at a time, stirring well after each addition. Add melted butter. Butter and flour a 2-quart cake form and pour batter into it. The batter should not fill form more than ⅔ full.

Bake in hot oven (425°F.) 5 minutes, open door of oven quickly and make a cross mark on top of cake with knife. Close oven door and continue baking at 425°F. 5 minutes longer. Lower heat to 375°F. and bake 45 minutes.

POLENTA GATEAU

1 cup butter, room temperature	2 tablespoons lukewarm water
5 egg yolks	¼ teaspoon salt
7 tablespoons sugar	5 tablespoons cornmeal
1 envelope yeast	5 egg whites, beaten stiff
	½ teaspoon grated lemon rind

Cream butter, add egg yolks one at a time, stirring well after each addition. Add sugar a little at a time, mixing well after each addition. Blend yeast with water and let stand 5 minutes. Add yeast, salt and cornmeal to other ingredients and mix until thoroughly blended and smooth. Fold in egg whites which have been beaten until stiff but not dry, and add lemon rind.

Butter and flour a 1-quart tubular cake pan, pour into it the cake batter and bake in moderate oven (375°F.) 45 minutes. Turn out on cake rack and cool.

RICOTTA PIE

1¼ pounds ricotta	1 tablespoon seedless raisins
very small pinch salt	1 tablespoon candied orange peel
1 tablespoon flour	
4 tablespoons sugar	2 egg whites, beaten stiff
4 egg yolks	2 tablespoons confectioners' sugar
1 teaspoon grated orange rind	1 teaspoon cinnamon

Mix together well the ricotta, salt, flour, sugar, egg yolks and orange rind. Mix for at least 5 minutes and add raisins and candied orange peel. Fold in gently the beaten egg whites. Butter and flour a deep cake pan and pour in batter, taking care not to fill the pan more than half full. Bake in moderate oven (375°F.) 35 minutes, or until firm. Remove from oven, turn onto dish and sprinkle with confectioners' sugar and cinnamon.

RUM BABA

1¾ cups pastry flour, sifted	¼ teaspoon salt
1 envelope yeast	1 tablespoon sugar
3 eggs	2 tablespoons seedless raisins
¾ cup butter, at room temperature	

Place 1¼ cups flour in bowl with yeast and enough lukewarm water to bring the mixture to the consistency of a paste. Cover and set in warm place. In about 15 minutes dough will be double in size.

Place remaining ½ cup flour in large bowl, add yeast dough, eggs, butter and salt and work well with hands, slapping dough on floured pastry board with force and working until dough is smooth, velvety and elastic. Work in sugar and seedless raisins.

Butter well a 1½-quart tubular cake pan and add dough. (The dough must not take up more than ⅓ of the pan.) Set dough in warm place and let rise 1½ hours, or until dough reaches top of pan. Place in hot oven (425°F.) and bake 25 minutes, or until toothpick inserted in cake comes out clean.

While cake is baking, make syrup with following ingredients:

½ cup water	3 jiggers rum
3 tablespoons sugar	

Place water and sugar in small saucepan, bring to boil, boil 3 minutes and remove from fire. Add rum.

Remove cake from oven, turn over in deep dish (to catch rum syrup) and pour syrup over it. Baste occasionally with syrup while baba is cooling. Serves 8.

SAND TART

1 cup butter, melted	1 teaspoon grated lemon rind
1¾ cups sugar	2 tablespoons pastry flour
4 egg yolks	2 tablespoons potato flour
3 eggs	

Strain melted butter through a very fine sieve, let cool a little and beat while adding first the sugar, then egg yolks, and then whole eggs. Beat until yellow and light. Add lemon rind. Sift the two flours together and add to egg mixture, beating until smooth. Butter and flour a 10-inch cake pan, pour in cake batter and bake in moderate oven

If the recipe calls for pastry flour, cake flour can be substituted.

(375°F.) 40 minutes. Turn onto cake rack and cool. This cake is better served the day after it is baked.

SAVOIA CAKE

5 egg yolks	½ teaspoon grated lemon rind
2¼ cups sugar	½ teaspoon vanilla
¾ cup potato flour	5 egg whites
½ cup pastry flour	

Separate eggs and save whites until later. Beat yolks and sugar with rotary beater 10 minutes. Sift together the two flours until well blended and add gradually to beaten egg yolks, mixing and blending thoroughly. Add lemon rind and vanilla and mix well. Beat egg whites until stiff but not dry and fold into cake batter until thoroughly mixed.

Butter and flour a high cake form of 2-quart capacity (the shape is immaterial). Pour in cake batter and bake in moderate oven (375°F.) 45 minutes.

SAVOIARDI (Lady Fingers)

3 egg yolks	3 egg whites
⅜ cup sugar	1 tablespoon confectioners'
⅜ cup pastry flour	sugar
dash of salt	½ tablespoon granulated sugar
½ teaspoon vanilla	

Beat egg yolks and sugar together until yellow and foamy. Add flour and salt and mix until smooth. Add vanilla. Beat egg whites until firm and fold into egg yolk mixture until thoroughly blended.

Butter baking sheet and sprinkle with flour. Drop batter by tablespoonfuls on baking sheet and shape into fingers 3 inches in length. Mix together confectioners' and granulated sugars and sprinkle half the combination over fingers. Let stand 10 minutes. Sprinkle with remaining half of sugar, let stand 5 minutes and bake in moderate oven (375°F.) 10 minutes, or until golden. Remove from pan and cool on cake rack. Makes about 24 lady fingers.

PIES AND PASTRY

BIGNE

4 cups water	½ teaspoon grated lemon rind
¼ cup butter	3 cups oil or vegetable
¼ teaspoon salt	shortening
3 cups pastry flour	1 cup confectioners' sugar
4 eggs	vanilla flavored
1 teaspoon sugar	

If the recipe calls for pastry flour, cake flour can be substituted.

Combine water, butter and salt and bring to a boil. Remove from fire, add flour, mix well and return to fire. Cook, stirring constantly, until mixture leaves pan and spoon clean (about a half hour).

Remove from fire and add eggs one at a time, mixing after the addition of each egg until completely absorbed in dough. When dough is smooth and velvety, add sugar and lemon rind, mix thoroughly, cover and let stand in cool place 30 minutes.

Heat oil or shortening in frying pan, drop in dough by spoonfuls and fry until golden. Do not fry more than 3 or 4 at a time. When golden brown, remove from pan, drain on paper and sprinkle with confectioners' sugar to which powdered vanilla has been added to give it additional flavor. Makes about 40 bignè.

CASTAGNACCIO FLORENTINE
(Chestnut Pie)

1½ cups chestnut flour	2 tablespoons white raisins
¼ teaspoon salt	2 tablespoons pine nuts
2 tablespoons olive oil	¼ teaspoon rosemary
1½ cups water	

Mix together flour, salt, oil, water and raisins. Mix thoroughly until smooth and pour into a well-oiled 8- or 9-inch pie plate. Sprinkle with pine nuts and rosemary and bake in moderate oven (375°F.) 45 minutes, or until top is crisp. Serves 6.

LARGE BRIOCHE

1 recipe of pasta brioche (see index)	1 tablespoon butter, melted
	1 egg, lightly beaten

Make a large ball of all the dough except for a piece about the size of a small apple. Butter a round and deep form and put in dough. (The dough must reach halfway to top of form.) Make a shallow cavity in center of dough. Brush dough with butter and egg. Put small ball of dough on top of cavity in center and brush with butter and egg. Let dough rise to top of form in warm place. Bake in hot oven (425°F.) 35 minutes, or until brioche is golden and crusty.

LITTLE BRIOCHES

1 recipe pasta brioche (see index)	2 tablespoons butter
	1 egg, lightly beaten

Roll dough on floured board. Butter well 20 small forms for brioches (large muffin tins will do). Make 1 long roll of dough 3 inches in diameter. Cut into 20 segments about 2 inches in length. Roll remaining dough to size of pencil in diameter and cut into 20 small pieces.

Place 1 large piece of dough in each tin and top with small piece as a head. Set in warm place and let rise 30 minutes. Brush lightly with egg and bake in hot oven (400°F.) 6 minutes, or until brioches are brown and crusty.

PANDORO DI VERONA (Golden Bread Verona Style)

1 tablespoon pastry flour	1⅓ cups pastry flour
1 envelope dry yeast	2 tablespoons sugar
1 tablespoon lukewarm	2 tablespoons butter, melted
water	1 egg
¾ cup pastry flour	2 egg yolks
1 tablespoon sugar	1 teaspoon vanilla
1 egg	¼ teaspoon salt
1 egg yolk	2 tablespoons pastry flour
1 tablespoon butter, melted	¾ cup butter

Place flour in bowl, add yeast and water and mix together well. Cover and let stand in warm place 20 minutes. In another bowl place ¾ cup flour, 1 tablespoon sugar, 1 egg, 1 egg yolk and 1 tablespoon melted butter. Mix together a little and add the yeast mixture. Work together well 5 minutes, cover bowl and let rise in warm place 1 hour, or until double in bulk.

Place on pastry board 1⅓ cups flour, 2 tablespoons sugar, 2 tablespoons melted butter, 1 egg, 2 egg yolks, vanilla and salt and mix together a little. Add yeast dough and work well with hands 10 minutes. Add 2 tablespoons flour and work well until dough does not stick to hands or board. Make a ball of dough and let rise in warm place 3 hours.

Roll dough into a sheet 2 inches thick and dot with ¾ cup butter which has been cut into little pieces. Fold dough over 3 times and roll out as before. Let stand 20 minutes, fold over 3 times again, roll flat and let stand 20 minutes. Repeat this procedure once again.

Grease a 2-quart cake form and sprinkle with a little granulated sugar. Place dough in form and let rise until dough reaches top edge of form. Bake in medium hot oven (400°F.) 15 minutes, lower heat to 350°F. and bake 30 minutes longer, or until toothpick inserted in center of cake comes away clean. Turn over on cake rack and cool. Sprinkle with confectioners' sugar.

If the recipe calls for pastry flour, cake flour can be substituted.

PASTA BRIOCHE

2 cups sifted pastry flour	2 tablespoons sugar
1 envelope dry yeast	¼ teaspoon salt
1 tablespoon lukewarm	¼ cup and 1 tablespoon butter
water	at room temperature
2 eggs	

Place ½ cup flour on pastry board and make a well in center. Dissolve yeast in lukewarm water and place in flour well. Work dough with hands until smooth and form into ball. Make 2 incisions in dough and wrap in towel. Set in warm place and let rise 20 minutes.

Make a well of remaining flour and place eggs, sugar and salt in well. Work this dough energetically, banging it on pastry board until smooth and all in one piece.

When the yeast dough has doubled in quantity, stretch it with hands into shape of pie crust. Do the same thing with the second piece of dough and work the two doughs together until well blended. Work in butter until butter is all absorbed and the dough is elastic and smooth.

Place dough in bowl in warm place 30 minutes. When dough starts to rise, push it down with hand. Cover bowl and place in refrigerator 7 hours. This is the secret of making extra fine brioche. This dough is the foundation for all types of brioches.

PASTA FROLLA

2 cups sifted pastry flour	½ cup butter, at room
1 cup sugar	temperature
small pinch salt	2 eggs
	½ teaspoon grated lemon rind

Sift together flour, sugar and salt. Make a well of dry ingredients on pastry board. Place butter, eggs and lemon rind in well and work dough with hands quickly. Do not add water. When smooth, shape into ball and chill 30 minutes. Frolla is now ready for use in many ways.

PASTA FROLLA ROMAN STYLE

2 cups sifted pastry flour	2 whole eggs, lightly beaten
½ teaspoon cinnamon	½ cup leaf lard
1 cup sugar	½ teaspoon lemon rind
small pinch salt	

Sift together flour, cinnamon, sugar and salt and make a well of dry ingredients on pastry board. Place eggs, lard and lemon rind in well and

If the recipe calls for pastry flour, cake flour can be substituted.

work with hands until smooth. Place in cool place and chill 30 minutes before using.

PASTA FROLLA WITHOUT EGGS

1 cup sifted flour	½ cup sugar
1 cup potato flour	1 teaspoon grated lemon rind
¾ cup butter	

Sift the two flours together until well blended. Cream butter, add sugar and lemon rind. Add flour, a little at a time, working well until flour is all absorbed. Chill 30 minutes before using. Use as a regular pasta frolla.

PASTA SFOGLIATA

1 cup sifted pastry flour	½ cup butter
tiny pinch salt	ice water

Sift flour with salt, cut in butter with pastry cutter and add ice water 1 tablespoon at a time until dough sticks to fingers. Be careful not to use too much water. Roll dough on floured pastry board into a strip 6 inches wide and about 15 inches long. Fold strip over 3 times (reducing length to 5 inches). Roll into strip again and again fold strip 3 times. Repeat this procedure 6 times. The sfogliata is now ready for cutting and using in different ways in various recipes.

PASTICCIO DI MACCHERONI ROMAN STYLE
(Macaroni Tart)

3 cups beef gravy (see braised beef in index)	1 recipe pasticciera cream (see index)
1 tablespoon butter	1 recipe pasta frolla Roman style (see index)
6 chicken livers, cut into small pieces	1½ pounds rigatoni macaroni
½ pound Italian sausage, minced	6 quarts boiling water
¼ pound chopped beef	2½ tablespoons salt
¼ pound mushrooms, minced	¼ cup butter
	½ cup grated Parmesan cheese
	1 egg, lightly beaten

Make sure that the beef gravy is devoid of fat. A good way to ensure this is to make the gravy the day before, chilling it and removing the fat that comes to the top.

Braise the livers in butter, add minced sausage, chopped beef and mushrooms, and 2 tablespoons beef gravy and cook 10 minutes.

Make cream pasticciera and cool. Prepare pasta frolla and chill.

If the recipe calls for pastry flour, cake flour can be substituted.

Cook macaroni in boiling salted water 15 minutes, or until tender, drain and add butter, Parmesan and gravy. Mix well and let cool.

Butter 12-inch cake pan. Divide pasta frolla into 2 parts, roll 1 part and cover bottom and sides of cake pan. Spread half the macaroni on the pasta, pour over it the sausage and mushroom mixture and spread evenly. Top with remaining macaroni, giving it a dome shape. Pour pasticciera cream over macaroni, making sure that every crevice is well filled. Roll the second half of the pasta frolla and cover the top of the pasticcio, making sure that bottom and top layers of pasta frolla close well. Trim off excess dough. Brush top of pasticcio with beaten egg and bake in moderate oven (375°F.) 45 minutes. Remove from oven, sprinkle with confectioners' sugar (optional), let cool and serve. Serves 8 or 10.

PASTIERA DI PASQUA (Easter Tart)

1½ cups pearl tapioca	6 egg yolks
2 cups hot milk	¼ teaspoon cinnamon
¼ teaspoon salt	¼ teaspoon grated lemon peel
¼ teaspoon grated lemon peel	½ cup candied citron and orange peel, diced fine
1 tablespoon sugar	4 egg whites, beaten stiff
¼ teaspoon cinnamon	1 recipe pasta frolla (see index)
1¼ pounds ricotta	2 tablespoons confectioners' sugar
2 cups sugar	

Soak tapioca in water the night before baking the tart. After soaking overnight, boil in water 15 minutes and drain. Add hot milk, salt, sugar, cinnamom, and half the lemon peel, and simmer until milk has completely evaporated. Remove from fire and cool.

Place ricotta in bowl and stir until very smooth. Add sugar and egg yolks, one at a time, stirring well after each addition. Add cinnamon, candied citron and candied orange peel, the rest of the lemon peel, and last of all the cooked tapioca. Mix together well and blend in egg whites which have been beaten until stiff but not dry.

Divide pasta frolla into 2 parts, one larger than the other and roll the larger piece to a thickness of ½ inch. Butter and flour a 10-inch cheese cake spring pan and line the bottom and sides with rolled-out piece of pastry, trimming edges. Pour in ricotta filling. Roll out smaller piece of pasta frolla and cut into 1-inch strips. Place strips criss-cross over cheese filling, trimming neatly around edges. Bake cake in moderate oven (375°F.) 45 minutes. Let cool in pan. When cool, push up bottom of spring pan, transfer tart to serving dish and sprinkle with confectioners' sugar. Serves 12.

PINZA BERTOLDESE

5 cups pastry flour, sifted	¼ cup cocoa
2 envelopes dry yeast	2 cups apricot jam
5 tablespoons lukewarm	⅜ cup butter, at room
water	temperature
1 cup mixed candied fruits,	2 tablespoons warm honey
cut fine	½ jigger rum
1 cup chopped almonds	
or walnuts	

Mix 1 cup flour with yeast and 3 tablespoons warm water. Mix well, cover and keep in warm place until dough has doubled in size.

Make a well of remaining flour (4 cups), place yeast dough in it, add 2 more tablespoons lukewarm water and work the flour in with the yeast dough. Work well, adding a little more water if needed, until dough is soft and all the flour has been absorbed. Let stand in warm place 2 hours.

Push dough with hands to deflate and work in fruits, nuts, cocoa, jam and butter. Work well into dough, shape as a ring and place on buttered baking sheet. Let rise 2½ hours in warm place.

Bake in hot oven (400°F.) 1 hour. Mix together warm honey and rum. Remove ring from oven and brush with honey and rum mixture.

CANNOLI

1⅓ cups flour	½ teaspoon sugar
1 tablespoon shortening	wine (sweet or dry)
pinch of salt	

Mix flour, shortening, salt and sugar. Add enough wine to make a stiff but workable dough. Roll into ball and let it stand for about 1 hour. Roll out dough ⅛″ thick. Cut into 5″ squares. Place cannoli tube† across the corners of the square. First fold one corner around the tube, then the other and press together. Fry in deep fat, one at a time, until dark golden brown. Remove cannoli carefully and let it cool before filling. Makes 12.   (For filling, see recipe below.)

SFINGI DI SAN GIUSEPPE*
(St. Joseph's Day Cream Puffs)

½ cup butter	4 eggs
dash salt	1 tablespoon sugar
1 cup water	½ teaspoon grated orange peel
1 cup pastry flour	½ teaspoon grated lemon peel

† Cannoli tubes can be purchased at specialty stores, or can be made by hardware stores from sheet aluminum. Tube should be 8″ long and 1″ in diameter.

If the recipe calls for pastry flour, cake flour can be substituted.

Combine butter, salt and water in saucepan and bring to a boil. Add flour all at one time and mix well until dough leaves sides of pan. Remove from stove and cool a little. Add eggs one at a time, mixing well after each addition. Add sugar, orange and lemon peel and mix thoroughly.

Drop by tablespoonfuls on greased baking sheet, leaving a 3-inch space between them. Bake in hot oven (400°F.) 10 minutes, reduce heat to 325°F. and bake 30 minutes or until golden brown. Makes about 16 sfingi.

Make a slit in side of each puff and fill with pasticciera cream (see index) or with ricotta filling (see recipe below).

RICOTTA FILLING

1 pound ricotta	1 jigger crème de cacao, or
2 tablespoons chocolate	any other liqueur to your
chips	liking
1 tablespoon candied	2 tablespoons sugar
orange peel, cut fine	

Cream ricotta well, add chocolate chips, orange peel, crème de cacao and sugar and mix very well. Fill puffs with ricotta filling.

SFOGLIATA DI RICOTTA
(Ricotta Pie)

¾ pound ricotta	1 egg yolk
4 tablespoons sugar	¼ cup flour
1 tablespoon vanilla	2 tablespoons sugar
1 tablespoon seedless white	1 recipe pasta sfogliata (see
raisins	index)
1 tablespoon candied	1 tablespoon beaten egg
orange peel, diced fine	2 tablespoons confectioners'
1½ tablespoons rum	sugar
1 cup milk	

Cream ricotta well. Add sugar and vanilla and mix until creamy and smooth. Soak raisins and orange peel in rum 30 minutes. Combine milk, egg yolk, flour and sugar and cook over low flame until a smooth cream is formed, stirring constantly. Remove from fire, add ricotta mixture and the raisins and orange peel with rum. Mix all together well.

Cut pasta sfogliata into 2 parts and roll out into rather thin sheets. Line pie plate with one sheet, pour in filling and cover with second sheet. Press top sheet around edge and trim off excess. Press together two edges all around. Brush top with a little beaten egg and bake in hot oven (400°F.) 20 minutes. Remove from oven, sprinkle with confectioners' sugar and return to oven for 4 minutes.

STIACCIATA FLORENTINA (Florentine Pie)

5 cups flour	1¼ cups sugar
2 envelopes dry yeast	1 tablespoon grated orange
¾ cup lukewarm water	peel
2 eggs, lightly beaten	1½ cups lard
¼ teaspoon salt	¼ cup confectioners' sugar,
	sifted

Sift and measure flour. Dilute yeast in water and slowly work all the flour into it. Work well with hands until dough does not stick to bowl. Cover and let rise in warm place 1 hour, or until double in bulk. Deflate with hand and add eggs, salt, sugar and peel. Continue working dough until all ingredients are absorbed and the dough is elastic (about 15 minutes). Add lard and work well.

Grease a 14- by 18-inch baking sheet and stretch dough over it. Cover and let rise 2 hours. Bake in hot oven (400°F.) 35 minutes. Allow to cool on cake rack and sprinkle with confectioners' sugar.

STRUFOLI (OR PIGNOLATA) NEAPOLITAN STYLE

2½ cups pastry flour	dash salt
4 eggs	½ teaspoon grated lemon peel
1 egg yolk	2 cups vegetable lard
¼ cup leaf lard	1½ cups honey
½ tablespoon sugar	1 teaspoon grated orange peel

Place pastry flour on board, make a well in center and place in well the eggs, egg yolk, leaf lard, sugar, salt and lemon peel. Mix well, working dough with hands, as in the making of noodles. Shape into very small balls the size of marbles and fry in hot lard, a few at a time, until golden brown.

Melt honey in saucepan and add grated orange peel. As soon as the little balls are fried, drop them into the honey mixture, take them up with a strainer and place on serving dish, piling them into conical mounds. Cool. Serves about 6.

ZEPPOLE NEAPOLITAN STYLE

1 cup water	2 tablespoons olive oil
¼ teaspoon salt	2 cups cooking or olive oil
1 jigger cognac or brandy	½ cup confectioners' sugar
1 cup pastry flour	

Combine water, salt and cognac and bring to a boil. Remove from fire, add flour all at one time and mix vigorously. Return to stove and continue mixing until dry and somewhat hard.

If the recipe calls for pastry flour, cake flour can be substituted.

Pour olive oil on pastry board, place dough on it and let cool. Roll dough, fold over and roll again, repeating procedure about 6 times until dough has absorbed all the oil and is elastic.

Roll dough and shape into long rope about the thickness of a finger. Cut rope into pieces about 6 inches long and form each section into a ring. Prick each ring with fork and fry in hot oil until golden and crisp. Do not fry too many at a time. Drain and sprinkle abundantly with confectioners' sugar. This recipe will make about 12 zeppole.

PUDDINGS AND CREAMS

CHOCOLATE PASTICCIERA CREAM

1 recipe pasticciera cream omitting lemon rind (see index)	2 squares cooking chocolate, grated

Add grated chocolate to cooked pasticceria cream and cook 1 minute longer, stirring constantly, until chocolate is blended in well. Cool. Serves 4.

CHOCOLATE RICOTTA PUDDING

¾ pound ricotta	2 tablespoons grated cooking chocolate
2 hard cooked egg yolks, strained	⅛ pound shelled, blanched almonds, chopped
4 tablespoons sugar	2 egg whites, beaten stiff
1 jigger rum	

Cream ricotta, add strained egg yolks, sugar, rum, chocolate and almonds and mix very well. Blend in egg whites.

Butter 1-quart tube mold, pour in mixture and place in pan of water in moderate oven (375°F.) and bake 1 hour. This is better served warm but it may also be served cold.

CREME ZABAIONE

1 recipe pasticciera cream (see index)	¼ cup dry Marsala wine

Add Marsala to warm, cooked pasticciera cream, mix well and cool. Serves 4.

PASTICCIERA CREAM

3 tablespoons sugar	½ teaspoon vanilla
3 egg yolks	2 cups milk
3 tablespoons flour	1 tablespoon butter
½ teaspoon grated lemon rind	

Place sugar, egg yolks, flour, lemon rind and vanilla in saucepan and mix together well. Scald milk and pour over mixture, beating constantly with rotary beater. Continue cooking on low flame, stirring with wooden spoon, until mixture reaches the boiling point. Cook 4 minutes longer, stirring constantly. Remove from fire, add butter and mix well. Pour into bowl and let cool, stirring occasionally to prevent skin from forming over top. Serves 4.

RICOTTA PUDDING

1¼ cups water	1 tablespoon candied orange
3 tablespoons semolina	peel
(Cream of Wheat)	1 tablespoon seedless white
1 pound ricotta	raisins
4 tablespoons sugar	1 jigger rum
1 egg	1 egg white, beaten stiff
1 egg yolk	½ cup bread crumbs

Cook semolina in boiling water, stirring constantly, until thickened. Cook 4 minutes longer, remove from fire and cool. Mix together well the ricotta, sugar, egg, egg yolk, candied orange peel, raisins and rum. Mix 5 minutes and blend in egg white. Add cooled semolina.

Butter a 1½-quart mold, sprinkle with bread crumbs and pour in mixture, taking care that it does not fill mold more than ⅔ full. Bake in moderate oven (375°F.) 1 hour. Remove from oven, let stand 10 minutes, turn out on plate, cool and sprinkle with confectioners' sugar.

SANGUINACCIO NEAPOLITAN STYLE

3 tablespoons pastry flour	¾ pound cooked pork blood
3 tablespoons sugar	(to be found in Italian
2 cups milk	meat shops)
3 egg yolks	2 squares cooking chocolate
½ teaspoon vanilla extract	1 tablespoon pine nuts
¼ cup butter	1 tablespoon candied fruit,
	diced

Combine flour, sugar, milk, egg yolks and vanilla in saucepan and cook over low flame, stirring constantly until thick and creamy. Add butter and mix well. Chop blood very fine, combine with cream mixture and strain. Melt chocolate over warm water and add to cream along with nuts and candied fruit. Mix thoroughly and serve cold in crystal cups.

If the recipe calls for pastry flour, cake flour can be substituted.

SEMOLINA TART

3 cups milk	¼ teaspoon salt
1½ cups semolina (Cream	¼ teaspoon grated lemon rind
of Wheat)	2 eggs
⅓ cup sugar	1 egg yolk
½ cup butter	2 tablespoons powdered sugar

Bring milk to boil and gradually add semolina, stirring well. Cook 5 minutes, stirring constantly. Add sugar and cook 3 minutes longer, stirring all the time. Remove from fire, pour in bowl, add butter, salt and lemon rind and mix well. Let cool. Add eggs and egg yolk and mix until well blended.

Butter and flour a deep 9-inch pan, pour in mixture and bake in medium oven (375°F.) 1 hour. Remove from oven, let stand 10 minutes and turn out on serving dish. Sprinkle with powdered sugar and serve either hot or cold.

ZUPPA INGLESE (English Soup)

1 recipe pan di Spagna	1 tablespoon candied fruit,
(sponge cake) (see index)	cut fine
1½ jiggers rum	3 egg whites
1½ jiggers crème de cacao	4 tablespoons sugar
1 recipe cool pasticciera	
cream (see index)	

Cut sponge cake into ½-inch slices. Sprinkle half the slices with rum and the other half with crème de cacao. Spread the bottom of a 10-inch heat-resistant dish with a little of the pasticciera cream and place on it 2 layers of the cake soaked with rum. Pour pasticciera cream over cake and sprinkle with candied fruit. Cover cream with 2 layers of cake soaked with crème de cacao. Beat egg whites until stiff, add sugar and beat again. Pile egg whites on cake and bake in slow oven (300°F.) 20 minutes. Cool before serving.

CANDY

TORRONE (Italian Christmas Nougat)

1 cup honey	½ pound hazel nuts, shelled
2 egg whites	and slightly toasted
1 cup sugar	1 teaspoon candied orange
2 tablespoons water	peel, cut into small pieces
1 pound almonds, shelled	½ teaspoon grated lemon rind
and blanched	

Place honey in top of double boiler over boiling water and stir with wooden spoon 1 hour, or until honey is caramelized. Beat egg whites until stiff and add to honey slowly, mixing well. The mixture will be fluffy and white.

Combine sugar with 2 tablespoons water in small saucepan and let boil, without stirring, until caramelized. Add caramelized sugar to honey mixture a little at a time, mixing well. Cook mixture a little longer and when a little dropped into cold water hardens, add nuts, candied fruit and grated rind. Mix well and quickly before mixture has time to harden.

Line 2 or 3 6x8-inch loaf pans with wafer† and pour in mixture about 2 inches deep. Cover top with wafers, let cool 20 minutes and cut each mold into 2 long rectangular pieces, cutting down the center lengthwise. Makes from 4 to 6 long pieces. Wrap in waxed paper to keep.

CHOCOLATE TORRONE (Italian Christmas Candy)

½ pound honey	2 tablespoons water
1 cup sugar	1 tablespoon sugar
2 tablespoons water	1¼ pounds shelled hazel nuts,
2 egg whites	slightly toasted
1¾ cups cocoa	

Place honey in top of double boiler over boiling water and stir constantly 1½ hours, or until caramelized. Combine sugar and water in small saucepan and let boil until caramelized. Beat egg whites until stiff and add to honey a little at a time, mixing well. Add sugar and mix well.

Combine cocoa with 2 tablespoons water and 1 tablespoon sugar and cook until creamy. Add cocoa and nuts to first mixture and mix.

Line 2 or 3 6x8-inch loaf pans with wafer* and pour in mixture to a depth of about 2 inches. Let cool and cut into 2 long rectangular pieces. Wrap in waxed paper to keep. Makes 4 to 6 pieces.

FRUIT

ITALIAN BAKED APPLES

8 cooking apples	¼ teaspoon grated lemon rind
¾ cup raisins	4 tablespoons sugar
1¼ cups white wine	1½ tablespoons butter

Core apples. Soak raisins in wine ½ hour. Stuff centers of apples with raisins, sprinkle with lemon rind and sugar, dot with butter and

† Very thin sheet-like unleavened wheat bread, known as *ostia*.

sprinkle with wine left over from raisins. Bake in moderate oven (375°F.) 45 minutes. Serve hot or cold. Serves 4 or 8.

ORANGES IN SOUFFLE

6 large oranges	6 tablespoons flour
2 cups milk	1/4 teaspoon vanilla extract
5 egg yolks	5 egg whites, beaten stiff
3/4 cup sugar	

Cut off tops of oranges and scoop out pulp. Scald milk. Mix together egg yolks and sugar, beat a little and add flour and vanilla. Add to scalded milk, cook gently until slightly thickened. Cool.

Add stiff, beaten egg whites and blend in thoroughly. Fill orange cups almost to the top with this mixture and place in hot oven (400°F.) 10 minutes. Serve hot, with or without the following sauce:

4 tablespoons apricot jam	4 tablespoons warm water
	1/2 jigger rum

Mix together thoroughly and serve warm.

PEACHES IN WINE*

4 large ripe peaches	8 ounces Asti Spumante
1/2 teaspoon sugar	(Italian champagne), chilled

Peel peaches and slice lengthwise in thin slices. Add sugar and mix well. Place in large crystal cups or sherbet glasses. Pour 2 ounces chilled Asti Spumante over peaches and serve. Serves 4. (Tiara's Gran Spumante may be used in place of the more expensive Asti Spumante.)

PEACHES PIEDMONT STYLE

7 peaches, medium size	5 macaroons, crushed
2 tablespoons sugar	1 egg yolk
1 1/4 tablespoons butter	

Cut 6 peaches in halves. Remove pits and scoop out a little of pulp from each half. Remove all pulp from extra peach and mash together with pulp removed from peach halves. Add sugar, butter, macaroons and egg yolk and mix well. Fill each peach half with pulp mixture, place in well-buttered baking dish and bake in moderate oven (375°F.) 1 hour. Serve hot or cold. Serves 6.

PEACHES WITH ZABAIONE SAUCE

4 peaches
½ cup water
2 tablespoons sugar
1 jigger crème de cacao,
    or any other liqueur

4 slices pan di Spagna (sponge
    cake) (see index)
8 maraschino cherries
2 cups zabaione sauce (see
    index)

Cut peaches in halves and remove pits. Mix together water, sugar and crème de cacao, pour over peach halves and let stand in warm place 1 hour.

Place 1 slice sponge cake on each serving dish, place 2 peach halves on each slice of sponge cake, top each peach half with maraschino cherry, pour some of the zabaione sauce over all and serve. Serves 4.

PEARS REGINA MARGHERITA

4 large pears
1 quart water
3 tablespoons sugar
¼ teaspoon vanilla extract

1 cup pasticciera cream (see
    index)
½ jigger rum

Peel pears and core carefully so as not to break the fruit. Boil gently in combined water, sugar and vanilla extract 15 minutes. Remove, drain and fill centers with pasticciera cream to which rum has been added. Serves 4.

STRAWBERRIES AND MARSALA

1 quart strawberries
2 tablespoons sugar

1 pint Marsala or sherry

Hull and wash strawberries, sprinkle with sugar and pour Marsala or sherry over them. Mix well, chill and serve. (In place of Marsala any sweet white wine or red wine may be used.) Serves 4 to 6.

SWEET FRIED BANANAS

4 large bananas
2 tablespoons sugar
2 teaspoons lemon juice
½ teaspoon grated orange
    peel
2 jiggers rum

2 tablespoons flour
½ cup water
1 tablespoon olive oil
1 egg white, beaten stiff
½ cup olive oil

Cut bananas into halves lengthwise, sprinkle with sugar, lemon juice, orange peel and rum and let stand 2 hours.

Make a batter of flour, water and 1 tablespoon oil, mixing well, and blend in stiff egg white.

Drain bananas, dip into batter and fry in hot olive oil only until golden in color. Sprinkle with sugar and serve hot. Serves 2 or 4.

SWEET FRIED CANTALOUPE

1 small cantaloupe (about 1½ pounds)	½ cup dry white wine
2 tablespoons powdered sugar	1½ teaspoons olive oil
2 jiggers crème de menthe	dash salt
liqueur (white, or your	1 egg white, beaten stiff
choice of a liqueur)	1 cup olive oil
2 tablespoons flour	1 tablespoon confectioners' sugar

Cut melon into thin slices, remove seeds and skin and sprinkle with powdered sugar and liqueur. Let stand for at least 1 hour.

Mix together flour, wine, 1½ teaspoons oil and salt and blend in stiff egg white. Dip melon slices into batter and fry in hot olive oil only until light gold in color. Sprinkle with confectioners' sugar. Serves 4.

ICINGS AND SAUCES

CAKE ICING WITH LIQUEUR

¾ cup butter	1 tablespoon cold pasticciera
4 tablespoons confectioners' sugar	cream (see index)
	1 jigger liqueur of your preference

Cream butter, add sugar and mix well. Add cream and mix. Add liqueur and mix until smooth. This will cover 1 layer of a 12-inch cake.

COFFEE ICING

1 cup confectioners' sugar, sifted	2 tablespoons strong Italian coffee

Mix sugar and coffee together well and beat until smooth and of the desired consistency. Makes enough icing for 1 layer of 12-inch cake.

LIQUEUR ICING

1 cup confectioners' sugar, sifted	1 tablespoon of a favorite liqueur
	1 tablespoon water (approximate)

Mix sugar well with liqueur and add water, a little at a time, until icing is of desired consistency. Beat until smooth. Makes enough icing to cover 1 layer of 12-inch cake.

MOCHA ICING

¾ cup butter
4 tablespoons confectioners'
sugar

1 tablespoon cold pasticciera
cream (see index)
¼ cup strong Italian coffee

Cream butter, add sugar and blend well. Add cream and mix. Add coffee and mix well. Chill 15 minutes. Covers 1 layer of 12-inch cake.

ROYAL ICING

2 cups confectioners'
sugar, sifted

½ teaspoon lemon juice
2 egg whites

Place all ingredients together in bowl and beat with rotary beater until stiff, but not dry. This icing is used for petit-fours or for trimming on fancy cakes.

PRINCE CREAM

2 squares sweet cooking
chocolate, grated

1 cup heavy cream

Place chocolate and cream in small saucepan and cook over very low flame, stirring with wooden spoon, until chocolate and cream are blended together well. Remove from fire and cool. Beat with rotary beater until of desired consistency. Excellent for icing cakes and small pastry. Makes enough for 1 layer of a cake.

WATER ICING

1 cup confectioners'
sugar, sifted

1 teaspoon apricot jam
2 tablespoons water

Place sugar in bowl, add jam; add water, 1 teaspoon at a time, mixing well after each addition of water. When icing reaches right consistency, stop adding water. Mix until icing is very smooth. One teaspoon vanilla or ½ teaspoon grated lemon rind may be substituted for apricot jam, if so desired. Makes enough icing for 1 layer of a 12-inch cake.

WINE SAUCE SYRACUSE

1 pint Moscato wine
½ cup raisins
2 cloves

½ teaspoon cinnamon
6 egg yolks

Combine wine, raisins, cloves and cinnamon in saucepan and cook until wine has evaporated to half original quantity. Strain wine and cool. Add egg yolks to wine, mix and place in top of double boiler. Cook until slightly thick, beating well. Makes 2½ cups sauce.

ZABAIONE

4 egg yolks	8 tablespoons Marsala
4 tablespoons sugar	¼ teaspoon vanilla

Combine all ingredients in top of double boiler, place over hot water and beat constantly until frothy, smooth and slightly thick. Serve plain or on sponge cake, either hot or cold. Serves 4.

ZABAIONE SAUCE

6 egg yolks	⅘ quart Marsala
1 tablespoon water	1 cup heavy cream
1¾ cups sugar	

Combine egg yolks, water, sugar and Marsala in top of double boiler, place over warm water and beat with rotary beater, increasing heat of water and continuing to beat until mixture is slightly thick and creamy. Remove from over hot water and continue beating until cool. Whip cream until thick, add to mixture and serve as sauce. Makes about 6 cups of sauce.

FROZEN DESSERTS

CASSATA ALLA SICILIANA (Sicilian Cream Cake)

1¼ pounds ricotta	1 tablespoon chocolate bits
2 cups sugar	2 tablespoons candied fruit,
1 teaspoon vanilla	cut into small pieces
1 jigger crème de cacao or	1 recipe pan di Spagna (sponge
any other favorite liqueur	cake) (see index)

Place ricotta, sugar, vanilla and crème de cacao in bowl and mix well with wooden spoon until smooth and fluffy (about 10 minutes). Add chocolate bits and fruit and mix well.

Cut sponge cake into 1-inch slices and line casserole bottom and sides with cake slices. Pour ricotta cream over cake, cover with more cake slices and keep in refrigerator overnight or for at least 4 hours. Turn over onto serving dish and sprinkle top with confectioners' sugar.

COFFEE ICE BOMBE

2 egg yolks	⅓ cup strong Italian coffee
¼ cup sugar	(see index)
1 teaspoon potato flour	1 tablespoon curaçao or cointreau
½ cup milk	½ teaspoon vanilla extract
	2 cups heavy cream

Combine egg yolks, sugar, potato flour, milk and coffee in saucepan and mix well. Place over low heat and cook, stirring constantly, until slightly thickened. Do not boil. Pour into bowl, add liqueur and vanilla, mix well and chill.

Whip heavy cream until stiff. Chill a spumoni mold or any ¾-quart mold and line inside of mold with ½ of the whipped cream. Mix remaining half of whipped cream with chilled coffee mixture and fill rest of mold carefully. Cover top of mold with waxed paper and freeze. Cut into 6 or 8 portions to serve.

CUP MACEDONIA

2 pears	6 tangerine sections
2 apples	¼ cup confectioners' sugar
2 peaches	2 jiggers Strega liqueur
2 bananas	1 pint vanilla ice cream
12 maraschino cherries	1 cup heavy cream, whipped
18 seedless grapes	

Peel and core the apples, pears and peaches and cut into cubes. Skin and slice the bananas. Add pitted cherries and grapes and tangerine sections, cut into pieces. Add confectioners' sugar and Strega liqueur, mix well and chill. Place fruit mixture in bottom of cup, top with ice cream and then with whipped cream. Serves 6.

GRANITA DI CAFFE CON PANNA (Coffee Sherbet with Cream)

¾ cup sugar	2 cups strong coffee
2 cups water	1 cup heavy cream, whipped

Melt sugar in water, add coffee and place in freezing tray. Freeze to a mush, stirring frequently. Serve in sherbet glasses, topped with whipped cream. Serves 6.

LEMON ICE

2 cups warm water	½ cup lemon juice
¾ cup sugar	1 teaspoon grated lemon rind

Melt sugar in warm water, add lemon juice and lemon rind and let stand 5 minutes. Strain, place in freezing tray and freeze, stirring frequently, until it reaches a mushy consistency. Serves 4.

LEMON ICE ROMAN STYLE

1½ cups sugar	1 egg white
1 quart water	¼ cup sugar
¾ cup lemon juice	2 jiggers rum

Combine sugar and water in saucepan and heat until sugar melts. Add lemon juice and strain through very fine sieve. Freeze until mushy, stirring frequently, and remove from freezer.

Add stiffly beaten egg white and ¼ cup sugar and mix well. Add rum and mix. Return to freezer and continue freezing to ice consistency, stirring very often. Serves 6.

MILADY'S SWEET SECRET

1 egg	¼ pound hazel nuts, toasted
¾ cup sugar	and chopped
¾ cup cocoa	¼ pound macaroons, or any
⅓ cup butter at room	other cookie you prefer
temperature	

Beat egg and sugar together 10 minutes, or until lemon-colored and fluffy. Add cocoa and continue whipping until well blended. Cream butter, add to cocoa mixture and beat together well. Add hazel nuts. Break up macaroons into very small pieces and add to mixture. Mix well and place in 1-quart casserole which has been lined with greased paper. Place in refrigerator for 2 hours. Turn over on serving dish and serve. Serves 8.

RICE AND STRAWBERRY TIMBALE

¼ cup rice	1 quart strawberries
¼ teaspoon salt	3 tablespoons sugar
2 cups milk	1 jigger rum
2 tablespoons sugar	1 jigger curaçao
½ teaspoon vanilla	2 cups heavy cream

Cook rice and salt in milk until rice is tender, add 2 tablespoons sugar, vanilla and place in refrigerator to cool. Hull and wash strawberries, add sugar and liqueurs and place in refrigerator 45 minutes.

Take 3 tablespoons strawberries, mash and strain. Whip cream until stiff, add strained strawberries and blend well.

Pour strawberries and liqueurs on chilled rice, top with whipped cream and serve. Serves 8.

SPUMONI

Spumoni is usually placed in molds especially made for the purpose. If you do not have these, a large ¾-quart jelly mold may be used. First mixture:

2 cups milk	½ teaspoon vanilla, or
¾ cup sugar	any other flavoring
5 egg yolks	you may prefer

Combine milk, sugar, egg yolks and vanilla in saucepan and cook over very low flame, stirring constantly, until thick. Cool, place in refrigerator tray and freeze medium hard (about 2 hours). It should be soft enough to be spooned out easily. Second mixture:

1 cup heavy cream, beaten stiff	1 tablespoon candied orange peel, cut fine
¼ cup sugar	8 shelled, blanched almonds,
8 maraschino cherries, cut into small pieces	cut into slivers

Mix all ingredients together gently and chill thoroughly in refrigerator.

Chill mold thoroughly. When first mixture is ready, remove from tray and line inside of mold with it, leaving hollow in center for second mixture. Fill the hollow with second mixture, cover top of mold with waxed paper and freeze 2 hours in freezing compartment of refrigerator. Dip mold briefly in warm water to unmold. Serves about 6.

SPUMONI ZABAIONE

3 egg yolks	½ cup Marsala wine
½ tablespoon water	¾ cup heavy cream
3 tablespoons sugar	

Combine egg yolks, water, sugar and Marsala in top of double boiler, over hot but not boiling water, and beat mixture until lukewarm. Remove from over hot water and continue beating until foamy and slightly thick. Beat cream until stiff and blend with egg mixture. Pour into a spumoni mold, or any 1-quart mold, cover and freeze. Cut into 6 or 8 portions.

STRAWBERRY GELATO (Sherbet)

1 quart strawberries	2½ cups sugar
½ cup lemon juice	2½ cups water
¼ cup orange juice	

Wash strawberries and pass them through a sieve. Add lemon juice and orange juice. Combine sugar and water in small saucepan and cook until syrupy. Cool and add to fruit mixture. Place in ice cream freezer or in refrigerator tray and freeze about 1 hour or until it has consistency of thick mush. If refrigerator is used, stir mixture frequently. Serves about 6.

STRAWBERRY SPUMONI

1 quart strawberries	2 cups heavy cream
1½ teaspoons lemon juice	½ cup confectioners' sugar
3 tablespoons sugar	

Wash, hull, crush and strain strawberries. Add lemon juice and sugar and mix well. Whip cream until stiff, adding confectioners' sugar slowly, and blend with strained strawberries. Place in spumoni mold or any similar quart mold and freeze. Cut into 6 or 8 portions.

ZABAIONE BISCUIT

3 egg yolks	2 egg whites, beaten stiff
6 tablespoons Marsala wine	1 cup heavy cream,
3 tablespoons sugar	beaten stiff

Combine egg yolks, Marsala and sugar in top of double boiler over hot but not boiling water, and beat well until foamy and slightly thickened. Remove from water and continue beating until cool. Add egg whites and whipped cream and blend in slowly and gently but thoroughly. Pour into 6 champagne cups or other dessert dishes and chill thoroughly. Serves 6.

Miscellaneous

CHEESE DESSERT*

The typical Italian dessert consists of a variety of cheeses, accompanied by fresh fruit. Here we give a list of cheeses best suited for this purpose.

Stracchino: A light yellow cheese, very tasty.

Provolone: A very popular cheese which comes in two varieties: very sharp (imported), or medium sharp (domestic). A safe cheese to serve to people not too fond of strange flavors.

Caciocavallo: A good, not too spicy cheese. Delicious with crackers or crusty bread.

Gorgonzola: A cheese for the gourmet. Creamy white with green mold. Not too safe a choice for people not used to foreign foods.

Bel Paese: A mild, rich, delicious cheese with a very distinctive flavor.

Provola Affumicata: A very mild cheese with a good smoky flavor.

We recommend serving cheese in large pieces and slicing it at the table as required.

SWEET OMELETTE IN FLAME

3 eggs	2 tablespoons apricot jam
dash salt	3 tablespoons confectioners'
¼ teaspoon grated lemon peel	sugar
¼ cup butter	2 jiggers rum

Beat eggs lightly with fork, add salt and lemon peel and mix well. Melt butter in frying pan, add egg mixture, form into omelette and brown gently on both sides. Remove from frying pan. Spread apricot jam over omelette, fold over and place in flame-proof serving dish. Sprinkle with confectioners' sugar, pour rum over it and set fire to the rum. Bring to table while gently flaming. Serves 2.

15. Beverages

AFTER-DINNER ITALIAN COFFEE*

The most commonly known Italian coffee drink is *Caffè Espresso.* Strictly speaking, this form of Italian coffee cannot be prepared in the home, for it requires a large urn in which steam under pressure is forced through the powdered coffee. The following recipes are devised for home preparation and come close to the favorite *Caffè Espresso.*

For the preparation of the following recipes it is possible to purchase a *Macchinetta da Caffè,* a special coffee maker that drips the coffee twice. These machines come in different sizes and with full instructions.

To make after-dinner coffee the proper coffee is the so-called "French-roasted" coffee. However, in Italian stores it is known as Italian-roasted. There are on the market several excellent brands of this type of black-roast coffee in 1-pound or ½-pound cans. The drip method is preferable for making coffee Italian style. It may be made very strong or not, according to your taste. We are giving you the medium-strong measurements for a regular drip coffee maker.

4 tablespoons coffee	sugar to taste
2 cups boiling water	

This makes 4 demitasses of coffee. Always serve after-dinner coffee very hot and in small cups. As a variation you may add a little twist of lemon peel in your cup if you like it. You may also vary it with ½ jigger of rum or with 1 jigger of Anisette liqueur (Roman style).

AFTER-DINNER COFFEE ITALIAN MACCHINETTA STYLE*
(Italian Coffee Maker Style)

3 tablespoons Italian-ground coffee	2 cups water
	sugar to taste

Place coffee in middle strainer section of coffee maker, put water in lower part and replace middle and top sections. Place over high flame. When water is boiling the steam will escape from a tiny hole in the bottom part of the coffee maker. Remove from flame and, holding both handles firmly, reverse entire *macchinetta.* Return it to hot stove and let drip. Dripping takes but a few minutes. Serve as hot as possible in demitasses.

For variation, add a twist of lemon peel to each cup, or ½ jigger of rum, or 1 jigger of Anisette liqueur (Roman style). Add sugar to taste.

WINES

Many Italian recipes call for the use of wine as a cooking ingredient. In addition, a perfect Italian meal calls for a drinking wine. The use of substitutes (water, coffee, tea, beer, strong liquor) is almost sure to detract from your enjoyment of Italian cookery.

Generally speaking, an aperitif of vermouth makes a perfect opener for an Italian dinner. An excellent combination is half sweet vermouth, half dry vermouth (both well iced), with a dash of bitters and a twist of lemon peel.

Dry white wines work out best with antipasto, soup, macaroni, fish and fowl. Dry red wines are best for meat courses. Dessert wines and/or sparkling wines come at the close of the meal, with the dessert or fruit.

Native Italian wines offer an extremely wide variety. Only a few of the better known names are listed below; most of them are available in the United States in those localities where the law permits the use of wine. Many of these imported varieties may be ordered from reliable wine importing firms.

In addition, there are available in the United States excellent American wines which are the equivalents of the various Italian types.

ITALIAN WINES WITH AMERICAN EQUIVALENT TYPES

Imported	*Domestic*
APERITIF WINES	
Marsala	Aperitif Wine
Dry Vermouth	Dry Vermouth
Sweet Vermouth	Sweet Vermouth
	Sherry
DRY WHITE WINES	
Albano	Chablis
Capri	Haute Sauterne
Chianti	Riesling
Cortese	Rhine
Est-Est-Est	Sauterne
Falerno	
Frascati	
Greco di Gerace	
Grottaferrata	

Lacrima Christi
Misilmeri
Montefiascone
Orvieto
Soave
Trebbiano

DRY RED WINES

Barbaresco   Burgundy
Barbera   Chianti
Barberone   Claret
Barolo   Barbera
Capri   Zinfandel
Chianti
Dolcetto
Falerno
Frascati
Freisa
Grignolino
Lacrima Christi
Lambrusco
Montepulciano
Nebiolo
San Gimignano

DESSERT WINES

Aleatico   Port
Farnese   Sherry
Marsala   Pale Dry Sherry
Passito   Muscatel
                      Tokay

SPARKLING WINES

Asti Spumante   Champagne
Nebiolo Spumante   Gran Spumante
Frascati Spumante   Pink Champagne
                      Sparkling Burgundy

GLOSSARY

abbacchio (ah-BAH-kyo) — Tender young spring lamb, often weighing no more than 6 pounds. *Abbacchio al forno* (oven-baked lamb) is one of the specialties of Rome.

affumicato (ah-foo-mee-KAH-toe) — Smoked.

agnolotti (ah-nyo-LO-tee) — "little big lambs." Dough dumplings stuffed with meat and other ingredients. A specialty of Turin.

al dente (ahl DEN-tay) — "to the tooth." Term used to indicate macaroni products which are not overcooked.

al forno (ahl FOR-no) — "in the oven."

amaretti (ah-mar-ET-tee) — "little bitter ones" (from *amaro*, "bitter"). Macaroons, usually made with almond paste.

anaci (AH-nah-chee) — Anise.

anguilla (ahn-GWEE-lah) — Eel.

antipasto (ahn-tee-PAH-sto) — "before meal." General term used for appetizers or hors-d'oeuvres.

arancini (ah-rahn-CHEE-nee) — "little oranges." Name given to a rice and meat dish of Sicily.

arista (AH-rees-tah) — Pork loin or back.

baccalà (bah-kah-LAH) — Dried and salted fish, usually cod. The Italian name goes back to Dutch *kabeljaauw*.

basilico (bah-SEE-lee-ko) — Sweet basil, an herb, derived from the Greek *basilikos*, "kingly," "royal." According to the Byzantine legend, St. Helena, mother of the Emperor Constantine, was informed that she would find the true cross in a spot where perfume filled the air. She found it under a mass of sweet basil.

bavette (bah-VET-tay) — "little foams." A delicate macaroni product.

bel paese (BEL pah-AY-say) — "beautiful country," the name of a semi-soft Italian cheese, which may be obtained in an imported or a domestic variety.

bignè (bee-NYAY) — A form of pastry.

biscotto (bee-SCUT-toe) — "twice-baked." Biscuit.

bistecca (bee-STEK-kah) — "beefsteak." The Italian word is borrowed from English.

bordolese (bor-doe-LAY-say) — "pertaining to the city of Bordeaux," in France.

brodetto (bro-DAY-toe). From *brodo*, "broth." Any dish (meat or fish) in which the main ingredient swims around in a thick, abundant gravy, usually based on eggs and lemon juice. Since this dish was known to the ancient Spartans, the Italian expression *antico quanto il brodetto*, "as ancient as brodetto," means very ancient indeed.

buon gusto (bwon GOOS-toe) — "good taste."

buridda (boo-REED-dah) — A fish dish of Genoa.

burro e parmigiano (BOOR-roe ay par-me-JAH-no) — "butter and Parmesan cheese." Macaroni is often eaten plain, with only these two seasonings.

cacciatora (kah-chyah-TOE-rah) — "hunter style." More precisely *alla cacciatora.*

cacciucco (kah-CHOO-ko) — A fish soup, made with various kinds of fish and shellfish, strongly peppered and spiced. A specialty of Leghorn.

caciocavallo (kah-cho-kah-VAH-lo) — "horse cheese." A cheese similar to provolone.

caffè e latte (kah-FAY ay LAH-tay) — "coffee and milk." The customary Italian breakfast beverage, consisting of half milk, half black-roast Italian coffee.

caffè espresso — See "espresso."

calzone (kahl-TSO-nay) — "trouser," "one leg of a pair of pants." A dish of dough, stuffed with meat, cheese and spices. A specialty of Naples.

cannelloni (kah-nay-LO-nee) — "big pipes." A large round macaroni product, usually stuffed with meat or other ingredients.

cannoli (kah-NO-lee) — "pipes." A Sicilian pastry.

capellini d'angelo (kah-pel-LEE-nee d'AHN-jay-lo) — "angel's hair." A thin, delicate macaroni product.

capitone (kah-pee-TOE-nay) — A variety of large eel, usually eaten at the Christmas Eve meatless supper.

capocollo (kah-po-KO-lo) — "head-neck." A pork product, similar to *coppa.*

caponatina (kah-po-nah-TEE-nah) — A Sicilian combination of pickled vegetables.

capozzella (kah-po-TSEL-lah) — Neapolitan dialect for "little head." Roasted lamb's head.

cappelletti (kah-pel-LAY-tee) — "little hats." A Roman variant of the Bologna *tortellini.*

capretto (kah-PRET-toe) — Young kid, from *capra,* "goat." Oven-baked *capretto* is one of the delicacies of Rome.

cardinale (kahr-dee-NAH-lay) — "cardinal," "cardinal style."

cassata (kah-SAH-tah) — An ice cream, similar to spumone.

cassata siciliana (see-chee-LYAH-nah) — A rich Sicilian cake.

castagnaccio (kah-stah-NYAH-cho) — From *castagna,* "chestnut." Chestnut flour pie, to which almonds, pine nuts, walnuts and raisins are added.

ceci (CHAY-chee) — Chick peas, *garbanzo* beans.

companatico (com-pah-NAH-tee-ko) — From *con*, "with" and *pane*, "bread." That which goes with bread, any sandwich filler.

coppa (KOH-pah) — A variety of salame made from the pig's head, muscles, feet and rind.

coratella (ko-rah-TEL-lah) — From *cuore*, "heart." Lamb's lung, heart and liver, combined in a single dish.

coteghino (koh-tay-GHEE-no) — From *cotica*, "rind," "pigskin." A variety of salame, generally cooked with beans, lentils and other legumes.

cotoletta (koh-toe-LET-tah) — Cutlet or chop.

cozza (KO-tsah) — Mussel.

crostino (crust-EE-no) — From *crosta*, "crust." Bread that is spread with anything and then toasted.

cruda (CREW-doe) — "raw"; *al crudo*, "in the raw."

cuscinetti (koo-she-NET-tee) — "little pillows," "little cushions." Baked cheese sandwiches.

espresso (es-PRESS-so) — "express," or "pressed out." *Caffè espresso* is Italian coffee made in a special machine in which steam under pressure is forced through the powdered coffee.

fagottino (fah-go-TEE-no) — "little bundle." A Venetian pastry.

filanti (fee-LAHN-tee) — From *filo*, "thread." Streaming, having threads.

finanziera (fee-nahn-TSYE-ra) — "financier"; *alla finanziera*, "financier style," a term derived from French cookery.

fondua (fun-DOO-ah) — Piedmontese dialect for "melted," "molten." A Piedmontese cheese and truffle dish.

fontina (fun-TEE-nah) — A soft cheese of Piedmont and the Alpine district.

(Fra) Diavolo (frah DYAH-vo-lo) — "Brother Devil." *Fra Diavolo* was an Italian bandit leader of the Robin Hood type, who stole from the rich and gave to the poor (not forgetting to take a commission on the transaction). He and his followers often disguised themselves as monks, whence the *Fra*.

fritto misto (FREE-toe MEES-toe) — Mixed fry.

fritto misto di pesce (dee-PAY-shay) — Mixed fish fry.

frittura piccata (free-TOO-rah peek-KAH-tah) — A veal fry.

garmugia (gar-MOO-jah) — A meat dish of Lucca.

gelato (jay-LAH-toe) — "frozen." Ice cream or sherbet.

gnocchi (NYOK-kee) — Dumplings made of wheat or potato flour.

gnummarielli (nyoo-mah-RYEL-lee) — Entrails of baby lamb, roasted on spit.

Gorgonzola (gor-gun-DZO-lah) — The name of a town in northern Italy, and of a cheese first produced there, which is of the same general type as the French Roquefort or the American Blue.

granatina (grah-nah-TEE-nah) — A chopped beef dish.

granita (gra-NEE-tah) — "granite." The name of the Italian ice.

grappa (GRAH-pah) — From the same root that gives us "grape." A distilled, highly alcoholic beverage produced from wine lees.

gratella (grah-TEL-lah) — Grate or griddle for broiling.

grissini (gree-SEE-nee) — Piedmontese dialect: bread sticks.

in bianco (een BYAHN-ko) — "in white." A term applied especially to fish which is boiled and served plain, with oil, lemon juice and parsley.

in bianco pesce (PAY-shay) — Boiled fish, served as above.

incanestrato (een-kah-nest-RAH-toe) — "basketed," "placed in a basket." A grating cheese. Usually comes in a reed basket or *canestra* (from the same Latin root as the Spanish *canasta*) and takes the shape of the container.

in carrozza (een kar-RO-tsah) — "in a carriage." Usually applied to a soft cheese, baked between slices of bread.

lasagne (lah-SA-nyay) — Giant noodles, over an inch wide, usually baked in the oven after boiling.

macaroni (*maccheroni* — mah-kay-ROE-nee) — For the origin of the term, see Introduction, p. xv. The current English form "macaroni" comes from the southern dialectal *maccaroni* rather than from the literary Italian *maccheroni*.

maccaroncini (mah-kah-run-CHEE-nee) — "little macaroni."

macchinetta (mah-kee-NET-tah) — "little machine." The Italian coffee making machine; more specifically, *machinetta da caffè*.

manicotti (mah-nee-KUT-tee) — "muffs." Large hollow tubes of delicate macaroni dough, stuffed with ricotta and other ingredients and baked in a baking dish with sauce.

Margherita (mar-gay-REE-tah) — "Margaret" or "Daisy." Name of the Queen-Mother under the long reign of Victor Emanuel III. Many dishes were named in her honor.

marinara (mah-ree-NAH-rah) — "sailor," "sailor style."

maritato (mah-ree-TAH-toe) — "married." As applied to a dish, it means "combined," "united."

maritozzo (mah-ree-TUT-so) — Dialectal for "big husband." A bun.

Marsala (mar-SAH-lah) — A heavy, semi-sweet dessert wine, produced in Sicily and named after the city of Marsala, in the western part of the island.

minestrone (mee-nest-ROE-nay) — "big soup," from *minestra*, "soup." A thick vegetable soup.

molinara (mo-lee-NAH-rah) — "miller," "miller style," from *molino*, "mill."

mortadella (mor-tah-DEL-lah) — From *mortaio*, "chopping bowl." A large variety of salame, made famous in the city of Bologna. *Mortadella di Bologna* is what gives rise to our abbreviated "boloney," a very different product.

mozzarella (mo-tsah-REL-lah) — Seemingly from *mozzare*, "to chop off." A fresh cheese.

nero (NAY-roe) — Black.

oliva (aw-LEE-vah) — Olive.

oregano (aw-RAY-gah-no) — The herb known in English as "origan."

ortica (or-TEA-kah) — "nettle"; *all' ortica,* "nettle style." The origin of the expression is obscure.

ossobuco (aw-so-BOO-ko) — "hollow-bone." A meat specialty of Milan.

pagnotta (pah-NYUT-tah) — "loaf," from *pane,* "bread." The term is generally reserved for the round loaf. The French loaf is called *filone,* "big thread."

pan di Spagna (pahn dee SPAH-nyah) — "bread of Spain." A cake.

pandorato (pahn-doe-RAH-toe) — "gilded bread." Bread, rolled in egg and fried.

pandoro (pahn-DOE-ro) — "golden bread." A cake of Verona.

panettone (pah-net-TOE-nay) — "big bread." A Milanese cake.

panforte (pahn-FOR-tay) — "strong bread." A pastry specialty of Siena, Tuscany.

panna (PAH-nah) — Whipped cream.

panzanella (pahn-tsah-NEL-lah) — "little paunch," or, according to another etymology, from *pantano,* "swamp," "marsh." A Roman lower-class dish of bread with a salad dressing.

parmigiana (par-mee-JAH-nah) — Parma style. Parma is a city in the northern region of Emilia. Parmesan cheese is *parmigiano.*

pasta (PAHS-tah) — Dough; also, a generic name for all macaroni products. Do not confuse with English "paste." (Tomato paste in Italian is *salsina di pomodoro.*)

pasta asciutta (ah-SHOOT-tah) — "dry dough." Macaroni in general.

pasta e ceci (ay CHAY-shee) — Macaroni and chick-peas.

pasta e fagioli (ay fah-JO-lee) — Macaroni and beans.

pasta frolla (FRAWL-lah) — "soft dough." A crumbly egg cake.

pasta sfogliata (sfo-LYAH-tah) — Dough "turned into leaves," rolled paper thin.

pastella (pahs-TEL-lah) — "little dough." Batter.

pasticceria (pahs-tee-chay-REE-ah) — "pastry" in general.

pasticciera (pahs-tee-CHAY-rah) — "pastry cook style."

pasticcio (pah-STEE-cho) — A piece of pastry, or timbale (particularly in the case of *pasticcio di maccheroni).*

pastiera (pah-STYAIR-ah) — A tart or pie, usually made with ricotta, and eaten at Easter time.

pastina (pah-STEEN-ah) — "little dough." Tiny macaroni for soup.

pennoni (pen-NO-nee) — "big pen-nibs," or "standards." A macaroni product.

pesce (PAY-shay) — Fish.

pesciolino (pay-shaw-LEE-no) — Little fish, whitebait.

pesto (PAY-stoe) — "mashed." A Genoese green sauce for macaroni, made with oil, garlic, herbs, anchovies, etc.

pignolata (pee-nyaw-LAH-tah) — Pine nut cake or nougat.

pignoli (pee-NYAW-lee) — From *pino,* "pine." Pine nuts.

pinza (PEEN-tsah) — "full," "stuffed." A cake of Bologna.

pizza (PEE-tsah) — "pie," "tart." Generic term for any bakery product that is flat and round.

pizzaiola (pee-tsah-YAW-lah) — Pizza style, with melted mozzarella and tomato sauce.

pizzeria (pee-tsay-REE-ah) — A shop where pizza is sold.

polenta (po-LEN-tah) — Cornmeal, cornmeal mush.

polpetta (pul-PET-tah) — From *polpa,* "pulp," "flesh." A meatball.

polpettone (pul-pay-TOE-nay) — Large *polpetta,* or meatloaf.

potacchio (po-TAH-kyo) — A codfish or meat stew, specialty of Ancona.

preziosa (pray-TSYO-sah) — "Precious," in the feminine gender. *Preziosa* is the title of the ladies' magazine directed by the author. Outside of its literal meaning, the term seems to refer to the *Précieuses* (French intellectual women of the post-Renaissance period, who also gave rise to the English "preciosity").

preziosini (pray-tsyo-SEE-nee) — "little precious ones." Bread crumb buns.

prosciutto (pro-SHOOT-toe) — Ham, prepared Italian style (dried, salted, spiced and pressed, but not sugar-cured or smoked).

provenzale (pro-vent-SAH-lay) — "Provençal." Provence is the southern region of France, intimately bound to northern Italy by cultural and gastronomic ties. The name *Provence* comes from the *Provincia* of the Romans, to whom southern Gaul was the best beloved province.

provinciale (pro-veen-CHAH-lay) — "provincial," "pertaining to the small towns," in contradistinction to the metropolis.

provola (PRO-vo-lah) — A soft, fresh cheese, similar to mozzarella.

provola affumicata (ah-foo-mee-KAH-tah) — Smoked provola.

provolone (pro-vo-LO-nay) — A hard, yellow cheese, usually creamy and piquant to the taste.

ravioli (rah-VYO-lee) — A dough preparation, stuffed with chopped meat, spinach, cheese, etc., boiled, and eaten with a sauce.

rete (RAY-tay) — "net." The membrane of the lamb's intestine, used to wrap pork livers.

riccio (REE-cho) — "curly." A variety of shellfish, the sea-urchin.

ricotta (ree-KUT-tah) — "re-cooked," "cooked again." A substance resembling cottage cheese, obtained by the repeated boiling of skimmed milk.

rigatoni (ree-gah-TOE-nee) — Large, grooved macaroni; from *riga*, "groove."

ripieno (ree-PYAY-no) — As an adjective: "stuffed"; as a noun: "stuffing."

risotto (ree-SUT-toe) — "big rice." Boiled rice, with a sauce, much favored in the northern regions of Italy.

salame (sah-LAH-may). From the root of *sale*, "salt." A salted and spiced pork product, to be eaten sliced. *Salami* is the plural form, and means several sticks of salame.

salametto (sah-lah-MET-toe) — "little *salame.*"

salamino (sah-lah-MEE-no) — "little *salame.*"

saltimbocca (sahl-teem-BO-kah) — "jump into the mouth." The name of a tasty Roman dish which is so good that it figuratively jumps into your mouth of its own accord.

sanguinaccio (sahn-gwee-NAH-cho) — Blutwurst, blood-pudding, blood-sausage.

savoiardi (sah-voy-AR-dee) — "Savoyards," "from the province of Savoy."

scaloppine (skal-lo-PEE-nay) — Thin slices of meat (usually veal), stewed or fried.

scamozza (skah-MO-tsah) — A fresh cheese.

scampo (SKAHM-po) — A variety of shrimp found in the Adriatic.

schiacciato (skyah-CHAH-toe) — Crushed.

scungilli (skoon-GEE-lee) — The conch, whose meat is extracted from the shell, boiled, and served with a hot sauce. The name comes from the Neapolitan dialect, and seems to be a corruption of the Italian *conchiglie.*

semolina (say-moe-LEE-nah) — Finely ground wheat.

sfingi (SFEEN-gee) — "sphinxes." Cakes or cookies.

sfogliatella (sfo-lyah-TEL-lah) — "little leaves." A delicate pastry similar to *Apfelstrudel* in structure, but not in taste.

soffritto (so-FREE-toe) — "underfried," "slightly fried." A base for soups and meat dishes consisting usually of oil or salt pork and chopped parsley, onion, celery, etc.

spaghetti (spah-GET-tee) — From *spago*, "cord." The thinner varieties of macaroni products.

spaghettini (spah-get-TEE-nee) — "little spaghetti," "thin spaghetti."

spumante (spoo-MAHN-tay) — "foaming." The generic term for sparkling, bubbling wines, mostly produced in the North.

spumone (spoo-MO-nay) — "big foam." An Italian variety of ice cream.

stiacciata (styah-CHAH-tah) — "crushed" or "flattened." A Tuscan type of cake.

stracchino (strah-KEE-no) — "little tired." A soft cheese of Milan. The name is said to refer to the cheese which was originally made with the milk of cows that were "tired out" after their trip from the mountains.

stracciatella (strah-chah-TEL-lah) — "little ragged" (from *stracci* "rags"). The Roman egg soup, in which flaked eggs resemble tiny fragments of rag.

strufoli (STROO-foe-lee) — "wads of cotton." A Neapolitan cake.

taglioline (tah-lyo-LEE-nay) — From *tagliare*, "to cut." Noodles cut into strips.

torrone (tor-RO-nay) — From Latin *torrere*, "to toast," "to roast." A nougat, made with honey, almonds, nuts, etc.

torta (TOR-tah) — Tart, pie.

tortellini (tor-tel-LEE-nee) — "little twisted ones." A macaroni product, usually stuffed with meat and other ingredients and served in soup. A specialty of Bologna.

trifolato (tree-foe-LAH-toe) — Trifoiled, or clover-shaped.

triglia (TREE-lyah) — The Mediterranean red mullet.

tufoli (TOO-fo-lee) — A macaroni variety.

vongole (VAWN-go-lay) — Mediterranean clams, smaller than our Cherrystone variety.

zabaione, zabajone (zah-bah-YO-nay) — Form of eggnog made of egg yolks, sugar and wine, used as dessert in liquid or semi-solid forms, hot or cold. Also known as *zabaglione*.

zampone (dzahm-PO-nay) — "big paw." The pig's paw hollowed out and stuffed with chopped, salted and spiced meat.

zeppole (DZEP-poe-lay) — A Neapolitan fritter.

ziti (DZEE-tee) — A large macaroni variety.

zuppa inglese (DZOO-pah een-GLAY-say) — literally, "English soup." A soft, gooey cake which is a Roman favorite.

INDEX

INDEX